WITHDRAWN

ELIZABETHAN TRIUMPHAL PROCESSIONS

For Christiane, Danny and Aaron

Elizabethan Triumphal Processions

WILLIAM LEAHY
Brunel University, London

ASHGATE

Published by
Ashgate Publishing Limited
Gower House
Croft Road
Aldershot
Hants GU11 3HR
England

Ashgate Publishing Company
Suite 420
101 Cherry Street
Burlington
Vermont, 05401–4405
USA

Ashgate website: http://www.ashgate.com

British Library Cataloguing in Publication Data
Elizabethan Triumphal Processions
    1. Elizabeth I, Queen of England, 1533–1603. 2. Processions – England – History – 16th century. 3. Power (Social sciences) – England – History – 16th century. 4. Great Britain – History – Elizabeth, 1558–1603. I. Title.
    942'.055

US Library of Congress Cataloging in Publication Data
Elizabethan Triumphal Processions / William Leahy.
      p.   cm.
    Includes bibliographical references and index.
    1. Elizabeth, Queen of England, 1533–1603 – Travel. 2. Processions – England – History – 16th century. 3. Rites and ceremonies – Great Britain – History – 16th century. 4. Visits of state – England – History – 16th century. 5. Monarchy – Great Britain – 16th century. 6. Royal visitors – England – History – 16th century – 7. England – Social life and customs – 16th century. 8. Great Britain – History – 1558–1603. I. Title.
    DA356.L44 2004
    394'.5'094209031–dc22

DA
356
L43

2004013248

ISBN 0 7546 3984 3

This book is printed on acid free paper.

Printed and bound in Great Britain by MPG Books Ltd, Bodmin, Cornwall

Contents

Acknowledgements

I would like to thank all those people who have helped and supported me in writing this book. First of all, I would like to thank my colleagues at Brunel University for creating a stimulating environment in which to work. I would especially like to thank Maureen Moran for her support. The administrative staff have also been very helpful, and I am particularly appreciative of the help given to me by Suzanne Wills and Sara Brown.

Nina Taunton has been both a great colleague and valued friend, and I would like to thank her for the close reading of each chapter she undertook, and the excellent advice she always proffered. I appreciate her perception and trust. I would also like to thank Tony Bromham, who was always ready to listen and to give constructive advice. Thanks are due also to David Fitchett for the companionship and the laughter. I owe a debt of gratitude to Erika Gaffney at Ashgate for her encouragement of the project and to Kirsten Weissenberg, also at Ashgate, for the technical support she provided.

Certain sections of the book have appeared in different forms in the following journals: *Shakespeare Jahrbuch* 138 (2002); *Parergon: Journal of the Australian and New Zealand Association for Medieval and Early Modern Studies* 20.2 (July 2003); *Early Modern Literary Studies* 9.1 (May 2003); and *Renaissance Renegotiations. EnterText* 3:1 (Spring 2003). I would like to thank the editors of these journals for their assistance. I would also like to thank Martin Coyle, Lisa Hopkins and the many students who have helped make teaching at Brunel University a great experience.

Finally, and most importantly, I would like to thank Christiane, Danny and Aaron for their love and support. Without their patience and understanding this work would not have been possible and I dedicate this book to them with love.

William Leahy
Brunel University

Introduction

'Triumphal Processions'

Processional practice took three major forms in early modern England, each with its own discrete defining characteristics, but sharing much common ground materially, textually, and ideologically. The royal entry and the royal progress were defined by the determining presence of the sovereign, the 'centre of the centre',[1] and form the two types of Elizabethan procession that will be the focus of this current study.[2] The processional form itself was not an innovation of the early modern period, but had its roots in the Roman triumphs that took place in order to celebrate the return of the victorious Roman army from a successful military campaign.[3] This triumphal function was still important during Elizabeth I's reign, but such processions had, by that time, broadened their purpose as well as their originating occasion. The essential hypothesis of both types of Elizabethan procession can be regarded as synonymous however: their exhibition of power. As David Bergeron writes: 'The theme that binds all the pageants, whether progress shows or royal entries, together is the celebration of Elizabeth's power, her spiritual, mystical, transforming power'.[4] The major contrast between them can be seen to be a geographical one, in the sense that royal entries were the urban manifestations of this desire to celebrate sovereign power, and royal progresses their primarily rural modes of representation. This was no small difference however and, as Bergeron goes on to say, resulted in the production of entertainments that reflected these particular locations: 'in the Elizabethan era mythology and romance dominate in the progress entertainments while historical subjects and moral allegory abound in the royal entries'.[5] The progress thus witnessed the production of a primarily pastoral mode of representation, whilst the entry invoked a more spectacular and historically specific mode of address. The inhabitants of London were presented with two of these magnificent urban spectacles during Elizabeth's reign, the first to mark her ascendancy to the throne, and the second to commemorate victory over the Spanish in 1588. Many other cities were host to an Elizabethan royal entry, such as Coventry, Warwick, Bristol, and Norwich, but never on the scale reserved for the two unique occasions in the capital.

During the summer months of her reign Elizabeth embarked upon royal progresses, visiting the private estates of the nobility and gentry, usually accompanied by a large part, or indeed the whole of her enormous court. These carefully plotted royal tours would proceed through the countryside, enabling the public to take advantage of the opportunity of having visual contact with the Queen. This visibility was seen to have positive propagandist value, the sovereign demonstrating her accessibility at the same time as she showed her love and concern for her subjects. Once she had reached the private estate of the honoured nobleman, entertainment in the form of celebratory pageants were often performed, the public again having the opportunity to view the Queen as spectators or even participants. This visual contemplation was one of the progresses' main functions, along with the desire to escape the dangers of the plague which was rife in London during the summer months, and the further desire to shift some of the costs of supporting both her governmental machinery and the Court itself onto her hosts. It is with the first of these aims – the propagandist value of Elizabethan processions – that this book is generally concerned, and with the ways in which procession and pageant analysis has traditionally conceived of this aim as having been successful. While it is quite clear that processions were indeed, among other things, public relations exercises, their success in achieving their aims, this book claims, is more ambiguous than has previously been suggested. Studies of Elizabethan processions and pageants have traditionally failed to register this ambivalence, and have instead regarded rural progresses and royal entries into cities as rituals that helped to strengthen Elizabeth's position of power. The examination of a specific example will outline this process and will, in many ways, articulate the general approach this book takes to Elizabethan processions and their transmission through history.

In the summer of 1568 the Spanish Ambassador to England, Guzman de Silva, accompanied Queen Elizabeth on one of her progresses through the countryside, an event that he later reported back to the King of Spain. This report remains one of the few eyewitness accounts of the public face of such a progress, and is therefore important evidence when attempting to perceive the nature of these processions. This is a fact recognised by Alison Plowden in her widely accessible study of Elizabethan England where, in her discussion of processions, she quotes the Ambassador's report as describing what she calls a 'typical scene':

> She was received everywhere ... with great acclamations and signs of joy, as is customary in this country; whereat she was extremely pleased and told me so, giving me to understand how beloved she was by her subjects and how highly she esteemed this, together with the fact that they were peaceful and contented, whilst her neighbours on all sides are in such trouble. She attributed it all to God's miraculous goodness. She ordered her carriage sometimes to be taken where the crowd seemed thickest and stood up and thanked the people.[6]

For Plowden this account conjures up the atmosphere of progresses in general, where always 'the Queen was assured of an enthusiastic welcome from the townspeople'.[7] Plowden perceives an evidently unproblematic unity between sovereign and people, each contented due to 'God's miraculous goodness'. In this piece of evidence, dated 10 July 1568, we seem to behold the reality of a wholly popular Queen moving comfortably amongst her adoring subjects, confident of her place in their hearts and minds, aware of the effect that this accessibility is having. The theatricality of her actions is noticeable, as is her reported gratitude for the ability to meet her subjects in such a manner. In this scenario, Elizabeth's presence contains no element of ambiguity or vulnerability as she passes through the countryside of her England and, through Plowden's intercession, into our world as a most popular, semi-mythical individual, responsible for the vitality of a glorious golden age.

A re-reading of the section of the Spanish Ambassador's report that Plowden has reproduced is enlightening as a re-figuring of the reported events becomes possible. Certainly Elizabeth's insistence on her popularity, on the esteem in which she is held by her subjects, is revealing, and insinuates perhaps her desire to reassure this foreign dignitary of the secure nature of her position politically, and more importantly religiously, as she was the head of a Protestant faith still in conflict with the Catholicism represented by the Spanish Ambassador, a conflict felt to be unresolved in her own country. A brief look at the *Calendar of State Papers (Spanish)*, from which the above quotation has been culled, enables the construction of a rather different scenario than that elucidated for us by Plowden, and suggests the possibility of irony on the part of the Spanish Ambassador. For, significantly, Plowden has chosen to omit the opening two sentences of the Ambassador's report, which seem to contradict the Queen's confidence, and which read as follows:

> The Queen arrived in this city on the 6th in good health and continued her progress which as I have said, *will only be in the neighbourhood, as she is careful to keep near at hand when troubles and disturbances exist in adjacent countries.* She came by the river as far as Reading, and thence through the country in a carriage, open on all sides, that she might be seen by the people, who flocked all along the roads as far as the duke of Norfolk's houses where she alighted. She was received ... (emphasis added).[8]

Even bearing in mind that the following year saw the eruption of the Northern Rebellion and it is therefore understandable that the Queen should be discerning as to where she went on progress, it is important that the Ambassador juxtaposes her fears and her confidence – demonstrating contradiction – and equally important that Plowden recognises neither these fears nor this contradiction. While, at first sight, it would seem that it is the Ambassador who is guilty of such contradiction if he holds that the Queen is both universally popular and unpopular, he can only be regarded in this manner if he is not being ironic. For, how can Elizabeth restrict her movements within her own realm and at the same time seriously regret the fact that 'her neighbours on all sides are in such trouble', whereas her own subjects are 'peaceful and contented'? Plowden's intentions in her failure to report this contradiction (or irony) are probably less ambiguous than the Ambassador's, and would seem to suggest a certain partiality evident in a study that characterises Elizabethan England as 'An Age of Adventure'.[9] Such a partiality is further emphasised by the fact that, in those two omitted opening sentences, it is shown that Elizabeth was on her way to visit the Duke of Norfolk, in whose name (among others) the Catholic rebellion of the Northern Earls erupted in 1569, and who was subsequently executed in 1572 for his involvement in the Ridolfi Plot. The Catholic minority in England posed a very real threat to the rule (and life) of the Queen, and Norfolk himself actively attempted to overthrow her and replace her with a Catholic monarch in the person of her great rival, Mary, Queen of Scots – a plot that required (and received) the support of the Spanish.

Alison Plowden's book is part of the 'Reader's Digest Life In Britain' series, and could therefore be regarded as popular rather than academic and thus unworthy of the consideration that it is being given here.[10] However, the kind of selective quotation in which Plowden indulges is not unique to such popular history, as is evidenced by the tendency for both historical and literary studies of every status to indulge themselves likewise. If Plowden is taken as a starting point, the use to which this historical document has been put can be determined in progressively scholarly studies that reproduce her practice. Neville Williams, for example, in a study that is less idealised and hagiographic than Plowden's, though is still highly accessible, quotes and omits precisely the same lines as Plowden, relating how the Ambassador 'dwelt on the popularity these personal appearances engendered'.[11] Zillah Dovey does the same in her exhaustive study of an Elizabethan progress, adding that the Spanish Ambassador's despatch confirms the fact that progresses were 'one of the Queen's major – and successful – policies'.[12] Further up the academic ladder, Christopher Haigh, in his famous biography of Elizabeth that many scholars believe demystifies the Queen and injects a good deal of realism and common sense into the study of her relationships with all levels of the contemporary population, reproduces and omits the same lines, and states that the enthusiasm with which she was greeted 'was the product of her own hard work and that of her propagandists'.[13] And Louis Montrose, one of the foremost practitioners of the New Historicism, does the same, mobilising the example as proof of the effectiveness of the Queen's presence on progress in cementing her relationship to the various social groups which made up the audience, confirming his model of Elizabeth as the consummate 'power-actor', as the embodiment of a demonstration of what Michel Foucault called dissymmetry.[14] Each of these studies is taken as a representative of the wide-ranging trend that marks the whole practice of the transmission of conventional knowledge.

This retrieval of the Spanish Ambassador's documentation shows that the Queen would seem to be articulating a great deal of anxiety in the presence of the Spanish Ambassador, an anxiety that would have been well-founded in the light of subsequent events. The Queen's words are indeed insecure, as they attempt to give credibility to a reality that even the Spanish Ambassador could see was contradictory. It is probably true that Elizabeth felt more threatened in the vicinity of both the Duke of Norfolk and the Spanish Ambassador than would normally have been the case, but this threat was in no way unique. For throughout her entire reign the Queen felt safe and popular in certain parts of her realm, and not in others. This is reflected in the fact that the Queen's progresses were always restricted in scope, never venturing 'further north than Stafford or further West than Bristol'.[15] According to Jean Wilson, Elizabeth kept 'to the parts of the country where there was little disaffection', the progresses being 'propaganda for the faithful, not gestures of goodwill to the potentially hostile'.[16] Mary Hill Cole supports such a view, stating that rather than 'using progresses to bring order to troubled regions', the Queen 'validated royal authority and social stability where it already existed'.[17] These observations at least recognise that the potentially hostile did exist, did pose a real threat to the Sovereign, and did dwell within the limits of her own domain. For the Queen was wise to 'remain in the neighbourhood', particularly in this period of her reign, and was wiser still to suspend progresses altogether during certain high-risk periods such as the 1580s. It is a wisdom that is not attested to in the work of many scholars who have reported upon this particular progress, however. Much is omitted, such as the possibility of discontent, insecurity and most significantly, contradiction. In these studies, the Spanish Ambassador joins the ordinary people of England in adoring the sovereign of a peaceful, contented, unified land.

The common people 'who flocked all along the roads' according to the Spanish Ambassador, are represented (in both his account and in the accounts of subsequent scholars) as a marginal conglomeration into which the Queen was driven 'in a carriage open on all sides', instinctively celebrating the passing of the sovereign. In the rebellion that did take place in the north of the country the following year, many of their class were forced to fight (that is to say they were pressed) on behalf of both parties, and in the aftermath, on the side of the rebels, 'some 600 men who had been sent by their villages to fight were hanged'.[18] One wonders if, given the fact that common men were continually pressed in this way, such a reality would indeed induce instinctive adulation. However, it is possible to state that both in the fact that the progress in 1568 took place, to an extent, in order to address these people, and that their volatile nature contributed to the restriction of the Queen's movements both at that moment and for the duration of her reign, there is a passing of their presence into a more central position in the ideological topography of such public events. This particular progress itself is the site of a movement of the marginal towards the centre, and the presence of the common audience can be recognised as, at the very least, important.

Plowden's interpretation of events underlines this reality in its construction of this presence as either acquiescent or invisible. The Queen, it should be remembered, was always heavily protected, especially when travelling in an open carriage.[19] And both the accessibility possible through the use of such an open carriage and its necessary protection are elements of the nature of the progress as influenced by the presence of the common people (as well as, for example, foreign agents). Plowden's subject is these same common people, conjuring them up as the consumers of spectacle and not as the (deferred) co-producers of such events. And therefore both her reading of this progress, and those of the many scholars who read it in the same fashion, contribute to it becoming one of those documents which, Foucault believed, are characterised by their 'carefully protected identities', which possess an 'essence ... fabricated in a piecemeal fashion',[20] and articulate a transmission of conventional, partial knowledge.

In the reading offered above, a process of recuperation is evident. Disunity and disruption are either glossed over, or made to function in order to strengthen the dominant ideology. Analyses of this royal progress of 1568 demonstrate a perceptible blindness, one induced, to paraphrase Walter Benjamin, by the light of cultural treasures transmitted through time from owner to owner in a triumphal procession.[21] Traditional analyses of Elizabethan processions generally, whether of the entries into cities or of the rural progresses, have regarded them as instances of the successful use of propaganda, the population at whom they were aimed being ideologically hailed in an attempt to maintain their loyalty, causing them to identify with a rigid hierarchical social structure of which they formed the base. In this study, I wish to read Elizabethan royal entries and progresses, and their respective literatures, in a way described by Walter Benjamin as one that attempts to 'brush history against the grain',[22] as one that will try to ascertain whether, and in what ways, they produced and negotiated the ideological effects prescribed to them, and to question if they were successful in their perceived normative functions. It takes seriously the claims made for these literary forms that they functioned in the service of state power and conventional notions of order, and ponders whether they were successful in fulfilling this function. More specifically, this book will subject both primary and secondary literature to Benjamin's further claim that all cultural artefacts that have been passed down to the present as such articulations of conventional order are participating in a 'triumphal procession' that occludes other potential meanings. Benjamin believed that these 'cultural treasures' must be viewed 'with cautious detachment', in order for the process of their transmission through time to be analysed both rationally and adequately.[23]

Given the profusion of Renaissance literary criticism, it is surprising that studies which examine literature that was produced for processions and progresses as a discrete literary form are scarce. In comparison to such areas of Renaissance literature as, for example, Shakespeare's history plays, pageant and procession literature has, to a great extent, been critically ignored.[24] I make the connection between the two literary forms deliberately, as the two separate genres of Shakespearean historical drama and pageant literature have traditionally been regarded as commensurate with each other. This commensurability has been seen to be unproblematic and evident, demonstrated by Andrew Cairncross, for example, who writes with reference to Shakespeare's first tetralogy: '*3 Henry VI* is much more than a pageant for the eye. It is part of a great all-embracing conception of a pageant in which England and man himself work out the expiation of an original crime [the removal from the throne of Richard II] towards the final reassertion of a divinely controlled universal order [the establishment of Henry VII as king]'.[25] The apotheosis of such a critical dynamic is reached in Marion Wynne-Davies's *The Renaissance: From 1500–1660*, part of the series of Bloomsbury's Guides to English Literature, and thus effectively a textbook. The final part of Davies's study provides an alphabetically ordered reference section in which, under the term 'Pageant' the following – which I quote at length – is entered:

> the traditions of the pageant are twofold: in one sense it is purely spectacle, but in another it may be a spectacle combined with the narrative of a conflict, which is dramatic only because the conflict is seen as symbolic of human experience.

This second sense of the pageant tradition is important for understanding Elizabethan history plays, especially those of Shakespeare. Thus, in *Henry IV, Part 1* the modern audience is inclined to see the drama as a conflict for the identity of Prince Hal, who on the one hand is faced with the temptations of self-indulgence through Falstaff, and on the other with the task of winning 'honour' from Hotspur. Yet the audience is misled by this approach, since in I. ii. Prince Hal declares that he is in no danger of yielding to Falstaff, and his acquisition of honour is also foreknown through the historical fact of the battle of Agincourt; Hal is thus not the hero of an inner moral and an outer physical conflict, at least in the sense that there is the smallest uncertainty in the audience's mind about the outcome. On the other hand, Falstaff and Hotspur – the self-indulgent favourite and the self-centred politician – are dangers to which any nation is everlastingly exposed. Thus the dramatic interest of the play is not Hal but the nation, and the play is essentially the re-enactment of a conflict to which the nation is perpetually exposed – a dramatic pageant in the mystery and morality tradition.[26]

It is clear in this definition that Davies perceives an evident affinity – indeed equivalence – between the ideological trajectory of pageant devices and Shakespeare's history plays. This project of equivalence has been detected by Michael Bristol, who writes in this respect:

> It has frequently been implied or suggested, that individual plays, and in the case of Shakespeare's 'tetralogies' whole cycles of plays, are organised in accordance with strategies similar to those of official pageantry. They consist of extended political anti-masques eventually routed by the appearance of a legitimate king.[27]

Bristol is delineating the Tillyardian conceit of 'order from disorder' that has characterised so much criticism of the history plays of Shakespeare, whereby all disorder appears only to be overcome by the norm of order itself, represented by the monarch as absolute and natural authority.[28] The notion of order has been perceived as the dominant coda of the history plays, and Shakespeare himself as the Elizabethan state's chief cultural ideologue. That this is a position which has been contested by any number of Renaissance critics is a sign of the centrality of Shakespearean studies within the literary institution, and signals the marginality of pageant and procession literature in comparison.[29] The history plays of Shakespeare, that category of critical plenitude, are widely regarded to be amongst the greatest cultural productions in the English language, indeed in any language, and are the site of an ongoing ideological struggle within the institution of Literature, a struggle that continually witnesses political realignments and regroupings in the light of vacillating theoretical developments. Dramatic pageant literature produced for Elizabethan royal entries and royal progresses on the other hand has been, to a large extent, critically abandoned in the sense that it has often been seen to be mechanically constructed and thus of limited literary interest, and as wholly transparent in its ideological desire and therefore worthless as a site of potential political contestation.[30] Despite this fact, in the analyses that do exist, pageant literature has, along with the actual public events it sought to commemorate, traditionally been held to be an unproblematic example of the state displaying sovereign power to the marginalised and suitably impressed subject.

It would seem to be evident that Elizabeth herself was keenly aware of the value of her processions as public relations exercises, not least by the fact that they were very well documented, many of the dramatic entertainments which took place in both city streets and on country estates appearing in print soon after they were performed.[31] Many of these entertainments, written by the likes of Richard Mulcaster, John Lyly, Thomas Churchyard and Sir Philip Sidney have been preserved, and can in fact be said to form a discrete literary sub-genre that can be examined in the broader totality of celebratory literature for the Queen. These celebratory texts were gathered together in one collection for the first time over 200 years after Elizabeth's death, in John Nichols' *The Progresses and Public Processions of Queen Elizabeth I*, published in 1788 and extensively revised in 1823, and very much the founding text of the genre of processional pageant literature. Nichols gathered together not only all of the various pamphlets that described the entertainments performed for Elizabeth, but also many letters and documents which tell of each procession's preparation and realisation. It is therefore an essential source of primary material, though a collection of data rather than a critique, having little to say about the function of pageants and progresses, and few words too regarding the nature of Elizabeth's reign.[32]

Even with the broadening of the area of research into Elizabethan court entertainments to include more exclusive forms of pageant literature such as court masques, tilts and tournaments, examples of processional analysis are not numerous. E. K. Chambers' *The Elizabethan Stage* and Glynne Wickham's *Early English Stages 1300–1660*, are two of the more comprehensive studies, both attempting in their own ways to analyse dramatic practice in its entirety within the temporal limits they set themselves. Chambers is the more interesting in terms of social and political contexts, and remains the only analyst to consistently cast a critical eye over processional practice in the Elizabethan era. Wickham, whose area of investigation is broader in that he examines drama over a period of three and a half centuries, concentrates much more on the development of theatrical practice as an enclosed cultural form, and has much of interest to say in terms of a perceived emblematic tradition.[33]

The first examination of the public generation of pageantry as a discrete cultural form was Robert Withington's *English Pageantry*, which appeared in 1918. Withington traces the development of pageantry in its public form since its inception in folk custom, and its subsequent determining encounter with the royal entry. While he has little to say about the processions of Elizabeth I, he does illuminate the evolution of public pageantry that came to characterise Elizabeth's reign. He writes:

> During the centuries from Edward I to Elizabeth this kind of entertainment was developing in London under the stimulus of the 'royal entry'. Without the hampering tradition of folk-custom, and with the conscious planning of poets and engineers, pageantry developed rapidly, drawing from folk, from history, from romance, the Bible, saint's legend and the tournament ... In 1432 Lydgate gave it

allegory, and soon – as a result of history and allegory – we find personification. Symbolism is almost inseparable from it; and with the necessity of explaining symbolism, speech appeared.[34]

This is the stage it had reached by the time of Elizabeth's pre-coronation 'Recognition March' of 14 January 1558, in which she became a central participant in the dramatic devices performed in her honour.

While Withington has much to say about the development of the royal entry, he does not consider, to any useful extent, royal progresses. This is true also of the next major work on public pageantry to appear, Sydney Anglo's *Spectacle, Pageantry, and Early Tudor Policy*. The fact that this was published in 1969, over 50 years after Withington's study, further underlines the relative invisibility of pageantry as a literary genre and, as indicated in Anglo's title, as a politically vibrant cultural practice. Anglo's attention is given to the productions of pageantry that occurred in the reigns of Elizabeth's ancestors, with a final chapter that, to a great extent, merely chronicles her pre-coronation procession as it appears in Nichols' earlier work. Anglo does however choose the term 'spectacle' in his description of royal entries, pre-empting Michel Foucault, whose formulation of the notion of the early modern period as a predominantly 'spectacular' one has become so important in modern literary critical practice. Foucault was later to conclude that royal processions were occasions very much determined by the desire to demonstrate a spectacular display of sovereign power.[35]

We enter what could be called the modern era of public pageant criticism with the appearance of David Bergeron's seminal *English Civic Pageantry 1558–1642*. Published in 1971, it is a work focused exclusively upon the royal entries and progresses of Elizabeth and James I, as well as the Lord Mayor's Shows that took place within those dates. Bergeron defines his area of interest as 'civic pageantry', which he says, 'refers to entertainments that, like the public theatre of Shakespeare's time, were generally accessible to the public, as contrasted with the private theatres or the court masques'.[36] This is reminiscent of the limits of John Nichols' founding text, a source that Bergeron frequently uses. His re-definition (or rather re-recognition) of these limits comes 150 years after Nichols' initial definition and, although his study is now over 30 years old, it remains the benchmark for critical analysis of English civic pageantry. Jean Wilson's excellent *Entertainments for Elizabeth I*, which focuses mainly on a number of specific progress entertainments, and the various general studies by Roy Strong, have added relatively little to our knowledge of Elizabethan public pageantry.[37] In fact, the only new or fresh critical evaluation of this processional practice has come from mainstream Renaissance literary studies and, more specifically, from the New Historicism.[38] That said, this school of criticism has tended to analyse Elizabethan processions in a rather piecemeal fashion, concentrating on a single event and then generalising the conclusions reached through this analysis. Indeed, the only sustained examination of these events by a New Historicist critic has been Mary Hill Cole's *The Portable Queen: Elizabeth I and the Politics of Ceremony*.[39] However, while Cole's book supplies much precious historical material regarding progresses, it has little new to say about these processions as cultural rituals and nothing at all to say about royal entries.

Although the availability of analysis is therefore limited, there is a conventional perception of both the ideological thrust of processions, and their success in achieving their ideological aims. John Nichols regards them as part of Elizabeth's 'plan of popularity',[40] while Christopher Haigh recognises them as 'major public relations exercises'.[41] The fulfilment of the official purpose of these exercises is never doubted, Neville Williams, for example, regarding the processions as effective means of winning 'the average subject's bonds of affection',[42] and Zillah Dovey declaring that they represented one of Elizabeth's 'successful policies'.[43] Their perceived normative effect is clear and unproblematic for these critics, the processions, according to Bergeron, 'winning additional loyalty and support',[44] for Elizabeth, Mary Hill Cole agreeing that they 'gave the queen a public stage on which to present herself as the people's sovereign and to interact with her subjects in a calculated attempt to keep their support'.[45] Indeed, Cole goes so far as to state that Elizabeth's progresses were 'intrinsic to her ability to govern'.[46]

Like Mary Hill Cole, New Historicist critics generally have tended to reproduce the notion of processions and progresses as such normative cultural practices. Although New Historicists such as Cole, Stephen Greenblatt, Leonard Tennenhouse, and Jonathan Goldberg are indebted to many social and cultural theorists and philosophers in their work, notably Clifford Geertz and Victor Turner and, more problematically Louis Althusser and Jacques Derrida, it is the work of the French philosopher Michel Foucault which can be regarded as the primary source in the construction of their theoretical architecture. More specifically, it is in his conception of early modern societies as being 'spectacular' in terms of the power relations between sovereign and subject, and of power continually exalting itself in such societies through the use of various techniques of visual display, that the New Historicists have found particularly enabling in their critical practice.[47] This concept of a normative aura surrounding forms of such visual display, coupled with the Geertzian concept of the 'textuality of reality', invited these literary critics to insert any form of public event into this category of display, the early modern theatre, for example, being a natural choice. Foucault himself regarded this theatre as a much more complex site of power relations, one which did not demonstrate the same spectacular characteristics as such practices as public executions.[48] One public event that he did regard as possessing a similar spectacular nature to that of the public execution was the royal entry, particularly one that coincided with a unique celebration. In *Discipline and Punish: The Birth of the Prison*, he writes that the 'public execution ... is a ceremonial by which a momentarily injured sovereignty is reconstituted', and that it 'belongs to a whole series of great rituals in which power is eclipsed and restored (coronation, entry of the king into a conquered city, the submission of rebellious subjects)'.[49] As such, he continues, 'it deploys before all eyes an invincible force', as its 'aim is ... to bring into play ... the dissymmetry between the subject ... and the all-powerful sovereign ... '.[50] Determining the equivalence of a coronation and public execution outlines the type of society Foucault regards the early modern one to have been, a society in which the absolute power of the sovereign was constituted through spectacular display, through the demonstration of the arbitrary nature of its force/violence, through its thorough 'dissymmetry'.[51] The coronation procession functioned therefore in a way that underlined and reconstituted a power that 'sought a renewal of its effect in the spectacle of its individual manifestations ... '.[52] In such a scenario then, public executions and royal entries shared a function that could be said to be propagandist and, in early modern society the social hierarchy itself was constituted and preserved by the effectiveness of this propaganda. Furthermore, the tradition of public-pageant analysis as a whole is one that not only generally considers Renaissance processional practice to be overtly propagandist and, in Foucauldian terms, spectacular, but also as having been successful in fulfilling its ideological aims. Accordingly, these processions have been analysed as functioning in an exemplary fashion, the populace being perceived as having submitted themselves to displays of hierarchy in which they form the lower level. In an Althusserian sense, these processions are interpreted as having successfully 'hailed', 'subjected' and 'interpellated' their common audience.[53] Simply put, the whole tradition of analysis of Elizabethan processions has regarded them as having accomplished their ideologically normative task.

For all their talk of the relationship between subject and sovereign, and of the mutual love that circulated there, analysts of Elizabethan entries and progresses have traditionally examined these dramatic/political formations exclusively from a position of, or commensurate with, that of the culturally dominant. This is evident in a number of more recent studies which have cast a critical eye over Elizabethan processions and pageants and, indeed, over the historical transmission of an evident 'cult' of Elizabeth. Critics such as Helen Hackett, Susan Doran, Philippa Berry, Susan Frye and Carole Levin have approached all aspects of Elizabeth's rule in a sceptical fashion and have argued persuasively for a reconsideration of many of the conventional beliefs regarding her reign.[54] However, what they have not done, an omission that distinguishes this current study from theirs (and previous studies), is consider the presence of the common people both at these specific public events and, indeed, more generally. Those at whom these instances of propaganda were aimed are rarely or, more usually, never included, or are merely regarded as Elizabeth's 'most loving People'.[55] This reality has arisen, to some extent, because many earlier scholars are themselves immersed in a cult of Elizabeth I, encouraging in them the conception of both panegyric and overt sycophancy as a social and cultural norm. The literary outpourings of a small group of poets and dramatists seeking patronage are, according to this reading, taken to represent the expression of a pervasive social reality, the reactions and behaviour of the whole contemporary population being collapsed into this condensed political truth.[56] Thus, a very narrow and selective use of texts, read partially, (re)produces a socially and culturally dominant trope.

It would seem to be true then, that procession and pageant analysts generally concern themselves with notions of sovereign power, the representatives of this sovereign power, and the means through which this power was successfully promoted and the social hierarchy preserved. What they do not consider however, at least not in any active sense, is that other side of the equation which is of great importance in this study, the recipients of the message, the audience. More specifically, they do not consider those subjects who, it was felt, needed to be targeted and constantly reminded of the dissymmetry in their relation to the sovereign.[57] Naturally these subjects would be the poorer section of society, the potentially disruptive section, the ordinary or common people who constituted a substantial section of the audiences of both royal processions and progresses. A formulation of the nature of the presence of the common people is, however, important in any compelling analysis of these public events. If royal entries and progresses are taken seriously as being instances of state propaganda, these common subjects, in their targeted reality, become a much greater (collective) subject of this propaganda. There was a perceived need by authority for such normative practices, and a clear perception of who needed to be targeted. This moment of dissymmetrical signification was forever renewed as, it seems, these people were felt to be so potentially disruptive by those who held power that they needed to be continually subjected.[58] What becomes clear in this light is that the question which traditional analysis has always failed to formulate is why, if Elizabeth was held in such high esteem and order was an essential part of the Elizabethan world picture, the state needed to continually attempt to (re)interpellate the masses?[59] Furthermore, the question that needs to be raised and posed to this traditional analysis is, given their nature as an important and defining presence at these public events, why have the common people been construed as marginal and wholly passive in both the city and the country?[60]

In the middle years of Elizabeth's reign, William Harrison, canon of Windsor, described the social structure of the country as it appeared to him, in his *Description of England*. He divided people into four classes: 'gentlemen, citizens or burgesses, yeomen, and artificers or labourers'.[61] Of this fourth category, who I shall call the ordinary or common people, he says that the 'fourth and last sort of people in England are the day labourers, poor husbandmen, and some retailers (which have no free land), copyholders, and all artificers, as tailors, shoemakers, carpenters, brickmakers, masons, etc.'.[62] In their commentary on the collection of documents in which Harrison's account appears, Joel Hurstfield and Alan Smith write, concerning this class:

> The fourth category of the population included the great bulk of the Queen's subjects, from respectable tradesmen and husbandmen to paupers. During good times the more prosperous members of this underprivileged mass of the people lived reasonably well, but even they seldom had any reserves to fall back on in times of trouble, and the great and growing number of paupers had no possessions at all.[63]

It is interesting that Harrison himself does not actually recognise the existence of paupers, and neither does he acknowledge the great numbers of vagrants, beggars, and discharged soldiers and sailors who were of great concern to the authorities. While Hurstfield and Smith do give some idea of the precariousness of ordinary people's lives in Elizabethan England, their definition also does not go far enough. Peter Burke's categorisation of 'ordinary Londoners' is perhaps more useful in this context:

> This large group of Londoners was of course neither socially nor culturally homogenous. It included not only shopkeepers and craftsmen (themselves divided into masters, journeymen and apprentices), but also servants, sailors, unskilled labourers, beggars and thieves; old and young, men and women, literate and illiterate.[64]

This group comprises the least wealthy of Elizabethan London, variously referred to at the time as 'the vulgar', 'the multitude', or 'the mob'.[65] For this study, this group – in all its heterogeneity – is defined as the common people, and constitutes that class or grouping of people at whom Elizabethan propaganda was aimed. This class, Harrison's identified fourth plus an unidentified fifth, were the targeted of these spectacular practices.

The basic question that arises from this movement towards the perception of the targeted subject (and which promotes the formulation of a connecting series of questions) is this: Did these attempts at regulation through spectacular display actually work? Given Foucault's belief, which has become conventional knowledge, that royal processions such as coronations and progresses functioned in the service of reconstituting sovereign power, were they successful in their aim? Were the targeted subjects, the common people, subjected? Or can the uses to which Foucault's formulations have been put be regarded as false in their very premise? Are these uses, like traditional pageant analysis, essentially partial views, ones that do not take into account the fact that the common people were unruly and unpredictable, and continued to be so despite these spectacular efforts? Did the common people remain, in fact, unimpressed? And given the New Historicism's immersion in Foucauldian notions of power relations, the same series of questions can be asked of it, regarding the belief in the effectiveness of royal entries and progresses. For with the knowledge that the British monarch was executed in 1649, it is questionable that such public events can be said to have successfully produced effective 'strategies for idealising power',[66] which enabled it to continually reconstitute itself.

The New Historicist conception of processions underwriting state/royal power bears a marked resemblance to the traditional thesis of them underwriting a shared and unproblematic notion of order.[67] This is a perception which has continued to hold sway in the most recent analyses of these events: the audience are cast in the role of passive, unthinking consumers, and are seen to be instructed/interpellated. Most of all they are, in all senses, marginal. This marginality characterises their presence, defines their material reality, and has continued to do so, in a historical process that can be said to constitute, in Benjaminian terms, a 'triumphal procession'. This being the case, there is an urgent need to re-process these early-modern discourses, to read them against the grain, in a way that can be described as adhering to Foucault's notion of genealogy, being 'an attempt to capture the exact essence of things, their purest possibilities, *their carefully protected identities*' (emphasis added).[68] Furthermore, much primary and secondary material concerning Elizabethan processions needs re-reading in the same way, to discover if 'their essence was fabricated in a piecemeal fashion from alien forms'.[69] There is little new evidence to be found that would reveal a dynamic opposed to conventional knowledge. What there is however, in those classic works on Elizabethan processions by John Nichols, E. K. Chambers and David Bergeron, as well as in the primary source material – such as eye-witness accounts, the records which survive in official sources such as the various *Calendar of State Papers* and *Acts of the Privy Council*, and the pageant literature produced for the processions – is a wealth of evidence that can be collated (for the first time), and used to present a different version of historical events.

As is evident from the preceding conceptualisation of the identified objects of analysis, a methodological model of centres and margins is of importance in this study (the defined lesser term is nothing but a position), concerned as it is with what have been considered to be the effects of representations of forms of dominant discourses (central), upon a section of the population that was/is dominated (marginal). In this, the unearthing of historically marginalised textual events is of great importance. As such, the overriding methodological concept is one of topography, the focus being upon a materially, textually and ideologically divided landscape. Within this landscape the line which divides the two groups is not always clearly definable, nor always static, which demonstrates an evident topographical instability. These theoretical issues will be examined in detail in Chapter 1 in order to clarify the approach taken in this study. Geertz's model of semiotics will be investigated, as will Foucauldian notions of dissymmetry and the spectacular, and the Althusserian formulation of interpellation/subjection. These examinations will of course suggest an ideological ambience regarding processions in general and the nature of contemporary negotiations of pageant and procession material will be investigated, considering to what extent their perceived normative effects are immersed in a pervasive modern cult of Elizabeth I, and how this cult disfigures such analysis. This will involve a detailed look at the work of both traditional analysis and that of the New Historicism, as well as more recent critical output. The philosophical and theoretical foundations of these approaches will be examined in order to determine precisely the ways in which they construct early modern English society and the function of public processions in that society. Use of primary, theoretical and original material will then demonstrate the ways in which processional analysis has been captivated by the central/dominant. The same evidence will be used in order to argue that it is likely that the common people were not, on the whole, successfully subjected by these spectacular displays.

Subsequently placed into this topographical area will be those textual materials mentioned above, materials which can be said to give a more complete analysis of the public events that were processions than could be achieved through reading of the primary documents – procession/pageant texts – alone. After examining the nature of Elizabethan entries and progresses in general, I will attempt to render the material realities of Elizabeth I's pre-coronation procession of 1558 and Victory procession of 1588 by processing the human inventory that is likely to have comprised these processions, the route they took, the materials used, and the individuals involved in their realisation. I will then attempt the same for her royal progresses, eventually concentrating on that to Sir Henry Lee's Ditchley estate in 1592. The splendid and magnificent reality of these processions will be delineated, focusing upon the ideological aim of the state to demonstrate its inviolable centrality. To contrast this, evidence will then be examined that could enable the construction of a tenable portrait of the common audience at a procession, bearing in mind that the spectacular effects of such a procession were aimed at them. Evidence of this sort is naturally scarce, as the reactions of the common people to such spectacles were very rarely processed in written form. However, it will be useful to analyse what is known about the nature and constitution of the common people at that time. Much evidence is available relating to the social and cultural conditions in which they lived, and it is possible to begin to picture the procession's audience through a reading of these records. Furthermore and importantly, I will consider records that could be said to undermine the idea that the common people were successfully interpellated by these processions, evidence that suggests that they could have been, conversely, either indifferent or in opposition to them. This material will form the substance of Chapter 2.

Chapter 3 will similarly see the investigation of the official texts produced for the pre-coronation procession and the Ditchley progress as well as that to the Earl of Leicester's estate at Kenilworth in 1575, examining the language and symbolism used, and again reviewing them from a position of their official ideological aims. I will then proceed to look at these same texts and attempt to perceive the extent to which the process of subjectification is occurring, to see if it is 'possible to trace the path which leads from the haunted work to that which haunts it'.[70] Allegory in these texts will be subjected to Walter Benjamin's dictum regarding this literary mode: 'Any person, any object, any relationship can mean absolutely anything else'.[71] Thus the allegorical displays and performances that structured these processions will be read in terms of their official meaning, as well as in ways that could be said to be alternative or, indeed, oppositional. Primary evidence will also be introduced to articulate the ways in which allegory is in many instances 'allegorised by reality'.[72] Finally, my conclusion will then bring all of these matters to bear on a specific painting of Elizabeth I on procession, enabling the perceptions reached throughout the study to be applied to a discrete and material cultural artefact.

When traditional criticism approaches Elizabethan pageants and processions, it discovers a Tillyardian dynamic characterised by the naturalness of harmony and consensus, a dynamic that is founded upon the notion of agreed order. This dynamic claims that disorder is created merely so that conventional, monarchical order can rout it and thereby strengthen itself. When the New Historicism approaches the same pageants, processions and progresses, it discovers the inescapability of state power and an artificially constructed disorder that is made to suffer defeat at the hands of conventional, monarchical power, which thereby strengthens itself. The New Historicist commitment to radical theorisation and methodology promises much in terms of radical readings, yet they essentially replicate the ideologically conservative trajectory of the older historicism. The promised radicalism does not materialise. When post-New Historicist criticism approaches these same processions, it follows the conventional practices of such analysis and simply fails to register the defining presence of the common people.

To a great extent this duplication of ideological trajectory is to be expected given that these cultural artefacts, as well as Elizabethan culture generally, are approached from a similar perspective. Traditional criticism reads dominant early modern culture as all of Elizabethan culture, and analyses all of its artefacts through the presence of the figurehead of this dominant culture, the monarch. The New Historicism articulates this same cult of authority in their obsession with the all-encompassing and determinate cultural presence of the sovereign. The older historicism prioritises the omnipresent monarch as the material reconstitution of God on earth. The New Historicism transfers Foucault's dissymmetrically resonant sovereign from the scaffold of the public execution to the street and the theatrical stage wholesale. In both instances, this sovereign is the register of all social, political, religious and cultural activity and works discursively to continually reproduce itself. Post-New Historicist criticism avoids many of the failings of the historicist schools in their recognition of conflict and disunity but, like them, fails to register and theorise the common people as important elements in these rituals. As will be demonstrated in the readings of the pageants, processions and progresses undertaken in this book, a plethora of ambiguities and discontinuities are articulated by these events, each of which needs to be taken on its own terms rather than subsumed into some greater thesis of the implicit and invisible functions of the early modern theatre-state, the hidden agenda of the pageant authors, the functionalist determination of a monolithic and unchanging power/order or as the manifestation of conflict between powerful individuals and groups.

This book sets out to demonstrate a process whereby certain identified cultural treasures have been transmitted to the present in a triumphal procession that constructs these treasures as always and un-problematically underwriting royal and state power. An attempt will be made to expose this process by regarding these treasures with cautious detachment, and reading them against the grain. This methodology is intended to enable the drawing of the critical gaze away from sovereign power and concentrate it upon the reception of these cultural events by any potential common audience.[73] This perceptible shift in the critical focus will hopefully clarify the triumphal procession in which traditional criticism, the New Historicism and procession critics writing subsequently have participated. Furthermore, this process of clarification will attempt to demonstrate the ambiguities and discontinuities that become apparent and resonant when it is seen that these forms of analysis fail to consider the main character of the common people, so spellbound are they by the spectacular presence of the sovereign and her nobles. A consideration of the common audience demonstrates the implications of the readings that continue to dominate the analysis of Elizabethan pageants and processions. In the consideration given to them here, it will become clear that, despite all claims to the contrary, 'the old brings in the new, which brings back the old'.[74] Such is the nature of the triumphal procession.

Notes

1. This is the term used by Clifford Geertz (with reference to, among other royal figureheads, Elizabeth I) in his essay on monarchical charisma, 'Centres, Kings, and Charisma: Reflections on the Symbolics of Power', *Local Knowledge* (London: Fontana, 1993) 121–46.
2. The third form, the annual Lord Mayor's Pageant, that took place every 29 October in London, demonstrates marked similarities to the royal pageants, with the Lord Mayor merely replacing the sovereign as the centre around which the procession was built. For extensive examinations of these civic pageants, see David M. Bergeron, *English Civic Pageantry 1558–1642* (London: Edward Arnold Ltd., 1971) and F. W. Fairholt, *Lord Mayors' Pageants*, 2 vols (London: Percy Society, 1843–4).
3. This is discussed in Glynne Wickham, *Early English Stages 1300–1660*, 4 vols (London: Routledge & Kegan Paul, 1959) 1:51–111.
4. Bergeron, *English Civic Pageantry* 11.
5. Ibid., 64.
6. Quoted in Alison Plowden, *Elizabethan England: Life in an Age of Adventure* (London: Reader's Digest, 1982) 53.
7. Ibid., 53.
8. *Calendar of State Papers & Manuscripts (Spanish) (1568–79)* 50–51. E. K Chambers believes that there has been a mistake in translation with regard to the location stated: '"*Vino por rio hasta Reder*"; the translation "Reading" ... is absurd; it might be Knightrider St' (*The Elizabethan Stage*, 4 vols (Oxford: Clarendon Press, 1923) 4:84). Chambers believes that the Spanish Ambassador actually accompanied the Queen to Charterhouse.
9. Plowden's book is replete with examples of a certain glossing-over of historical realities, not least in its chapter on 'The New Found Lands', where the actualities of emergent colonialism are regarded as 'adventure' rather than 'conquest' (200–233).
10. While the fact that Plowden's book is part of the 'Reader's Digest Life In Britain' series, it is precisely because of its popularity that it is worth examining. In the London Borough of Hillingdon, where I presently live, this book is held by 11 of the Borough's 17 libraries. This being the case, not only is it the most common study of the Elizabethan era, it is, in many of the smaller libraries, the only work covering that historical period (often accompanied by one biography of the Queen herself). For many people it therefore represents their sole source of information regarding this period and, presented as it is as history, is read by the public generally as a work that can give them some kind of access to the real Elizabethan era. Its very pervasiveness is therefore, I would argue, the major reason for reading it sceptically.
11. Neville Williams, *The Courts of Europe: Politics, Patronage and Royalty 1400–1800*, ed. A. G Dickens (London: Thames and Hudson, 1977) 147–67:165.
12. Zillah Dovey, *An Elizabethan Progress: The Queen's Journey into East Anglia, 1578* (Stroud: Alan Sutton Publishing Ltd, 1996) 1.
13. Christopher Haigh, *Elizabeth I*, 2nd edn (London: Longman, 1998) 156–7.
14. Louis Montrose, '"Eliza, Queene of shepheardes," and the Pastoral of Power', *English Literary Renaissance* 10.2. (Spring 1980): 153–82.
15. Jean Wilson, *Entertainments for Elizabeth I* (Woodbridge: D. S. Brewer, 1980) 143.

16. Ibid., 143.
17. Mary Hill Cole, *The Portable Queen: Elizabeth I and the Politics of Ceremony* (Amherst: University of Massachusetts Press, 1999) 24.
18. Helen Hackett, *Virgin Mother, Maiden Queen: Elizabeth I and the Cult of the Virgin Mary* (Basingstoke: Macmillan, 1995) 74–5.
19. This is clear in the painting of Elizabeth on procession (see Fig.1) and which currently hangs in Sherbourne Castle. This is also evident in a manuscript drawing of her coronation procession held in the British Library (MS 3320, Egerton, BL), where Elizabeth is shown to be surrounded by armed guards.
20. Michel Foucault, 'Nietzsche, Genealogy, History', *The Foucault Reader*, ed. Paul Rabinow (Harmondsworth: Penguin Books 1987) 76–100:78.
21. Walter Benjamin, 'Theses On The Philosophy Of History', *Illuminations*, trans. Harry Zohn, ed. and intro., Hannah Arendt (London: Fontana Press, 1992) 245–55.
22. Ibid., 248. This formulation of historical practice by Benjamin has been highly influential since the 1970s, and can be regarded as one of the founding principles of a broadly Marxist approach to investigations of the past, such as the approach to literature and history generally termed Cultural Materialism. The works of such critics as Terry Eagleton, Alan Sinfield, Jonathan Dollimore and Francis Barker, among others, all acknowledge a debt to Benjamin. See for example: Terry Eagleton, *Walter Benjamin: Towards a Revolutionary Criticism* (London: Verso, 1981); Alan Sinfield, *Faultlines: Cultural Materialism and the Politics of Dissident Reading* (Oxford: Clarendon Press, 1992); Jonathan Dollimore, *Radical Tragedy: Religion, Ideology and Power in the Drama of Shakespeare and his Contemporaries* (Brighton: Harvester, 1984); Francis Barker, *The Culture Of Violence: Essays on Tragedy and History* (Manchester: Manchester University Press, 1993).
23. Benjamin, 'Theses' 248.
24. Until the 1980s, literary criticism in general was to a great extent geared to what was perceived to be 'enduring' literature, rather than 'occasional' literature such as pageants and court masques. Some of the important studies of procession literature include the following: John Nichols, *The Progresses and Public Processions of Queen Elizabeth I*, 3 vols (1823; New York: AMS Press, 1977); Robert Withington, *English Pageantry: An Historical Outline*, 2 vols (Cambridge, Mass: Harvard University Press, 1918–20); Sydney Anglo, *Spectacle, Pageantry and Early Tudor Policy* (Oxford: Clarendon Press, 1969); David M. Bergeron, *English Civic Pageantry 1558–1642*; Jean Wilson, *Entertainments for Elizabeth I*; Roy Strong, *The Cult of Elizabeth: Elizabethan Portraiture and Pageantry* (Wallop: Thames and Hudson, 1977) and *Splendour at Court* (London: Weidenfield and Nicolson, 1973); Mary Hill Cole, *The Portable Queen: Elizabeth I and the Politics of Ceremony*. Large sections of the following are also devoted to processions: E. K. Chambers, *The Elizabethan Stage*, 1:106–48 and 4:60–130; Glynne Wickham, *Early English Stages 1300–1660*, 1:51–111 and 2:206–44. The list of critical texts dealing with Shakespeare's history plays is too long to outline here in detail, but some of the major studies include the following: E. M. W. Tillyard, *Shakespeare's History Plays* (1944; London: Chatto and Windus, 1966); Lily B. Campbell, *Shakespeare's 'Histories': Mirrors of Elizabethan Policy* (1947; London: Methuen & Co, 1977); H. A. Kelly, *Divine Providence in the England of Shakespeare's Histories* (Cambridge, Mass: Harvard University Press, 1970); John Wilders, *The Lost Garden: A View of Shakespeare's English and Roman History Plays* (Totowa, New Jersey: Rowman & Littlefield, 1978); Phyllis Rackin, *Stages of History: Shakespeare's English Chronicles* (London: Routledge, 1991); Graham Holderness, *Shakespeare Recycled: The Making of Historical Drama* (Hemel Hempstead: Harvester Wheatsheaf, 1992);

Jean E. Howard and Phyllis Rackin, *Engendering a Nation: A Feminist Account of Shakespeare's English Histories* (London: Routledge, 1997). It is also necessary to acknowledge the importance of two essays which appeared in the 1980s, Stephen Greenblatt's 'Invisible Bullets: Renaissance Authority and its Subversion, *Henry IV* and *Henry V*', and Leonard Tennenhouse's 'Strategies of State and Political Plays: *A Midsummer Night's Dream, Henry IV, Henry V, Henry VIII*', both of which are contained in Alan Sinfield and Jonathan Dollimore, eds., *Political Shakespeare: Essays in Cultural Materialism* (Manchester: Manchester University Press, 1985) 18–47 and 109–28 respectively. A plethora of single play studies also exists.

25. Andrew S Cairncross, ed., introduction, *3 Henry VI*, by William Shakespeare, The Arden Shakespeare (London: Methuen & Co, 1964) xiii–lxvi:lxvi.

26. Marion Wynne-Davies, ed., *The Renaissance: From 1500 to 1660* (London: Bloomsbury, 1992) 216.

27. Michael D. Bristol, *Carnival and Theatre: Plebeian Culture and the Structure of Authority in Renaissance England* (London: Methuen & Co. Ltd, 1985) 198.

28. I shall deal with the subject of E.M.W. Tillyard's conceptualisation of early modern society and culture in the following chapter.

29. All of the studies of Shakespeare's history plays listed above generally hold such a position. However, this position has been questioned since the early 1980s and the position of Shakespeare in our society is now a contested one. Two particular collections of essays can be regarded as the foundational texts for this questioning: John Drakakis, ed., *Alternative Shakespeares* (London: Routledge, 1985) and Alan Sinfield and Jonathan Dollimore, eds., *Political Shakespeare: Essays in Cultural Materialism*. The fact that this is a contested field is evident in the plethora of studies that take this questioning as their starting point. See for example: Ivo Kamps, ed., *Shakespeare Left and Right* (London: Routledge, Chapman & Hall, 1991); Graham Holderness, ed., *The Shakespeare Myth* (Manchester: Manchester University Press, 1988); Patricia Parker and Geoffrey Harman, eds., *Shakespeare and the Question of Theory* (London: Methuen, 1985).

30. With the exception of the works listed above, analysis of processions and processional literature has never figured as part of mainstream Renaissance criticism. This situation has altered somewhat recently, mainly due to the importance given by the New Historicism to incidents of Elizabeth parading herself in public and the effects of these royal displays. See for example: Stephen Greenblatt, *Renaissance Self-Fashioning: From More to Shakespeare* (1980; Chicago: The University of Chicago Press, 1984); Leonard Tennenhouse, *Power on Display: The Politics of Shakespeare's Genres* (London: Methuen, 1986); Stephen Orgel, *The Illusion of Power: Political Theatre in the English Renaissance* (Berkeley: University of California Press, 1975); Jonathan Goldberg, *James I and the Politics of Literature* (Baltimore: Johns Hopkins University Press, 1983). All of these studies are heavily influenced by the work of Michel Foucault, particularly his theorisation of Renaissance public display in *Discipline and Punish: The Birth of the Prison* (1975; Harmondsworth: Penguin Books, 1982).

31. The documents relating to the movements of the Court and entertainments performed in the monarch's presence are various and dispersed, and include a number of dispatches from foreign ambassadors also collected in several editions of the *Calendar of State Papers*. These accounts are too numerous to list here in their entirety, as there are records referring to many examples for most years of Elizabeth's reign. However, important examples exist in *Calendar of State Papers & Manuscripts (Spanish) (1568–69)* 50–51 and 611; *Calendar of State Papers (Venetian) (1558–80)* 12–16. Also important is Raphael Holinshed, *Holinshed's Chronicles of England,*

Scotland, and Ireland, 6 vols (London: J. Johnson, 1807) 4:159–75. It is also worth noting the many references made to processions in J. G. Nichols, ed., *The Diary of Henry Machyn, Citizen and Merchant-Taylor of London: From A.D. 1550 to A.D. 1563* (London: Camden Society, 1848). E. K. Chambers has collected together the vast majority of these documents and has formed a 'Court Calendar' for the years 1558–1616 in *The Elizabethan Stage* 4:75–130. The entertainments themselves were frequently published – often anonymously, sometimes under the name of the author – by the noble upon whose estate the entertainment was performed. See, for example, George Gascoigne, *The Princely Pleasures at the Courte at Kenelwoorth. That is to saye, The Copies of all such Verses, proses, or poetical inventions, and other Devices of Pleasure, as were there deuised, and presented by sundry Gentlemen, before the Quene's Majestie ...*, in Nichols, *Elizabeth*, 1:485–523; John Lyly, *The Complete Works of John Lyly*, ed. R. Warwick Bond, 3 vols (1902; Oxford: Clarendon Press, 1973) 1:403–504; Nichols, *Elizabeth* 2:136–78, 179–213, and 533–99.

32. Whilst the seven volumes that comprise Nichols' examination of processions (as well as the three regarding Queen Elizabeth and an additional four on the reign of James I) are exhaustive, it is worth noting that very little of the author himself comes through. Nichols rather adopts the role of compiler of the (invaluable) material he has gathered together. See also *The Progresses and Public Processions of James I*, 4 vols (1828; New York, AMS Press, 1977).

33. Wickham outlines a continuum from the Roman triumphal processions to Renaissance processions, providing interesting insights into how embedded these public events were in the relationship between sovereign/ruler and subject; see for example, 1:51–63. I shall be examining this continuity in Chapter 1. A particularly interesting aspect of Wickham's research is his study of the traditions of pageant emblems (2:206–36).

34. Withington 1:84.

35. See particularly the first two chapters of *Discipline and Punish*, in which Foucault outlines the subject/sovereign relationship that he believes characterised early modern 'spectacular' societies. I shall be dealing with Foucault's theories in the following chapter.

36. Bergeron, *English Civic Pageantry* 2.

37. Jean Wilson, *Entertainments for Elizabeth I*; Roy Strong, *The Cult of Elizabeth* and *Splendour at Court*. Each of these studies provides a conventional view of processions, and consequently adds little to Bergeron. Strong's *Splendour at Court* is, however, useful with regard to his examination of a perceived tradition of public processions.

38. This treatment has, however, been brief: see Goldberg 32–3; Greenblatt, 'Invisible Bullets', 44, and *Renaissance Self-Fashioning* 166–7; Tennenhouse, *Power on Display* 102; Montrose, '"Eliza, Queene of shepheardes"', *English Literary Renaissance* 153–82.

39. Mary Hill Cole, *The Portable Queen*. It is Cole's use of Victor Turner's cultural theories regarding the 'interplay between structure and anti-structure', which sees her mobilising New Historicist methodologies, in that she believes these theories explain the need for the progresses, as Elizabeth 'created disorder through travel and used that chaos to facilitate her ability to rule' (6). For the original theory, see Victor Turner, *The Ritual Process: Structure and Anti-structure* (Ithaca: Cornell University Press, 1969).

40. Nichols, *Elizabeth* 1:xi.

41. Haigh, *Elizabeth I* 152.

42. Williams, *The Courts of Europe* 164.

43. Dovey 1.

44. Bergeron, *English Civic Pageantry* 9.
45. Mary Hill Cole, *The Portable Queen* 1.
46. Ibid., 1.
47. Foucault's broadly functionalist definition of the nature of power in *The History of Sexuality: An Introduction* (1976; Harmondsworth: Penguin Books, 1984) can be regarded as particularly important in this latter respect: 'Power is everywhere; not because it embraces everything, but because it comes from everywhere' (93). Greenblatt himself has rarely acknowledged his debt to Foucault other than in conversational asides: 'the presence of Michel Foucault on the Berkeley campus for extended visits during the last five or six years of his life ... has helped to shape my own literary critical practice' ('Towards A Poetics Of Culture', *The New Historicism*, ed. H. Aram Veeser (London: Routledge, 1989) 1–14:1).
48. However, it is clear that Foucault's conceptualisation of power in *The History of Sexuality*, together with a Geertzian model of semiotics, beckoned such a theoretical move. Foucault's 'soft' conceptualisation of power is that which appears in *The History of Sexuality*, and contrasts importantly with his more theoretically rigorous conceptualisation in *Discipline and Punish*. Compare, for example, the quote from Foucault in the above footnote with what he says in *Discipline and Punish*: 'power is exercised rather than possessed; it is not the "privilege", acquired or preserved, of the dominant class, but the overall effect of its strategic positions – an effect that is manifested and sometimes extended by the position of those who are dominated' (26–7). While I will cover this subject in some detail in a later chapter, it is worth saying now that this formulation, in contrast to that in *The History of Sexuality*, does allow for agency, as well as effective opposition. A clear and detailed exposition of the work of Clifford Geertz, an American cultural anthropologist, will be undertaken in Chapter 1. For now, it is worth stating that Geertz has, to a great extent, been responsible for the constitution of New Historicist methodology and theoretical paradigms. It is a particular essay by Geertz, 'Thick Description: Towards An Interpretive Theory Of Culture', *The Interpretation of Cultures* (1973; London: Fontana, 1993) 3–30, that has been so influential. This essay has allowed for a New Historicist Geertzian critical output which substitutes textuality for reality and contingency for any notion of truth. For a more detailed and more compelling study of the relationship between Geertz and Greenblatt, see Francis Barker's seminal 'A Wilderness Of Tigers: *Titus Andronicus*, Anthropology and the Occlusion of Violence', *The Culture of Violence* 143–206. Various essays in the collection *The New Historicism* examine Greenblatt's indebtedness to both Geertz and Foucault: see for example, 'The Limits of Local Knowledge', by Vincent P. Pecora 243–76, and Frank Lentricchia's 'Foucault's Legacy – A New Historicism', 231–42. For a consideration of the ideological implications of Geertz's methodologies, see Edward Said's essay 'Representing the Colonised: Anthropology's Interlocutors', *Critical Inquiry* 15 (Winter 1989) 205–25.
49. Foucault, *Discipline and Punish* 48.
50. Ibid., 48–9.
51. Ibid., 57. The term 'dissymmetry' can be regarded as a convenient rubric for Foucault's 'hard' conceptualisation of power (in this book) as a relationship rather than a negative force held by one side (the dominant) and not by the other (the oppressed). Here power is exercised rather than possessed, though there is no denial that one side has the ability to exercise more than the other.
52. Ibid., 57.

53. Louis Althusser, *Essays on Ideology* (London: Verso, 1984) 46–50. For Althusser all of these terms are interchangeable, and they define the ways in which individuals subject themselves to social processes that are not in their interests.

54. See the following, for example: Susan Doran, *Monarchy and Matrimony: The Courtships of Elizabeth I* (London: Routledge, 1996); Susan Frye, *Elizabeth I: The Competition for Representation* (Oxford: Oxford University Press, 1993) and 'The Myth of Elizabeth at Tilbury', *Sixteenth Century Journal* 23 (1992) 95–114; Carole Levin, *The Heart and Stomach of a King: Elizabeth I and the Politics of Sex and Power* (Philadelphia: University of Pennsylvania Press, 1994); Julia M. Walker, ed., *Dissing Elizabeth: Negative Representations of Gloriana* (Durham & London: Duke University Press, 1998); Sandra Logan, 'Making History: The Rhetorical and Historical Occasion of Elizabeth Tudor's Coronation Entry', *The Journal of Medieval and Early Modern Studies* 31:2 (Spring 2001) 251–92; Helen Hackett, *Virgin Mother, Maiden Queen*; Philippa Berry, *Of Chastity and Power: Elizabethan Literature and the Unmarried Queen* (London: Routledge, 1989); Carole Levin, Jo Eldridge Carney and Debra Barrett-Graves, eds., *Elizabeth I: Always Her Own Woman* (Aldershot: Ashgate, 2003).

55. They are constantly referred to as such in the pamphlet produced to coincide with the pre-coronation procession, attributed to Richard Mulcaster, entitled *The Passage Of Our Most Drad Soveraigne Lady Quene Elyzabeth Through The Citie Of London To Westminster The Daye Before Her Coronation*, Nichols, *Elizabeth* 1:38–60.

56. Roy Strong is perhaps the analyst most immersed in this cult: see for example, his book *The Cult of Elizabeth*. Other examples include: Roy Strong and Julia T. Oman, *Elizabeth R* (London: Secker & Warburg, 1971); J. E. Neale, *Queen Elizabeth I* (1934; Harmondsworth: Penguin, 1971); Frances Yates, *Astraea: The Imperial Theme in the Sixteenth Century* (London and Boston: Routledge & Kegan Paul, 1975).

57. An enormous amount of work has been done on the constitution and nature of the common people in early modern England, particularly regarding London. However, it is imperative to note that most of this work has been done by historians, and not by literary or cultural critics. Furthermore, most of these studies have not been consulted, to any great extent, by literary critics. It is generally true to say that traditional Shakespearean criticism and the New Historicism use historical evidence to underline the success of Elizabeth I and her government in all areas of early modern life, and do not deal with the reality of the lives of the common people in a sustained manner. The following studies by historians are particularly relevant: V. Pearl, 'Change And Stability In Seventeenth Century London', *London Journal* 5:1 (Spring 1979) 3–34, and 'Social Policy in Early Modern London', *History and Imagination: Essays in Honour of H. R. Trevor-Roper*, eds. H. Lloyd-Jones, B. Worden and V. Pearl (London: Duckworth, 1981) 115–31; Steve Rappaport, *Worlds Within Worlds: Structures of Life in Sixteenth-Century London* (Cambridge: Cambridge University Press, 1991); Paul Slack, *Poverty and Policy in Tudor and Stuart England* (Harlow: Longman, 1988); Paul Clark and Paul Slack, introduction, *Crisis and Order in English Towns, 1500–1700: Essays In Urban History*, eds. Clark and Slack (London: Routledge & Kegan Paul, 1972) 1–55; Paul Clark and Paul Slack, *English Towns in Transition 1500–1700* (Oxford: Oxford University Press, 1976); A. L. Beier, 'Vagrants and the Social Order in Elizabethan England', *Past And Present* 64 (August 1974) 3–29, and *Masterless Men: The Vagrancy Problem in London 1560–1640* (London: Methuen, 1985); A. L. Beier and R Finlay, eds., *London, 1500–1700: The Making of the Metropolis* (Harlow: Longman, 1986); Ian W Archer, *The Pursuit of Stability: Social Relations in Elizabethan London* (Cambridge: Cambridge University Press, 1991); Martin Holmes, *Elizabethan London* (London: Cassell, 1969).

58. In *The Culture of Violence* (201–2), Francis Barker shows that such discipline took the form of actual physical violence, as well as representations of power. That is, representations of power, whether cultural or social, were part of a greater system of domination. They were not the overriding part of that system, as is claimed by the New Historicism.
59. And indeed, as Barker points out, exterminate them (*The Culture of Violence* 202).
60. The common audience is given very little presence in both traditional and New Historicist procession analysis.
61. William Harrison, *A Description of England*, reproduced (in part) in *Elizabethan People: State and Society*, eds. J. Hurstfield & A.G.R. Smith (London: Edward Arnold, 1972) 18.
62. Ibid., 18.
63. Hurstfield and Smith, introduction, *Elizabethan People*, 2–8:2.
64. Peter Burke, 'Popular Culture in Seventeenth Century London', *London Journal* 3.2. (November 1977) 143–62:143.
65. Ibid., 143.
66. Tennenhouse, 'Strategies Of State' 125.
67. See E. M. W. Tillyard, *Shakespeare's History Plays* and *The Elizabethan World Picture*.
68. Michel Foucault, 'Nietzsche' 78.
69. Foucault, 'Nietzsche' 78.
70. Pierre Macherey, *A Theory of Literary Production* (1978; London: Routledge & Kegan Paul, 1989) 94.
71. Walter Benjamin, *The Origin Of German Tragic Drama*, trans. John Osborne, intro. George Steiner (1977; London: Verso, 1990) 175.
72. This statement appears in Julian Roberts, *Walter Benjamin* (London: Macmillan, 1982) 150. Roberts is paraphrasing Benjamin's conclusions regarding the nature of allegory in *The Origin of German Tragic Drama* 232–3.
73. Another study which reads early modern cultural events through the (in this case female) audience is Stephen Orgel, *Impersonations* (Cambridge: Cambridge University Press, 1996).
74. Phillipe Ivornel, 'Paris, Capital of the Popular Front or the Posthumous Life of the 19th Century', *New German Critique* 39 (Fall 1986) 61–84:75.

Chapter 1

Theorising Processions

In his influential essay on Elizabethan progresses, '"Eliza, Queene of shepheardes", and the Pastoral of Power', the New Historicist critic, Louis Montrose, states that the Renaissance pastoral form (which included the progress entertainments), was a 'symbolic mediation of social relationships … [which] are, intrinsically, relationships of power'.[1] He regards this cultural exchange as a very knowing one, claiming that the 'repertoire of pastoral form … was exploited and elaborated by Elizabethan poets and politicians, by sycophants and ideologues, by the Queen herself' (153). While he acknowledges the possibility of tensions between different groups within Elizabethan society, Montrose perceives the celebratory presence of the common people in this pastoral territory, outlining the ideological constitution of this pastoral landscape:

> in a context in which the commons were actually present … pageants … might fortify loyalty toward the crown among those whose relationship to the landlords … was one of endemic suspicion or resentment …. Thus the pastoral pageants … might affirm a benign relationship of mutual interest between the Queen and the lowly, between the Queen and the great, and among them all (179).

In this playing off of one class against another in such a way, Montrose seems to be claiming that the progress entertainments in fact secured and maintained order through the mystification of social relationships. Furthermore, this mystification is regarded as having achieved its aims, in the sense that Montrose regards the progress entertainments as having suitably impressed the common people. Thus he can state that the pageant entertainments functioned 'to transcend socio-economic stratification in "a beautiful relation between rich and poor"' (179).

While this may seem to be an attempt at interpreting such rituals from the perspective of the common people, a closer inspection of Montrose's methodology demonstrates certain problems with such a view. For, in order to enable the inclusion of the entire population in his equation (a crucial factor in the construction of his thesis), Montrose must find an example of the uninhibited celebration of these events by the common people. The example he finds is precisely that which opened this book, the report of the Spanish ambassador of 1568, a report that has been the subject of misrepresentation throughout history.[2] It may be recalled that analyses of Elizabethan progresses to date have failed to reproduce the initial two sentences of the Ambassador's report in which the popularity of Elizabeth is questioned, proceeding rather to merely reproduce that part of the document that shows the common people unambiguously celebrating the Queen. This has seen these studies endlessly reproduce such evidence as the following: 'She was received everywhere with great acclamations and signs of joy, as is customary ...'.[3] These same studies have failed to reproduce other evidence that immediately precedes these sentences: 'her progress ... will only be in the neighbourhood, as she is careful to keep near at hand when troubles and disturbances exist ...'.[4] Montrose fails to reproduce these opening two sentences, enabling him to build his thesis upon a perception of the monolithic and celebratory presence of the common people. This presence is included in what Montrose regards as the demonstration of unbridled celebration of the monarch by the entire population, and thus to his wider thesis concerning both progresses and pastoral in general.

This short examination of Montrose's theoretical trajectory helps to construct two very important areas of investigation for this book. First, it outlines the kind of conclusions reached in critical analyses of Elizabethan progresses that have been undertaken to date. Montrose's analysis is entirely in line with the tradition of progress and pageant criticism in finding the entertainments performed, as well as the material procession itself, to be successful celebrations of the Queen and of the dominant culture. Second, when the presence of the common people is included in analysis – which is rare – then they are found to be successfully interpellated by these rituals, successfully won over in 'a beautiful relation between rich and poor'. In this chapter I will attempt, by looking at traditional and New Historicist studies, as well as at more recent criticism, to deal at length with the nature and repercussions of previous analyses of Elizabethan processions and demonstrate their methodological and ideological trajectories. Considering each of these critical approaches in turn, and at length, will allow for a theoretical space to be cleared, into which the approach taken by this study will be inserted. This approach is based in an attempt to deal with the second problem outlined above when considering the Montrose essay, namely the perceived success of these rituals as propaganda, their success in cementing what he calls 'a bond of reciprocal devotion and charity between lowly subjects and sovereign' (180). Clearly then, there is a sense in which a topographical shift can be perceived in writing about historical events through the experience of the common people. My desire here is to re-figure Elizabethan processions so that the common people concerned in their realisation become more central than has been previously theorised. My aim is to question this marginalisation of the common people, positing that such a marginalisation represents a material realisation of Walter Benjamin's theorisation of 'triumphal processions'.

Marginality as a concept has to a great extent been a most important focus of twentieth century theory, not least because of the discovery of the human body as the proposed site of transcendental meaning.[5] More specifically, it is rooted in the revelations of Freud, and his naming of the unconscious. The unconscious clearly relates to any marginal presence, being that entity by which the central defines itself, that Other which is not the centre's binary opposite but is rather the very condition upon which that centre is based. This marginal presence is an Otherness that defines a boundary that has been manipulated in order to form a threshold of transgression. It is the boundary that marks a meeting of conscious/unconscious, Subject/Other, light/dark, order/chaos, centre/margin. It is, for this study, the boundary between the targets of public spectacle – the common people – and the elite group in Elizabethan society who felt this larger group needed to be constantly interpellated. Furthermore, it is the boundary between an over-determined and hidden history, as it marks the site where traditional procession analysis has always become silent or, alternatively, over-emphatic.

The naming of the unconscious in a literary context naturally suggests the work of the French critic Pierre Macherey, particularly *A Theory of Literary Production*.[6] For Macherey, and in opposition to both traditional literary criticism and more modern approaches such as the New Historicism, the task of the critic is not to seek unity in any cultural artefact, as this is an illusory task. The task of the critic is rather the determination of a 'conflict of meaning', a conflict which 'reveals the inscription of an otherness in the work, through which it maintains a relationship with that which it is not, that which happens at its margins' (79). Despite what the author might want to say consciously, any text is full of contradictions, silences and absences that emanate from the unconscious of both author and the society in which they write – only certain things are allowed to be said, and only in certain ways – and this reality denies the possibility of any work existing as a unified, unproblematic whole. Any work is suffused with latent meaning, and 'the latent is not another meaning which ultimately and miraculously *dispels* the first (manifest) meaning', for 'meaning is in the *relation* between the implicit and the explicit' (87). Macherey clarifies the nature of this relationship: 'the explicit requires the implicit: for in order to say anything, there are other things *which must not be said*' (85). While this naturally beckons the work of Freud, Macherey immerses his own study in the presence of ideology. Terry Eagleton, reading Macherey, is thus able to write the following:

> The text is, as it were, ideologically forbidden to say certain things; in trying to tell the truth in his own way, for example, the author finds himself forced to reveal the limits of the ideology within which he writes. He is forced to reveal its gaps and silences, what it is unable to articulate.[7]

For Macherey, the critic's task is to reveal these absences, these silences, and then to proceed in making them speak in order to reveal an ideological conflict.[8]

The desire to 'show a sort of splitting within the work' where 'this division is *its* unconscious' (94), can be regarded as pre-empting much of the work of Jacques Derrida, who has not only demonstrated the illusory nature of first principles, but also the fact that the first principles which we delude ourselves into believing do exist, and upon which we have built our thought/knowledge systems, are founded as much upon what they are not as upon what we consider them to consist of/in.[9] They are, according to him, always shot through with the traces of what they have excluded, and indeed define themselves by that excluded opposite. Thus any one thing's identity is determined as much by what it is not as what it is, and is also traced with past and future identities of that thing.[10] Thus, outside is as much not-inside as it is outside, and the term itself has shifting, multiple meaning(s) determined by both its historical and potential uses. In the text itself therefore, we see a constant flickering of meaning, a surplus that resembles Macherey's absences, a differing and deferring that mirrors his notion of the effects of the unconscious. We can detect a constant movement across the frontier that marks the division, a continual return of the repressed. Thus, if a certain procession/pageant is studied, no inherent unity would be found there unless one were willed into existence, and which would however remain founded upon a false premise. For, according to Macherey, in the work would be discovered that division, that unconscious 'which is history, the play of history beyond its edges, encroaching on those edges ...' (94).[11]

It is interesting that twentieth-century theory has been so involved with such notions of de-centredness, and interesting too that much of it is expressed in terms of the spatial, in terms that suggest a topography.[12] This is clarified by Toril Moi in her study of the important theoretical works of the French critics Hélène Cixous, Luce Irigaray and Julia Kristeva, and is useful in this context. Moi formulates the existence of what is a theoretically demarcated landscape, a geography that prioritises centres and margins as representative and constitutive of a divided symbolic order. She writes:

> If, as Cixous and Irigaray have shown, femininity is defined as lack, negativity, absence of meaning, irrationality, chaos, darkness – in short, as non-Being – Kristeva's emphasis on marginality allows us to view this repression of the feminine in terms of *positionality* rather than of essences.[13]

Such a theorisation is important for this current study, if we substitute the common people here for feminine/femininity as the lesser term. The dominant symbolic order defines the common people as this darkness and chaos, and positions them on the margins of order, construing 'them as the *limit* or borderline of that order' (167). They become the frontier between order and chaos, and 'because of their very marginality they will also always seem to recede into and merge with the chaos of the outside' (167).[14] When the common people are therefore seen as the limit of the symbolic order, they can be regarded as both inside and outside or as neither inside nor outside. This allows them to be either vilified as representing this darkness and chaos, or alternatively elevated as pure and innocent. Moi makes precisely this point when she says that in 'the first instance the borderline is seen as part of the chaotic wilderness outside, and in the second it is seen as an inherent part of the inside: the part that protects and shields the symbolic order from the imaginary chaos' (167).

This is clearly demonstrable in terms of Elizabethan England where, depending upon circumstances, the common people were dismissed as 'the rabble', 'the mob' or 'the multitude', or were venerated as the sovereign's 'most loving People'.[15] And if we allow for the fact that, as the mob or the rabble, the common people are 'lack, negativity, absence of being, chaos and darkness', then definition (in terms of who is allowed to define) is the important term. The common people are defined as such by that group who deem themselves to be not these things – that is, plenitude, positivity, being, rationality, order and light. These are the dominant groups in society, whether they are those who constituted the material centre of Elizabethan processions, or those who have subsequently defined these processions as being examples of all these positive terms.

The methodology that will be pursued in this study then is one that seeks to explain certain identified absences and omissions. Such an approach attempts to indicate lapses and occlusions in traditional criticism while at the same time displaying ways in which these lapses function in a wider social sense, which will necessarily work towards conclusions regarding both that critical practice and the object of its gaze (the processions) that question their theoretical trajectories.[16] However, it is important to emphasise that any critical practice that admits to its profoundly ideological nature is no more or less ideological in itself than a practice that either does not admit any ideological implications or that, alternatively, attempts to by-pass ideology altogether. A critical practice that seeks to be entirely formalist, for example, will produce readings of texts every bit as ideologically resonant as one that adheres itself to a defined political commitment, the difference being merely that the ideological orientation of the former is implicit, while that of the latter is explicit. Traditional criticism, in its identification of the naturalness of consensus and harmony in Elizabethan processions as well as, generally, in Elizabethan society, will be seen to produce certain (implicit) ideological projections, ones that adhere to notions of order which effectively allow its opposite, disorder, no ontological status.[17] In this conception, disorder is a floating signifier, constructed merely to be denied by its opposite term and thus strengthen an identified pervasive order. Furthermore, even if a critical practice does indeed acknowledge its ideological nature, the repercussions of its readings are not guaranteed to be what they claim to be. Thus while many New Historicist critics would regard themselves as being politically 'on the left', a certain critical projection can be identified in their practice whereby any commitment to a radical (or even liberal) politics is subsumed by a greater commitment to a radical textualism. They therefore find themselves pushing back all kinds of boundaries in formalist and theoretical terms, while producing readings that have ideological repercussions every bit as conservative as those of the practice they in fact wished to displace, the older form of historicism.[18]

Examining, in what follows, the ways in which the various critical approaches theorise Elizabethan processions, demonstrates their location in an ideologically demarcated landscape. After briefly investigating the ways in which traditional criticism theorises these cultural practices, I will show, in an extended analysis of its practice how the New Historicism, as the most significant and influential modern school of criticism in Renaissance studies, deals specifically with Elizabethan processions. Initially an attempt will be made to detect the sources of the New Historicism's methodological landscape, in order to understand their semiotic reading of culture. By examining the ways in which this school of criticism reads Elizabethan processions, their emphasis on the success of spectacular display through Elizabeth's embodiment of dissymmetry will be seen to be central to their analysis. I will then immerse these findings in an oppositional theoretical landscape, drawing out the ideological implications of the New

Historicist project. This immersion will suggest ways of reading these same events and practices that could be said to emphasise a more historical approach, while at the same time clarifying certain lacks in New Historicist analyses. Such an examination will attempt to display that New Historicism clearly takes up a position in culture's triumphal processions, and shows the ways in which it is the ideological inheritor of traditional criticism rather than its nemesis.

The strength and longevity of the New Historicism, as well as its centrality in studies of Elizabethan processions, is evidenced by the fact that the latest comprehensive study of these cultural events, Mary Hill Cole's *The Portable Queen: Elizabeth I and the Politics of Ceremony*, is one that positions itself within the ideological ambit of this school of criticism. Despite claims that the New Historicism is no longer alive as an identifiable critical practice in Renaissance studies generally, it is important to accept that, in the case of procession analysis, this is evidently not so. New Historicism is therefore analysed in this current study as an existent critical tradition, continuing to produce work of central importance in the field of Elizabeth processions. The diffuse studies of processions that could generally be said to have appeared since the highpoint of New Historicism in the 1980s and 1990s, yet are not identifiably of that school, will also be briefly addressed in what follows. A short review of these studies will demonstrate the ways in which these critics reproduce the views of the previous analyses of processions in their almost total disregard for the targets of spectacular display, the common people.

'The collective mind'

The vast majority of existing critical works on processions are demonstrably similar in their conception of Elizabethan England, a conception that consists of an agreed order and hierarchy throughout most of the reign. These analyses perceive the existence of a rigid social order based on an identifiable structural unity. Just such a social structure was theorised in 1943 by E. M. W. Tillyard in his important study, *The Elizabethan World Picture*, where his reading of the literature of the period allowed him to declare that in the Elizabethan age, 'the conception of order is so taken for granted, so much part of the collective mind of the people, that it is hardly mentioned except in explicitly didactic passages'.[19] Tillyard's construction of monolithic concepts such as 'the collective mind' and 'the people' bears the weight of a very definite ideological burden, one that originates in a conception of both culture and society which replicates that of the dominant forces in that society. Tillyard reads the literary output of the (in number very small) educated class in Elizabethan England, and not only regards it as reflecting and determining the values of the entire population, but takes this literature, including panegyric, at its word. For him, these works reflect an entire reality.

Tillyard grounds his conception of the social order in what he identifies as a Renaissance belief in cosmic order, one which governed all natural phenomena, including human institutions. This order is, he believes, most apparent in the overwhelming presence of disorder in Renaissance culture as a whole and in

Shakespeare's history plays specifically. Generally, he perceives a disorder with little or no ontological status being produced or dramatised merely so it can be routed by a given, reconstituted order. Such a thesis naturally beckons the much later New Historicist work of Stephen Greenblatt, particularly his essay, 'Invisible Bullets: Renaissance Authority and its Subversion, *Henry IV* and *Henry V*',[20] whereby subversion is summoned by state power in order to contain it and thus strengthen itself. The model of order that Tillyard conceives is also the same one taken to be displayed in traditional analyses of Elizabethan state processions, a model conceived of by the dominant forces in Elizabethan society and which defines their ideal social structure based upon an imaginary notion of (real) consensus. In this sense, Tillyard's notion of ideal order is what Richard Wilson calls a 'Platonised image of Elizabethan culture',[21] one that, as in a state procession, positively regarded an idealised hierarchy. Moreover, it is one that perceived the naturalness of such a hierarchy in the consciousness of every member of the Elizabethan population. As Jonathan Dollimore says, Tillyard regarded this 'metaphysic of order' as a consolidating force, and as 'socially cohesive in the positive sense of transcending sectional interests and articulating a genuinely shared culture and cosmology, characterised by harmony, stability and unity.'[22] This conception of harmony was based on readings of the cultural artefacts produced by the dominant sections of society, and instilled a belief in the real existence of the hierarchy valorised by them. As in processions, in this hierarchy the Queen (after God) was the centre of meaning itself, through the court, the state machinery, and then into the realms of the common people whose values were assumed and imagined to be those of the dominant. With the sovereign as the resplendent centre of meaning, the common people are seen to exist on the edges of meaning(lessness) itself, though convinced of the naturalness of their marginalised position.

This construction of the common people as being overwhelmed by and passive in the face of the naturalness of a hierarchical system of which they formed the base is a familiar one in the works of processional literature, both in the original documents and in those later analyses that utilise such original artefacts. In the processional document produced for Elizabeth, *The Passage Of Our Most Drad Soveraigne Lady Quene Elyzabeth Through The Citie Of London To Westminster The Daye Before Her Coronacion*,[23] commissioned by the London Corporation and attributed to Richard Mulcaster, we constantly read of the Queen's 'most loving subjects', and their unstinting adulation as she progressed through the city. Holinshed reproduces this tract and its delineation of the responses of the common audience word for word in his 1577 *Chronicle*,[24] while John Nichols, in also reproducing the pamphlet, writes that the common people were indeed passive consumers of the spectacle because a 'superstitious awe of Majesty produced unmanly adulation and servile attentions'.[25] Such behaviour had many reasons according to procession analysts however, not merely superstition. R. Malcolm Smuts believes that an 'ordinary Londoner who witnessed a royal entry would ... be forcefully reminded of his subordination to a massive, multi-layered system of authority ...',[26] while David Birt believes that 'such spectacles ... helped increase in onlookers a sense of the wealth, power and glory of the monarch – providing a

focus of national unity among Englishmen ...'.[27] Continuing in this vein, Jean
Wilson states that the common people were won over by their need for
reassurance, as for 'the Queen to be entertained by a town assured the townspeople
of their own importance'.[28] In such analyses, the progresses and processions are
thus seen as microcosms of Elizabethan society itself, in the sense that, as Alice S.
Venezky writes, '... the common denominator of all the entertainments – offerings
of the towns visited on progress, the shows presented by the country people and the
pageants displayed in London – was the earnest desire of the people themselves to
demonstrate their good will toward the honoured sovereign'.[29] This desire to
please, according to Roy Strong, came from the wish to gratify an all-knowing
Queen: 'The Elizabethan monarchy, by dodging and leaving unanswered many
crucial issues, by exploiting ... a remarkable woman, was able to cut across this
fundamental divisiveness and find in the Crown an ambiguous symbol which held
the hearts and minds of all its peoples'.[30]

Generally, the orientation of such work can be seen in the analysis of Alison
Plowden's construction of Elizabeth I on progress with which this book began. Put
simply, this kind of work can be seen to be immersed in a view of culture and
society from above. Discourses such as Plowden's are part of the *Weltanschauung*
that goes to comprise the views of the dominant forces within society, forces which
valorise order, unity, and stability, and underwrite the notion that such order is the
natural condition of any society. Hence the marginalisation of any perceived forces
of common disorder or anxiety. The emergence of the New Historicism was hailed
as a break with such a monolithic conception of society, steeped as it claimed it
was, in the post-modern perception of disruption and disintegration. However, an
examination of New Historicist analysis that deals with Elizabethan processions
demonstrates their tendency to reproduce instead the model of power conceived by
Tillyard at his time of writing in the 1940s.

'Royal glory and theatrical violence'

In their wide-ranging perusal of Renaissance experiences and events in search of
'texts' with which to identify a certain 'circulation' of cultural 'energy' that allows
for the 'negotiation' of literary texts, New Historicist critics regard the royal entry
and rural progress as spectacular events that successfully interpellated the
Elizabethan population through magnificent display.[31] In this context, the figure of
Queen Elizabeth, as the embodiment of Renaissance power, is a fascinating one for
this school of criticism, a leader who according to Stephen Greenblatt harnessed
the power of myth itself in order to rule her realm absolutely. In his essay 'To
Fashion A Gentleman: Spenser And The Destruction Of The Bower Of Bliss',
Greenblatt writes that 'Elizabeth's exercise of power was closely bound up with
her use of fictions', that she 'believed deeply ... in display, ceremony, and
decorum, the whole theatrical apparatus of royal power', and that she regarded 'her
identity as at least in part a *persona ficta* and her world as a theatre'.[32] Leonard
Tennenhouse believes that 'Elizabeth Tudor knew the power of display',[33] and did
so in 'a system where the power of the monarch was immanent in the official

symbols of the state' (105). In the same vein, Mary Hill Cole states that the progresses Elizabeth undertook 'were an important part of her efforts to fashion a public image'.[34] Tennenhouse and Cole would no doubt agree with Greenblatt when he suggests, in his seminal *Renaissance Self-Fashioning*, that Elizabeth was one of a 'handful of arresting figures' (31) who demonstrate the process of self-fashioning in the Renaissance, realising, as Thomas More did about himself, that personality was to a great extent 'a narrative fiction' (6). Consequently, according to Greenblatt, Elizabeth's 'whole public character was formed very early, then to be played and replayed with few changes for the next forty years' (167) much like, one assumes, a character or actor in the theatre. Indeed, he believes that 'kingship always involves fictions, theatricalism' (167). He attributes to Elizabeth a belief in the determining power of the dramatic, as even her 'ordinary public appearances were theatrically impressive' (166), and in his essay 'Invisible Bullets', goes as far as to regard her as 'a ruler whose power is constituted in theatrical celebrations of royal glory and theatrical violence visited upon the enemies of that glory' (44). The force of the dramatic is thus seen to be determining, as Greenblatt believes that it was indeed in the symbolic that Elizabeth's real power lay rather than in material institutions, stating that she was 'a ruler without a standing army, without a highly developed bureaucracy, without an effective police force ...' (44). As such, Greenblatt believes that her power lay entirely in persuasive symbolism, reliant 'upon its privileged visibility' for, just as 'in a theatre, the audience must be powerfully engaged by this visible presence ...' (44). According to Greenblatt, this 'privileged visibility' was manifested in precisely those royal processions and state pageants that form the subject of this current study, as well as in the body (politic) of the Queen herself.

Greenblatt's is a paradigmatically post-modern methodology in which previously discrete cultural and social practices are collapsed together, with spectacular processions being placed in a context of equivalence with the (similarly spectacular) Renaissance theatre, as well as the spectacular public execution. He believes that 'Royal power is manifested to its subjects as in a theatre, and the subjects are at once absorbed by the instructive, delightful, or terrible spectacles ...' (44). While this construction of the subjects of royal power being instructed recalls Tillyard,[35] it is in the naming of the 'terrible spectacles' that we find reference to the public execution, and in the 'delightful' that we find reference to the royal procession.

In terms of the nature of the New Historicist conception of the Renaissance theatre as an institution of power, its theorised equivalence to these other state institutions is necessarily important. However, it is interesting to find that, with the exception of Mary Hill Cole, this school of criticism has in fact very little to say with regard to Elizabethan processions. Though these practices are regarded as successful in normative terms, very few New Historicist critics have actually written about them at length. One major reason for this fact is that it is rather the person of Elizabeth herself in these processions, as the personification of Renaissance power that has become the object of the New Historicist gaze. This comes as no surprise perhaps in a practice for which (monolithic) power is such an important concept. For the New Historicists, Elizabeth I is the prime example of

normative and successful royal power, Greenblatt referring to her as 'the sole
legitimate possessor of absolute charismatic authority'.[36] Similarly, in the context
of royal progresses, Louis Montrose believes that their success was due to the
'charisma of Queen Elizabeth', figured in her ability to play the role that each
section of society wanted her to represent.[37] And R. Malcolm Smuts examines
royal processions in terms of Elizabeth's 'charismatic authority', pondering
whether the decline of the royal entry itself under the Stuarts was due to their lack
of such authority, which worked to 'weaken the royal charisma'.[38] The use of
'charisma' and 'charismatic authority' by these critics is important, as these terms
are regarded as articulating the nature of Elizabethan power, embodied in the
monarch, and realised through symbolic display. Although unacknowledged by
Montrose and Greenblatt, this conception of charisma stems (as does much else in
their work) from the writings of Clifford Geertz. Charisma is one aspect of
Geertz's semiotic conception of culture that has, to a great extent, been the
conception that New Historicism has taken up and used in its analysis of early
modern culture. It is worth investigating Geertz's conception, as in it lies the
implications such a semiotic definition of culture has, particularly with regard to
the conclusions reached in New Historicist discussions of Elizabethan processions.

While the work of Michel Foucault could be said to have fixed and situated the
New Historicist approach to the type of culture that existed in the early modern
period in England,[39] it is Geertz, an American cultural anthropologist, who has
been responsible for the constitution of the New Historicist methodology and
theoretical paradigms in terms of a general cultural analysis.[40] Geertz believes in a
semiotic conception of culture, stating 'that man is an animal suspended in webs of
significance he himself has spun, I take culture to be those webs'.[41] According to
this conceptualisation, reality is always grasped metaphorically, some thing always
symbolising or signifying something else. As such, experience itself is regarded as
existing in the realms of representation, a formulation which allows all cultural
events to be construed as texts to be read. The synecdochic interpretive models
Geertz establishes from this conceptualisation typify the work of the New
Historicists, who follow his perception of culture as consisting of purely symbolic
action in which 'both particular cultures and the observers of these cultures are
inevitably drawn to a metaphorical grasp of reality ...'.[42]

The defining influence of Geertz is supported by the fact that the New
Historicists have sought specific theoretical inspiration from him, the earlier
mentioned concept of charisma being a case in point. The uses to which this
concept is put enable Greenblatt, Smuts and Montrose to discover the material
realisation of power through official symbolism, and to perceive the dynamic of a
successfully interpellative cultural practice. The theme of Geertz's essay on the
subject of processions, 'Centres, Kings, and Charisma: Reflections on the
Symbolics of Power',[43] is typical of these general interests, concerned as it is with
'the symbolic construction of authority'.[44] His central interest (charisma), is taken
from Max Weber's theorisation of authority in his *Wirtschaft und Gesellschaft*, and
is applied to certain identified absolute monarchs, Elizabeth I being among them.[45]
In the introduction to his essay, Geertz informs us that charisma is a term that

originated in Christian theology and referred to the 'God-given capacity to perform miracles', and was later adapted by Weber 'as a label for the I-Am-The-Man type of leadership ...' (13). Geertz uses this as a basis for a semiotic reading of early modern society whereby, in her pre-coronation procession, Elizabeth I acts as the inscription of the 'connection between the symbolic value individuals possess and their relation to the active centres of the social order' (122). This is an important focus for Geertz's subsequent cultural semiotics, as he believes that these centres are 'essentially concentrated loci of serious acts' (122). It is these 'serious acts', cultural productions such as progresses and royal entries that represent and maintain authority in a society. In this context, Geertz writes that 'At the political centre of any complexly organised society ... there is both a governing elite and a set of symbolic forms expressing the fact that it is in truth governing' (124). These symbolic forms are all important for Geertz, for this governing elite 'justify their existence and order their actions in terms of a collection of stories, ceremonies, insignia, formalities ...' (124). These forms underpin what Geertz calls the 'inherent sacredness of sovereign power' (123), as well as ensuring the legitimacy of such power: 'It is ... crowns and coronations ... that mark the centre as centre and give what goes on there its aura of being not merely important but in some odd fashion connected with the way the world is built' (124). Geertz regards the royal entry and progress generally, and the pre-coronation procession specifically in this manner, as part of a number of symbolic actions which 'locate the society's centre and affirm its connection with transcendent things ...' (125).

It is clear that in his immersion in semiotics, Geertz lacks any theorisation of the operation of coercion in the process of authority maintaining itself in Elizabethan England, as well as maintaining an obvious belief in the success of these symbolic actions. According to Geertz, power not only manifests itself through ritual and symbol; it maintains itself through them also. Such a belief is clear in his theorisation of Elizabethan power as it manifested itself in her pre-coronation procession:

> Elizabeth was Chastity, Wisdom, Peace, Perfect Beauty, and Pure Religion as well as queen ... and being queen she was these things. Her whole public life ... was transformed into a kind of philosophical masque in which everything stood for some vast idea and nothing took place unburdened with parable (129).

This echoes Greenblatt's belief, expressed in *Renaissance Self-Fashioning*, that in 'the official spectacles and pageants, everything was calculated to enhance her transformation into an almost magical being, a creature of infinite beauty, wisdom and power' (167). And while such perceptions do not contravene either theorist's insistence on the power of representations, they clearly articulate their immersion in an adherence to what Geertz terms 'the inherent sacredness of central authority' (146). In other words, it would seem that Geertz's theorisation of the charisma of Elizabeth I, used significantly by the New Historicism, is none other than an alternative term for the cult of Elizabeth as it exists in traditional and present day analyses of her as a Platonic heroine.[46] Such analyses include those of her public processions.

This immersion in the belief in Elizabeth as the carrier of charismatic authority defines the work of Geertz. For around the notion of charismatic authority Geertz builds his semiotic conceptualisation of Elizabethan power, believing that such power was sustained and strengthened by symbolic forms alone. The idea that Geertz is seduced by the notion of the exceptional personality of the charismatic leader as it relates to Elizabeth I would seem to bear more than a little truth. For in his reading of the pre-coronation procession, and of Elizabethan processions in general, Geertz regards Elizabeth as one who ruled due to the stories that she told her audience regarding the legitimacy of her rule. She transmitted these stories through the idiom of allegory, Geertz stating that it 'was allegory that lent her magic, and allegory repeated that sustained it' (129). Such a formulation not only remains blind to any potential alternative readings of the audiences' reactions, it also reads allegory generally as successfully conveying its desired and monolithic message. Furthermore, it regards Elizabethan society as unified and stable, and this due to the success of allegory's ability to transmit this desired monolithic meaning. Finally, it regards Elizabeth herself as a stable entity, and representations of her as wholly and universally successful in the portrayal of her in positive terms. In the following chapters I will demonstrate the questionable nature of each of the above assertions.[47] Despite their problematic status, however, each of these assertions has been adopted by the New Historicism.

The most concise transferral of Geertz's theory of the symbolics of power to Elizabethan society is that made by Greenblatt. In his statement that in Elizabethan England 'power is constituted in theatrical celebrations of royal glory', Greenblatt is referring to both the public theatre and processions/pageants. He is stating that Elizabethan power was constituted by/in symbolic forms alone, a formulation that again lacks any notion of a theory of coercion or force. Of the New Historicists, Greenblatt is not alone in such a theorisation of the nature of power, nor is he alone in relying upon Geertz to supply the dynamic for such a formulation. In his *James I and the Politics of Literature*, Jonathan Goldberg examines the royal entries of both Elizabeth and James through a use of Geertz's work.[48] Goldberg theorises these processions in terms of 'the symbolic dimensions of state power', which are, he continues, 'real forces' (33). This theorisation of the symbolic nature of real power enables Goldberg to state that power itself 'is not brute force' (33). Thus, any notion of a coercive conception of power 'is just that – a conception of power, not a natural fact nor inherent to it' (33). Leonard Tennenhouse's delineation of power is similar, stating that Elizabethan society was in the thrall of Elizabeth's symbolic body, the display of this symbolic body being 'so essential to maintaining the power of the state', that Elizabeth needed to undertake progresses and processions as her body was identified 'with English power in all its manifestations'.[49] Mary Hill Cole makes precisely this connection when stating that in 'displaying her image as queen around the southern part of England, she worked to validate the social and political hierarchies while shaping and protecting her established church'.[50]

In one defining sense, the ideological problems of each of these New Historicist critics are located in an evident lack or partiality. The point which they constantly stress, that power is manifested in symbolic display, is not a controversial (nor indeed particularly profound) one. What is controversial, and ideologically problematic, is their belief that power is delineated and maintained by symbolic display *alone*. It is the pervasive failure to theorise coercion, or indeed to acknowledge the use and importance of force at all that jeopardises their theoretical trajectories. Moreover, it is their parallel belief in the success of these displays in achieving their ideological aims that further problematises these trajectories. I shall return to the problematic nature of the implications of this immersion in a semiotic notion of culture presently. Before doing so, I wish to examine this notion of dissymmetrical success. The New Historicist readings of processions have regarded them as symbolic manifestations of power which were wholly successful (from that dominant culture's point of view), by using the work of the French theorist, Michel Foucault. It is worth looking at this work in more detail.

Foucault's theorisation of the perceived equivalence of the royal entry and the public execution in spectacular terms, both displaying and re-enacting the dissymmetry of power in early modern society, has been influential in the study of this period. Foucault believes that the 'public execution ... belongs to a whole series of great rituals in which power is eclipsed and restored (coronation, entry of king into a conquered city ...)'.[51] He perceives the ritual of brutal, public torture to be a manifestation of the rule of the sovereign, as a stark display of the arbitrary power that they could wield over subjects who have in some way disturbed or transgressed upon the limits of that power. This ritual of spectacular punishment signalled to the population the nature and extent of the sovereign power, and acted as a regulatory device in the reassertion of sovereignty itself. Foucault theorises that this practice of 'exquisite torture' in fact can be said to characterise early modern society, in the sense that political intervention in everyday life was infrequent but dramatic. According to this theorisation, Foucault believes that the royal procession represents such a political intervention, one that also attempted to function as such a regulatory device. New Historicists agree with this formulation, Greenblatt stating that the 'idea of the "notable spectacle", the "theatre of God's judgements", extended quite naturally to ... homilies and hangings, royal progresses and rote learning'.[52] Following Foucault, the New Historicists see the necessity for the visibility of power use, the theatricality of the spectacle (whether execution or procession), being used to coerce the population. Where Foucault and the New Historicism differ, however, is in their perception of the effectiveness of these spectacular practices, in their ability to achieve the desired regulation through their visibility.

The underlying principle upon which the New Historicism bases its readings of such spectacular practices as public execution and royal processions is that they were effective in this interpellative sense, that they were successful in achieving their ideological aims. This is typified by Jonathan Goldberg's reading of such practices of torture in the reign of Elizabeth:

> It was one way in which the power of the monarch was displayed, inscribing itself on the body of the condemned. Those brought to trial and punishment became emblems of power, and their broken bodies testified to the overwhelming truth represented by the queen (2).

This New Historicist belief in the 'truth' of the Queen as manifested through such rituals, already shown in the works of Greenblatt, Tennenhouse and Montrose, clearly indicates a perception of their undeniable success in terms of interpellative desire. Quite simply, the New Historicists hold that these practices successfully hailed the population, causing them to accept the contemporary social hierarchy as evidently God-given and (thus) unchangeable. What such a perception clarifies, however, is a theoretical dynamic that sees Foucault's theories of early modern power taken up by the New Historicism in an identifiably partial manner, one that ignores essential elements of the theories which they have attempted to put to use. A closer look at Foucault's work on early modern public execution, bearing in mind its interpellative equivalence with royal processions, will enable a clearer delineation of this New Historicist partiality.

Foucault's notorious opening of his *Discipline and Punish*, in which he details the horrific public torture and (eventual) execution of the regicide Damiens, and upon which he builds his theory of early modern spectacular power, is an important moment for New Historicist criticism, and allows for the conceptual model of this power to be mobilised in the way typified by Goldberg above. Using the example of Damiens, the New Historicists continually valorise the interpellative effect that such a public display of dissymmetry embodies, finding in it, according to Scott Wilson, 'the seamless ubiquity of Elizabethan theatrical and political "power on display".'[53] This notion of the truth of the monarch, manifested in spectacular judgements like that of Damiens, or indeed in a royal entry is questionable, however. For as Wilson goes on to say:

> the odd thing about the opening to *Discipline and Punish* is that far from exhibiting the seamless, overwhelming truth of the monarch's power, the public execution of the regicide Damiens is an appallingly *botched* affair. If anything is exhibited here it is not the omnipotent sovereignty of power, but its disgusting ineptitude (138).

As an example of the effect of such a spectacular interpellative display therefore, this execution is unsuccessful. Rather than demonstrating any overwhelming dissymmetry, this event delineates an immense inefficiency in power's attempt to successfully reproduce itself. Foucault describes the abortive attempts by the executioners to dispatch Damiens, as well as the punishment he endured being perceived as far outweighing his crime.[54] The representatives of the sovereign are seen through their actions to demonstrate inefficiency in the dissymmetrical relationship itself, undermining the success of the ritual and thus undermining its desired effects.

One important factor that needs to be taken into account is that Foucault himself states that this sort of inefficiency was inherent in these practices, and that they were indeed unsuccessful; that is why they were replaced by other methods of control. Foucault theorises this at length in the opening two chapters of *Discipline and Punish*, demonstrating that such spectacular events did not (indeed could not) function in the ways that New Historicism claims they did. In a conscious re-focusing of interest in this context Foucault writes that in 'the ceremonies of the public execution, the main character was the people, whose real and immediate presence was required for the performance' (57). Foucault draws his gaze away from the monarch, and begins instead to theorise the presence of those for whom the performance was taking place. The people were called to observe in order to valorise the 'vengeance of the sovereign' (59), to demonstrate their allegiance to them. However, what Foucault demonstrates most clearly is the ambiguous nature of this presence, manifested in both a carnivalesque atmosphere and occasional outbreaks of actual disorder. The summoning of this presence in order for it to underpin the sovereign power often saw, according to Foucault, a refusal of that power, whereby 'the people, drawn to the spectacle intended to terrorise it, could express its rejection of the punitive power and sometimes revolt' (59). The immersion of the common people in a tradition of carnival frequently saw them act in ways opposite to those officially desired where 'rules were inverted, authority mocked and criminals transformed into heroes' (61). Rather than the constant successful reactivation of the overwhelming truth of the sovereign and sovereign power which the New Historicists find in these rituals, Foucault finds the opposite:

> It was evident that the great spectacle of punishment ran the risk of being rejected by the very people to whom it was addressed. In fact, the terror of the public execution created centres of illegality: on execution days, work stopped, the taverns were full, the authorities were abused ... (63).

Furthermore, rather than the sovereign power gaining from such an 'uncertain festival in which violence was instantaneously reversible' (63), it was the 'solidarity of a whole section of the population ... that was likely to emerge with redoubled strength' (63).[55] The kind of dynamic being articulated here, in which the population summoned to underwrite their own subjectification to the existing hierarchical structure of society conversely rejects official ideological desire, evidently occurred also in Elizabethan London. Official records for 1592, for example, tell of an 'execucion don of an offender that had killed an officier', which was witness to a riot by 'dysorderlie persons',[56] and stresses 'how manie of these dysorders have of late been commytted in divers places of the cyttie of London'.[57]

It can be assumed, given the real evidence for the rejection of official symbolic actions and events such as public executions, that a similar reading of the spectacular events of royal progresses and entries is possible. That is not to say that there were riots or that there was disorder. Rather it is to say that such spectacular displays were not defined by their monolithic demonstration of successful dissymmetry, but rather that the scepticism of a large section of the audience was possible in such processions. This is a reality emphasised by the reaction of the crowd during the procession which celebrated the accession of Anne Boleyn, where according to a witness present, just such scepticism was evident. He writes that during her 'coronation entry in 1533, the crowd stood mute. When a servant of the Queen exhorted the spectators to cheer he was told that "no one could force the people's hearts, not even the King"'.[58] In this case, the symbolic display of dissymmetry fails, and the audience are not hailed. In spite of the claims of Geertz and the New Historicism, this 'serious act' is not successful in its ideological desire. Indeed, the witness (writing in French) stresses that the crowd demonstrated their displeasure in many ways:

> Despite the English custom of making obeisance before the King and Queen on their entry, and of crying *"Dieu gard le roy, Dieu gard la royne"*, there was nobody, says the observer, who greeted them in this way. And when one of the Queen's servants asked the Mayor to order the people to give the customary welcome, *"lequel luy respondit que ne seroit contraindre les cuoeurs de gens et que le roy mesme ne seroit que fere"*. Moreover, the coincidence of the letters H. and A. interlaced, signifying Henry and Anne, painted everywhere as decoration, was seized upon everywhere derisively *"par interjection comique ha, ha, ha"* – such was the slight esteem in which the new Queen was held by the populace.[59]

This witness was a foreigner – Chapuys, the imperial ambassador, writing to Charles V – and thus it is evidence which needs to be read sceptically. However, even with this knowledge, it is clear that such evidence undermines conventional readings of royal processions and, to a great extent, severely undermines the New Historicist notion of the power of theatrical display. For, given their belief in the success of royal entries in achieving their ideological aims, they would surely find the audience reaction to Anne Boleyn's coronation procession puzzling.

The inherent ambiguity of these displays is further clarified if Foucault's comments regarding the physical ceremony of the execution are related to the pre-coronation procession. According to him, a 'whole military machine surrounded the scaffold: cavalry ... archers, guardsmen, soldiers. This was intended ... to prevent any escape or show of force ...' (50). Importantly however, it was also present 'to prevent any outburst of sympathy or anger on the part of the people ...' (50). As in the pre-coronation and coronation processions for Elizabeth, (more than merely symbolic) weapons were drawn, were held aloft, were clearly discernible in the hands of her bodyguards, aware of the threat of the procession's main character, the people. This is clear in a manuscript drawing of the actual coronation procession held in the British Library (MS 3320, Egerton, BL). On one page of the drawing, 17 Gentlemen Pensioners and 14 footguards stand in close proximity on either side of the Queen's carriage, each brandishing a weapon. In all, the Queen is surrounded by 34 Gentlemen Pensioners with halberds, and 28 footguards with short-swords drawn. A total of 62 men and weapons therefore encircle and protect Elizabeth.

The defining difference between Foucault's reading of early modern spectacular displays is that which sees him calling them 'ambiguous rituals' (65), whereas for the New Historicism these same events are always unambiguously successful in their official ideological desire. Their partial readings render theories of transformation and ambiguity ineffectual in any terms other than ones which will produce interesting stories that make no claims for themselves other than semiotic ones. Such a process leaves the New Historicism in a quandary however, in the sense that in its belief in the success of these symbolic rituals it is unable, for example, to account for the actions of the audience at Anne Boleyn's coronation entry. Indeed, in the same way, it is unable to account for the execution of Charles

I in 1649, unless it resorts to regarding it as a personal failure on the part of that particular monarch to mobilise an indefinable and ineffable quality entitled charisma. Its valorisation of this quality of charisma, along with its belief in the success of spectacular cultural events at the expense of any recognition of the existence of material forces of control in early modern England, seriously compromise any perceptible theoretical landscape which the New Historicism has carved out for itself. An adherence to a belief in the omnipotence of symbolic forms lies at the foundation of its theoretical and methodological shortcomings, articulated in the essay by Louis Montrose on Elizabethan progresses referred to at the beginning of this chapter. A closer examination of this essay will enable the shortcomings of such a methodology to be displayed in a similar way to those of traditional criticism which were demonstrated through the examination of Alison Plowden's reading of Elizabeth on progress.

In an essentially uncontroversial beginning to his essay '"Eliza, Queene of shepheardes", and the Pastoral of Power', it will be remembered that Montrose states that the Renaissance pastoral form represented a 'symbolic mediation of social relationships ... [which] are, intrinsically, relationships of power' (153). Hence the title of his essay, the 'Pastoral of Power', in which he proceeds to claim that the progress entertainments themselves were precisely such mediations and negotiations. As stated, he regards this relationship as one fully controlled by the powerful, stating that the 'repertoire of pastoral form ... was exploited and elaborated by Elizabethan poets and politicians, by sycophants and ideologues, by the Queen herself' (153). It is of the utmost importance to the construction of his thesis that the entire population are included in his analysis, and so Montrose seeks and finds an example of the celebratory presence of the common people in this pastoral territory. The example he uses of Elizabeth on progress is that of the report of the Spanish Ambassador of 1568, a report that has, as shown in the opening chapter, been traditionally misrepresented. Analysis of Elizabethan progresses have continually failed to reproduce the initial two sentences of the Ambassador's report in which the popularity of Elizabeth is questioned, proceeding rather to merely reproduce that part of the document that shows the common people unambiguously celebrating the Queen; a failure Montrose similarly reproduces.

In a typically Geertzian formulation, Montrose suggests that the 'images and metaphors; conventions of person, place, and diction; and distinctive generic features and their combinations' (153), together with the ability of the Queen as actress, ensured the continuation of charismatic authority. He believes that the repertoire of pastoral form in conjunction with 'Elizabeth [who] did not need to be provided with acting parts – she merely played herself' (170), sustained the Elizabethan social order itself. Montrose uses the Sudeley entertainment of 1592 (as representative of entertainments generally) to demonstrate the compelling nature of this (semiotic) reality:

> in a context in which the commons were actually present as performers or as spectators, pageants like the one at Sudeley might fortify loyalty toward the crown among those whose relationship to the landlords who were their immediate and

tangible superiors was one of endemic suspicion or resentment ... . Thus the
pastoral pageants at Sudeley and others like them might affirm a benign
relationship of mutual interest between the Queen and the lowly, between the
Queen and the great, and among them all (179).

Montrose thus plays one class off against another in such a way, claiming that the
progress entertainments allegorised reality, and that social order itself was secured
and maintained through this process. Needless to say, this process is regarded as
having been successful, the progress entertainments having suitably impressed the
common people. In a thesis that resembles that of Geertz, and also those of
Greenblatt and Tennenhouse, it would seem that real problems and inequalities are
deferred and indeed resolved through symbolic actions. Montrose's evidence
demonstrates the successful nature of such a symbolic practice in interpellative
terms. Thus he states that the pageant entertainments asserted 'a bond of reciprocal
devotion and charity between lowly subjects and sovereign' (180).

What becomes apparent in the readings of Montrose and Greenblatt is that the
dynamic of their theorisations point toward a Tillyardian notion of Elizabethan
society and its cultural practices. This is clearly articulated by Montrose:

> The 'symbolic formation' of pastoral provided an ideal meeting ground for Queen
> and subjects, a mediation of her greatness and their lowness; it fostered the
> illusion that she was approachable and knowable, loveable and loving, to lords and
> peasants, courtiers and citizens alike (180).

The defining characteristic of these cultural practices, as in Tillyard, is the
valorisation of order and rank – an aim that, according to Montrose, although based
on a partial reading of evidence, was successfully achieved. In the New Historicist
reading, the sovereign is given a cult-like omniscience in this play of social
relationships, the only individual truly wise to the operation of power. The wisdom
of the sovereign is to be found in the borrowings of the Geertzian formulation
whereby the 'charisma of Queen Elizabeth was not compromised but rather was
enhanced by royal pastoral's awesome intimacy' (180). Montrose sees Elizabeth
herself as 'the cynosure of ... Elizabethan pastoralism' (154), whereby she
effectively rules her country through the symbolic underwriting of her power in the
pastoral form. In this reading, the Queen successfully maintained her power
through the strategic mobilisation of a literary form that demonstrated her
greatness in contrast to her subjects' lowness, and demonstrated further the
naturalness of this hierarchy. As such, Montrose believes these 'pastorals were
minor masterpieces of a poetics of power' (180), and from 'every angle, the
political dynamic was advantageous to Eliza, Queen of shepherds' (180).

The repercussions of an analysis determined by Geertzian semiotics are
worrying in their inability to deal with material practices that are more than merely
symbolic, as are those of a critical practice such as Montrose's, which builds an
enormous theory of both Elizabethan pastoral and the society that produced it on
the misreading of a single document. This reading states that a monolithic common
people were subject to cultural practices which effectively and successfully

mystified their social status, and made them celebrate the structure of a hierarchy of which they formed the base. Yet a consideration of Montrose's methodology in reaching such a conclusion is enlightening. For these conclusions are built upon a partial reading of all of his influences and sources. Thus not only is there a lack of scrutiny with regard to primary material (the Spanish Ambassador's report), but Montrose's understanding of early modern culture is defined by emptied-out theories of Foucault, and a denial of the real in favour of the exclusively semiotic. However, if evidence which questions the semiotic findings of Montrose is considered at this point, problems with the whole New Historicist methodology can be perceived, and can lead into an alternative theorisation of Elizabethan society and, in turn, processions and pageants.

After its emergence in the early 1980s, and its elevation to a position of academic convention in the following decade, the New Historicism found itself the subject of an increasing amount of scrutiny in the 1990s.[60] While there were those who questioned its methodological and theoretical parameters, as well as its ideological trajectory, throughout its emergence few critics have, to my knowledge, immersed specific New Historicist statements/conclusions in an empirical landscape in order to see if they bear any relation to existent historical records.[61] Vincent P. Pecora, in his essay 'The Limits of Local Knowledge', is one example of such an empirical study, placing Clifford Geertz's conclusions regarding the presence and function of violence in modern Indonesian society into a factual backdrop of the military take-over of that country in the autumn of 1965. Consequently, Pecora finds Geertz's semiotic reading of Indonesian culture severely wanting in terms of its political trajectory.[62] Another such study, and one relevant to this book, is Francis Barker's 'A Wilderness of Tigers: *Titus Andronicus*, Anthropology and the Occlusion of Violence'.[63] In this essay, Barker delineates the Geertz/Greenblatt critical approach regarding an exclusively semiotic interpretation of culture, and questions whether, when such an assertion is juxtaposed with a detailing of actual examples of material power at work in early modern England, it can remain anything other than an 'aestheticisation of politics' (200). Centring around Greenblatt's belief that Elizabethan power was symbolic rather than material, Barker takes execution as the manifestation of symbolic power and subjects it to a reading of the historical records regarding 'death by hanging (and other related causes)' (169) in Elizabethan and Stuart England and Wales. After trawling through these records, Barker emerges with a startling series of statistics regarding early modern execution, which he suggests are, in all probability 'radical underestimations of the numbers of people actually put to death ...' (179). He writes:

> estimated national totals for England and Wales ... are as follows: 24,147.4 men and women hanged; 516.21 pressed to death, and 11,440.52 dead in gaol; or, on average at least 371.5 were put to death by hanging, 7.94 were killed by the *peine forte et dure* and a further 176 probably died in gaol in each and every one of the 65 years of the reigns of Elizabeth and James (178).

In order that the reader should grasp the full significance of these figures, Barker then scales them up to modern-day equivalents: 'if a similar proportion of the present day population were put to death, at least 4,599.17 people on average would be executed as convicted felons each year, a further 98.29 would be pressed to death without plea, and 2,178.88 would die in gaol' (178–9).

While it is not possible to do full justice to Barker's methodology in arriving at such figures in this current study, it should be emphasised that, on the evidence presented, his results are convincing. Prompted by the representation of the ease with which a common person is executed in Shakespeare's *Titus Andronicus*,[64] Barker explicates a cultural phenomenon – the widespread execution of common people in early modern England and Wales – founded in factual evidence. It is what he does with this evidence in relation to the New Historicism and Geertz that is most interesting, however.

For Francis Barker, the 'sense of the theatricality of power' theorised by Greenblatt very much 'approximates to the view that if there was social control in early modern England, it was achieved by essentially benign social – that is, "cultural" – means' (200). While he does not wish to deny that power operates in this way, Barker wants to stress that it does not operate in this way alone. If Greenblatt believes (as he indeed seems to and as does Geertz) 'that power is itself a metaphor', he seems to further believe that it is '*no more than a metaphor*' (200). And thus, as Barker goes on to stress, 'a wholly appropriate attention to the power of representation can, it seems, easily topple over into figuring power as *merely* invested in the representational' (200). Greenblatt's thesis regarding the symbolics of Elizabethan power is contrasted to Barker's 'record of death by hanging', which he goes on to say, 'suggests there was an extensive, ruthless and effective coercive apparatus that was putting to death vast numbers of the people, overwhelmingly the low-born and the poor' (201). Clinching his argument in a forceful manner and taking the practitioners of cultural semiotics to task, Barker makes it clear that with regard to this large majority of the population, means 'were available not so much to impress them with theatrical celebrations as to kill them' (202). If the fate of a certain Bartholomew Steere is considered here, Barker's thesis would seem to contain a good deal of credibility.

In 1596, a number of employees of Lord Norris and other Oxfordshire landholders attempted an uprising, in order to kill their employers and relieve their own hunger and poverty. These common men proclaimed 'they would murder Mr Power, as also Mr Berry ... Sir Hen. Lee, Sir Wm. Spencer, Mr Frere, and Lord Norris, and then go to London', there to meet up with 'the London apprentices [who] would join them'.[65] Four years earlier, in 1592, Queen Elizabeth and her court had visited the Oxfordshire countryside on progress, and had indeed stayed with a number of these landholders, including Lord Norris and Sir Henry Lee.[66] As employees of these landholders, each of the rebels is likely to have witnessed this progress, many of them, including Bartholomew Steere, also probably being present during the performance of entertainments produced for the Queen. If these facts are placed in the semiotic theorisations of Greenblatt, Montrose and Geertz, certain contradictions arise. For their belief that Elizabethan power was embodied in spectacular display alone, and their further belief that such display was effective, would not countenance uprisings by those at whom such display was aimed. Simply put, Greenblatt, Montrose and Geertz would contend that Steere and his followers must, of necessity, have been interpellated by the symbolic resonance of the Queen and her progress procession. As such, the rebels could not have rebelled because of their recognition of dissymmetry, their recognition of and subjectification to Elizabeth's charismatic authority. However, though their uprising was abortive, they did attempt to rebel, and they did, it would seem, remain unimpressed by the symbolism embodied in the Queen and her procession.

The rebels were subsequently captured, imprisoned, brought to London and tortured. Steere, it would seem, was tortured to death, while two other rebels were executed on Enslow Hill, the initial meeting place of the rebels.[67] The individuals responsible for their torture and execution were a number of Oxfordshire landholders, including Lord Norris, his son Sir Henry Norris, and William Frere.[68] Greenblatt's claim that Elizabeth was 'a ruler whose power is constituted in theatrical celebrations of royal glory and theatrical violence visited upon the enemies of that glory' does not fit comfortably with this example of material violence, however. In the case of Steere and his followers, the constitution of this symbolic power was ineffective, and the violence visited upon them was not merely theatrical but was real. As Barker clarifies, the means to impress and interpellate the common population were not merely symbolic, but existed also in material institutions of coercion.

Although Barker's essay is prompted by an analysis of Shakespearean theatre, his thesis is important for the conclusions its reaches regarding the nature of early modern power itself, and the place of other cultural practices within this society. He writes in a way that encourages the impression that he does not believe he is making a particularly profound point that he has 'tried to suggest that Elizabethan power certainly did not operate by theatrical spectacle, cultural display or circulation and exchange alone' (203). And yet Geertz, Greenblatt, Tennenhouse, Goldberg and Montrose suggest that early modern power functioned in precisely this way: through symbolic action alone. Barker's point is that power functions through material as well as symbolic actions, and not in a material way through symbolic actions alone. The success of any spectacular cultural practice, such as processions, lies in a combination of theatrical representations of potential violence and material representations of the threat of real violence. Barker regards the New Historicist immersion in cultural semiotics as an occlusion of real violence, their readings of the symbolic nature of power resulting in an occlusion of the material manifestations of that power, creating an ideological trajectory that celebrates the dominant culture.[69] The result of this immersion in cultural semiotics is the production of academic work that, though technically innovative, replicates the ideological paradigms of an older form of historicism. Thus the conclusions reached by New Historicists with regard to Elizabethan processions are essentially no different to those of the likes of J. Nichols, J. Neale, Roy Strong and David Bergeron. Similarly, the ideological trajectories of the New Historicism as a whole replicate a traditional form of processional analysis, blinded by the aura of Elizabeth, convinced of the power of allegory and display in achieving its ideological aims. For this is a critical practice that, like the older historicism's inability to countenance the existence of real disorder/discontent, is founded in partiality. It attempts to explain the past using theoretical tools that are essentially incomplete. A more considered use of these tools, such as primary material, the theories of Foucault and the existence of material as well as symbolic practices, would enable a more complete explanation/negotiation of this past, and produce knowledge with a recognition of ambiguity, disunity and complexity. Knowledge that would admit, for example, that Elizabethan processions were complex cultural events, produced and received in a complex society that was constituted by more than its governing class.

'Sex and power'

Analyses of Elizabethan processions produced in the aftermath of the New Historicism – by the likes of Helen Hackett, Susan Frye, Susan Doran, Philippa Berry, Carole Levin, Susan Logan and John N. King – view them more critically than earlier studies and do not reproduce these events as unified or as unproblematic in political terms. Berry, Hackett, Levin, King and Doran concentrate upon the symbolism used to represent Elizabeth at various points in her reign, with particular reference to the kinds of mythological figures mobilised during the progress entertainments. Generally, these critics find a gendering process to be of great significance in terms of Elizabeth's realisation of power, a struggle being perceived between how she attempted to represent herself and how she was represented by those powerful men around her. Frye is specifically interested in this kind of representation with regard to the Kenilworth entertainment of 1575 and is equally interested in the ways in which Elizabeth was represented during her royal entry into the city to celebrate her coronation. Frye terms the perceived differences a 'competition for representation'. The accession of Elizabeth also interests Susan Logan in a different context where she compares the various manuscript descriptions of the pre-coronation procession that are in existence and sees an apparent religious conflict between them.[70] With the exception of this latter essay, all of these critics are interested in the representations of Elizabeth as a woman in a patriarchal society and the ways in which those responsible dealt with the challenge of an initially unmarried, virginal and, eventually aging queen in their myth-making. Generally, these analyses are gender-related and take as their object of study the tensions and anxieties felt between Elizabeth and her courtiers in a world of *realpolitik* that relied so heavily on allegory and symbolism. Though important and enlightening in these terms, these analyses remain essentially partial as they fail, like traditional and New Historicist analysis, to consider the targets of the spectacular rituals themselves, the common people. They are too diffuse in their interests to address in detail here, but it is possible to say that this one deficiency unites them. Like previous analyses of processions, they too consider these events according to the *Weltanshauung* of the dominant ideology, the common people being essentially invisible and/or merely passive. This being the case, and although each of them will be referred to in the following chapters, a coherent critique of them as a whole would serve no purpose for this current study. The important point to establish in this context is the simple but defining one that the common people are not regarded as having any importance whatever, whether in terms of their responses to these rituals or, indeed, as the targeted subject of Elizabethan pageants, progresses and processions.

Notes

1. Montrose, "'Eliza, Queene of shepheardes'", *English Literary Renaissance* 153.
2. See Chapter 1.
3. *CSP (Spanish) (1568–79)* 51.
4. Ibid., 50.
5. This discovery is meant in those terms outlined by Foucault in *The History of Sexuality*, in which the human body itself becomes (in modernity) the site of scientific investigation.
6. Pierre Macherey, *A Theory of Literary Production* (1978; London: Routledge & Kegan Paul, 1989).
7. Terry Eagleton, *Marxism and Literary Criticism* (London: Methuen, 1976) 35.
8. Macherey himself writes: 'To explain the work is to show that, contrary to appearances, it is not independent, but bears in its material substance the imprint of a determinate absence which is also the principle of its identity' (79–80).
9. See particularly Derrida's deconstructionist work in *Of Grammatology*, trans. Gayatri Chakravorty Spivak (Baltimore: John Hopkins University Press, 1976), and *Writing and Difference*, trans. Alan Bass (London: Routledge and Kegan Paul, 1978).
10. This in turn naturally echoes the work of Simone de Beauvoir and her recognition of the female Other. For her, Man himself is such a first principle, defined as much by the exclusion of Woman as by what it consists of/in itself. Man is an (ideological) product of a (patriarchal) thought system that excludes its defined opposite, and is thus shot through with the presence of that opposite. For de Beauvoir this exclusion is a banishment, a repression of that which Man needs in order to maintain his identity, the process by which he can set himself up as a founding principle. See the seminal *The Second Sex*, trans. and ed. H. M. Parshley (1953; Harmondsworth: Penguin Modern Classics, 1987).
11. The illusory nature of the task that traditional criticism has set itself (the identification of unity) and that the New Historicism has sought (the discovery of unified cultural laws) suggests too the work of Jacques Lacan. The practices of these schools of criticism can be seen to reflect Lacan's perception of the ability to achieve unity on the imaginary level. These schools continue to search for a final, single meaning that is no longer achievable in a world where language, an endless process of difference, disallows any meaning to be fully present. The turbulence of the symbolic world denies the possibility of monolithic meaning, and produces ambivalence. What we are attempting to signify is never completely true or genuine as, according to Lacan, the unconscious disallows the absolute knowledge of what our signifiers are actually signifying. In the symbolic world in which we exist, these signifiers can never represent truth fully, are always the subject of difference, and therefore contain those same traces of what they are not. Thus, it is never possible to say precisely what we mean. See particularly Jacques Lacan, *Ecrits: A Selection*, trans. Alan Sheridan (London: Tavistock, 1977).

12. 'Thus we must go beyond the work and explain it, must say what it does not and could not say; *just as the triangle remains silent over the sum of its angles*' (Macherey 77; emphasis added).
13. Toril Moi, *Sexual Textual Politics: Feminist Literary Theory* (London: Methuen, 1985) 166. Particularly relevant also are two extracts which appear in *The Feminist Reader: Essays in Gender and the Politics of Literary Criticism*, eds. Catherine Belsey and Jane Moore (London: Macmillan, 1989): Helene Cixous, 'Sorties: Out and Out: Attacks/Ways/Out/Forays' 101–16, and Julia Kristeva, 'Women's Time' 197–217. See also Luce Irigaray, *The Sex Which Is Not One*, trans. C. Porter (New York: Cornell University Press, 1985).
14. This substitution of the category common people for feminine/femininity is equivalent to Evelyn O'Callaghan's substitution of the category black people in Moi's formulation, demonstrating the presence of many groups positioned on the margins of the (dominant) symbolic order. See her *Woman Version: Theoretical Approaches to West Indian Fiction by Women* (London: Macmillan Caribbean, 1993) 104–5 particularly. This substitution is possible precisely because Kristeva refuses to actually define femininity, considering it primarily as a position; one which is marginal to the dominant symbolic order. This being the case, it is possible to view the common people or black people in the same way, as being defined in terms of the relational, as a position; again, a marginal one in relation to the dominant.
15. An important point being of course that they were not allowed/able to define themselves for/to themselves.
16. The criticism to which I refer here is the tradition beginning with Mulcaster, *The Passage Of Our Most Drad Soveraigne* (1558), through Holinshed, *Chronicles* (1577), Nichols, *Elizabeth* (1823), Withington, *English Pageantry* (1918–20), Wickham, *Early English Stages* (1959) to Anglo, *Spectacle, Pageantry and Early Tudor Policy* (1969). It has continued to the present through Strong, *The Cult of Elizabeth* (1977) and *Splendour at Court* (1973), Bergeron, *English Civic Pageantry 1558–1642* (1971) and Wilson, *Entertainments for Elizabeth I* (1980).
17. Bristol, *Carnival and Theatre* 9.
18. There are a number of programmatic statements by New Historicist critics, most of which set themselves out against the older brand of historicism as practised by the likes of Tillyard. The most relevant ones to this current study are the following: Stephen Greenblatt, introduction, *Renaissance Self-Fashioning* 1–9; his introduction, *The Forms of Power and the Power of Forms in the Renaissance*, *Genre* 15.1–2 (Spring and Summer 1982) 3–6; his essay 'The Circulation of Social Energy', *Shakespearean Negotiations* 1–20; and his 'Towards a Poetics of Culture', *The New Historicism* 1–14. The same collection contains Louis A. Montrose's important essay in this respect, 'Professing the Renaissance: The Poetics and Politics of Culture', 15–36. Montrose confronts similar issues in his 'Renaissance Literary Studies and the Subject of History', *English Literary Renaissance* 16.1 (Winter 1986) 5–12, and in his 'The Purpose of Playing: Reflections on a Shakespearean Anthropology', *Helios* 7 (1980) 51–74. For an excellent overview of the New Historicism in this regard, see Jean E. Howard, 'The New Historicism in Renaissance Studies', *English Literary Renaissance* 16.1 (Winter 1986) 13–43.
19. Tillyard, *The Elizabethan World Picture* 18.
20. Greenblatt, *Political Shakespeare* 18–47.
21. Richard Wilson, *Will Power: Essays on Shakespearean Authority* (London: Harvester Wheatsheaf, 1993) 6.
22. Jonathan Dollimore, introduction, 'Shakespeare, Cultural Materialism and the New Historicism', *Political Shakespeare* 2–17:10.

23. Nichols, *Elizabeth* 1:38–60.
24. Holinshed 4:159–76.
25. Nichols, *Elizabeth* 1:vi.
26. R. Malcolm Smuts, 'Public Ceremony and Royal Charisma: the English Royal Entry in London, 1485–1642', *The First Modern Society: Essays in English History in Honour of Lawrence Stone*. eds A. L. Beier, David Cannadine and James M. Rosenbaum. (Cambridge: Cambridge UP, 1989) 65–93:74.
27. David Birt, *Elizabeth's England* (Harlow: Longman, 1981) 41.
28. Jean Wilson 39.
29. Alice S.Venezky, *Pageantry on the Shakespearean Stage* (New York: Twayne, 1951) 91.
30. Strong, *Cult* 116.
31. The terminology used here is that of Stephen Greenblatt in his seminal 'The Circulation of Social Energy', an essay that attempted to outline the theoretical and methodological parameters of his critical practice.
32. Greenblatt, *Renaissance Self-Fashioning* 166–7.
33. Tennenhouse, *Power on Display* 102.
34. Cole, *Portable Queen* 10.
35. 'The conception of order is ... so much part of the collective mind of the people ... ' (Tillyard, *The Elizabethan World Picture* 18).
36. Greenblatt, 'Shakespeare And The Exorcists', *Shakespearean Negotiations* 94–128:97.
37. Montrose, '"Eliza, Queene of shepheardes"', *English Literary Renaissance* 180.
38. Smuts 68.
39. These issues relating to Foucault are dealt with in detail on pp. 37–41.
40. For direct uses of Geertz's theories in New Historicist work, see R. Malcolm Smuts, 'Public Ceremony' 65–93, Goldberg, *James I*, and Greenblatt's epilogue, *Renaissance Self-Fashioning* 255–7.
41. Geertz, 'Thick Description', *The Interpretation of Cultures* 5.
42. Greenblatt, introduction, *Renaissance Self-Fashioning* 4.
43. Geertz, 'Charisma', *Local Knowledge* 121–46.
44. Geertz, introduction, *Local Knowledge* 3–16:5.
45. Weber theorised three types of authority, the 'traditional', the 'charismatic', and the 'legal-rational' or 'bureaucratic'. In Weberian terms, charismatic authority exists in the exceptional abilities of an individual which causes them to be followed, these exceptional abilities demonstrating their right to lead. This definition of charismatic authority demonstrates its dialectical nature – a ruler is seen to be competent by her subjects by the fact that she rules – as well as clarifying a certain identifiable functionalism. That is to say that, as Weber himself states, it 'is recognition on the part of those subject to authority which is decisive for the validity of charisma' (359), so that charismatic authority is legitimised simply by those subject to it recognising its legitimacy: see Max Weber, *The Theory of Social and Economic Organisation*, trans. A. M. Henderson and Talcott Parsons, ed. Talcott Parsons (New York: Oxford University Press, 1947). This is in fact a translation of the first part of Weber's *Wirtschaft und Gesellschaft* which in turn was published as the third part of his *Grundriss der Sozialökonomik*.
46. This cult to which I refer is that which has emerged in the twentieth century particularly, rather than the panegyric circle that surrounded Elizabeth in her own lifetime. Traditional procession analysis, in its valorisation of the interpellative success of Elizabethan symbolic events, as well as in its readings of panegyric as merely expressing personal feelings rather than as politically motivated (public and personal) propaganda, is part of a wider cultural grouping that comprises a modern cult of

Elizabeth I. The immersion in a form of historical reading that reproduces Tillyardian nostalgia, and the critical blindness induced by the bright aura of the monarch, has contributed to the belief in Elizabeth as a figure of ultimate glamour. This cult is based upon J. E. Neale's initial biography of Elizabeth, is consolidated in the Tillyardian influences of E. C. Wilson's *England's Eliza* (London: Frank Cass & Co, 1966), and Frances Yates's *Astraea*, and completed in many senses by Yates's pupil Roy Strong in his *Splendour at Court* and *The Cult of Elizabeth*. For all of these writers, Elizabeth is the embodiment of a lost golden age, a symbol of social unity, of political order, and the cynosure of the most civilised culture. For them, she is indeed a charismatic figure. Modern procession analysts such as Jean Wilson (in *Entertainments for Elizabeth I*) and David Bergeron (in *English Civic Pageantry*) regard Elizabeth in just such a light, the central point of a unified society, one that maintained this unity through symbolic rituals rather than (other) material practices. Such an immersion in a cult has deformed twentieth century processional analysis, resulting in readings of them that are partial and which occlude social, cultural and political complexities, and realities. These analyses form a representation of an ideal order which comprises part of a dominant ideology.

47. See Chapters 2 and 3.
48. Goldberg, *James* 32–3. Goldberg uses another of Geertz's ethnographies in *Negara: The Theatre State in Nineteenth Century Bali* (Princeton; Oxford: Princeton University Press, 1980).
49. Tennenhouse, *Power on Display* 105–6.
50. Cole, *Portable Queen* 9.
51. Foucault, *Discipline and Punish* 48.
52. Greenblatt, *Renaissance Self-Fashioning* 201. This school of criticism has of course taken the further step (which Foucault himself refused to do) of equating the early modern theatre with such spectacular practices.
53. Scott Wilson, *Cultural Materialism: Theory and Practice* (Oxford: Blackwell, 1995) 137.
54. Foucault, *Discipline and Punish* 3–6.
55. The importance of this cannot be underestimated, for as Foucault writes: 'And it was the breaking up of this solidarity that was becoming the aim of penal and police repression'(63).
56. *Acts of the Privy Council (1592)* 242.
57. Ibid., 242.
58. Quoted in Smuts 75–6.
59. Anglo 259.
60. Such studies are too numerous to mention here, though almost any critical study that attempts to read the early modern period theoretically has to do so through the New Historicism.
61. Important essays appeared at the time of this emergence such as Jean E. Howard's 'The New Historicism in Renaissance Studies', *English Literary Renaissance*. There are also a number of such essays in the collection *The New Historicism*, particularly the following: 'The History of the Anecdote: Fiction and Fiction' by Joel Fineman, 49–76; 'The Asylums of Antaeus: Women, War, and Madness – Is there a Feminist Fetishism?' by Jane Marcus, 132–51; 'Co-optation' by Gerald Graff, 168–81; 'The Limits of Local Knowledge' by Vincent P. Pecora, 243–76; 'The New Historicism and Other Old-fashioned Topics' by Brook Thomas, 182–203; and, finally, 'Foucault's Legacy: A New Historicism?' by Frank Lentricchia, 231–42. Though collected in 1989, many of these essays initially appeared earlier.
62. Pecora, 'The Limits of Local Knowledge', *The New Historicism* 243–76.

63. Barker, *The Culture of Violence* 143–206.
64. Ibid., 165–8.
65. *CSP (Dom) (1595–97)* 345.
66. See Chapter 3 for an extended examination of this event.
67. *CSP (Dom) (1595–97)* 316–8.
68. Ibid., 342–5 and 316–18. See also John Walter, 'A "Rising of The People"? The Oxfordshire Rising of 1596', *Past And Present* 107 (May 1985) 90–143:125–9; and Roger B. Manning, *Village Revolts: Social Protest and Popular Disturbance in England 1509–1640* (Oxford: Claredon Press, 1988) 220–29:226–7.
69. For an equally sceptical assessment of the New Historicism, though one which approaches it from an alternative ideological direction, see Brian Vickers, *Appropriating Shakespeare: Contemporary Critical Quarrels* (New Haven & London: Yale University Press, 1993) 214–71.
70. See Susan Doran, *Monarchy and Matrimony: The Courtships of Elizabeth I*; Susan Frye, *Elizabeth I: The Competition for Representation* and 'The Myth of Elizabeth at Tilbury', *Sixteenth Century Journal* 23; Carole Levin, *The Heart and Stomach of a King: Elizabeth I and the Politics of Sex and Power*; Sandra Logan, 'Making History: The Rhetorical and Historical Occasion of Elizabeth Tudor's Coronation Entry', *The Journal of Medieval and Early Modern Studies* 31:2; Helen Hackett, *Virgin Mother, Maiden Queen*; Philippa Berry, *Of Chastity and Power: Elizabethan Literature and the Unmarried Queen*; John N. King, 'Queen Elizabeth I: Representations of the Virgin Queen', *Renaissance Quarterly* 43:1 (Spring 1990) 30–74.

Chapter 2

'Her spiritual, mystical, transforming power': Elizabeth on Procession and the Common Audience

In medieval Europe, the processional entry into a city traditionally functioned as the most public of royal theatrical displays, always containing some element of triumph and, after a military victory, being to a great extent constituted by a form of thanks-giving. Indeed, such a triumphal function defined the earlier Roman notion of entry, and this purely processional form existed until the middle of the fourteenth century.[1] Already the important events in a monarch's reign – coronation, accession, marriage, the birth of children, death – were celebrated in such a processional manner, enabling the monarch 'to manifest himself at his most magnificent in the sight of his subjects'.[2] The Roman triumphal form had thus been appropriated and extended to these important events in the life of the nation's ruler, and for specific reasons. 'At the root of the matter', notes Glynne Wickham, 'lies the delicate balance of relationships between ruler and subject in medieval Europe' (1:52), relationships that, due to a Christian world-view, necessarily modified the basic assumptions implicit in the Roman triumphs. Wickham believes this led to a desire 'to imply acknowledgement by the subject that the particular ruler is the representative in their midst, chosen by God for their own good as a figurehead and arbiter of justice' (1:52). Already inherent in these medieval processions was an allegorical leap, the monarch in procession representing something other than themselves and embodying something greater than a mere barrier to foreign threat or invasion.

By the end of the fourteenth century, such urban processions saw the introduction of street pageant devices, organised by the trade guilds of the city and enabling a further process of allegorical subjectification through sovereign representation of itself as spiritual figurehead and as all virtue personified.[3] The following two hundred years saw a continued evolution in these theatrical devices, in many senses culminating in the grandiose entry into London of James I for his coronation in 1604.[4] Already by the mid-sixteenth century, however, the mixture of moral, religious, and historical allegory, with the monarch as the principal participant in their own glorification, can be seen to typify royal entries into cities. The pre-coronation procession of Elizabeth I that took place on 14 January 1558 is a perfect example.

The procession that occurred the day before Elizabeth's coronation can be regarded as a typical royal entry of the period in that it 'reflected the achievements of the present and reviewed those of the past while turning an optimistic eye to the future'.[5] Its production forms one of the two major London processions undertaken by Elizabeth, the other being more conventional (and therefore less allegorical) in its celebration of a military victory. The 1558 procession was, in fact, the penultimate act in an event that comprised a number of processions through the city prior to the day of the actual coronation on 15 January. As well as stoking the fires of expectation in the capital's population as the day approached, the procession witnessed the visible staking of a legitimate, Protestant claim to the recently vacated throne. Each procession within this aggregation attempted to fulfil just such a function, culminating in this Recognition March through the very heart of the city. This was the grandest and most important of the processions, whereby in a number of pageant devices the sovereign authority was symbolically offered to Elizabeth (which she naturally accepted). In 1588 a structurally similar procession passed through the streets of the capital in commemoration of the defeat of the Spanish Armada, an occasion that required little pre-emptive stimulation, representing as it did the overwhelming of a dangerous foreign invader.

Despite this difference, it is important for my purposes here to recognise that the material formation of the two actual processions themselves was, in terms of the human topographical pattern, almost wholly identical. The topography of status delineated by the two processions is the same, and the spectacular presence manifested through colour, configuration, affluence and sheer size is shared by both. The two examples of spectacle are therefore uniform in terms of this material presence.[6] This topography has been preserved in the form of an official inventory, listing the participants of the so-called Victory procession of 1588 (see Appendix 1), which demonstrates the grandeur and great size of the procession. The spectacular centrality of the procession's participants is clearly outlined, and bears witness to an impressive mobile presence through the streets of London. A similar reality is articulated in the inventory recording the details of the 1558 coronation preparations existent in the *Records of the Lord Chamberlain*.[7] This document lists the vast amount of cloth that had to be ordered for the coronation, as well as listing the members of the household who needed to be present for the subsequent banquet and those required to attend the coronation itself. Page after page is given over to these lists, which describe a most elaborate demonstration of affluence.[8]

Such an impressive reality is also visible in the drawing that survives of Elizabeth's actual coronation procession itself – referred to in the Lord Chamberlain's document – and which took place on the 15 January 1558. Though much smaller than both the Victory and the pre-coronation processions, the pictorial evidence of this spectacular display does enable a further glimpse at the nature of Elizabethan processional practice. The drawing is believed to be the work of one of the Heralds present at the coronation,[9] and represents the procession as it proceeded from Westminster Hall to the Abbey Church of St Peter. The manuscript (MS 3320, Egerton, BL) delineates 338 people in all, 171 horses, 3 carriages, and the litter in which the Queen was transported. On each side of her are Gentlemen Pensioners, as well as 14 foot-guards with drawn short-swords. The procession is stretched out over 28 pages, beginning with the Yeomen of the Guard leaving Westminster Hall, and ending with the preparations for the crowning of the Queen in the Abbey Church. The manuscript, like the 1588 inventory, enables the conceptualisation of the splendour of such an event. Closer inspection of the various descriptions of the pre-coronation procession encourages a similar perception of that particular spectacular display.

'The centre of the centre'

The pre-coronation procession of 1558, which 'epitomises the chief characteristics to be found in all royal entries and represents a high achievement of this dramatic form',[10] was well documented at the time both by educated observers and in authorised descriptions such as that credited to Richard Mulcaster.[11] David Bergeron believes Mulcaster's document 'is a marvellous piece of propaganda in addition to providing a record of the events'.[12] While Mulcaster's pamphlet does indeed provide us with a precise record of the route taken and describes too the various pageant devices performed, the letters of the Venetian Ambassador to England of the time, Il Schifanoya, to the Castellan of Mantua, enable us to determine the approximate size of the procession. He estimated the number of horses preceding the Queen to be one thousand, a total that is not unimaginable when contemplating the human inventory of the 1588 procession.[13] He goes on to write that the houses along the route were decorated in the Queen's honour, and that lining this route were 'merchants and artisans of every trade ... in long black gowns lined with hoods of red and black cloth ... with all their ensigns, banners, and standards, which were innumerable, and made a very fine show' (12). Each participant in the procession also displayed their symbols of office – keys, chains, pennants, and various uniforms of status and affluence. The Queen's ceremonial guards were all dressed in crimson silk, and there was also much satin, velvet, and fur in evidence. The Queen herself, he says, appeared in 'an open litter, trimmed down to the ground with gold brocade' (12), and that she was 'dressed in a royal robe of very rich cloth of gold, with a double-raised stiff pile, and on her head over a coif of cloth of gold, beneath which was her hair, a plain gold crown without lace ... covered with jewels ...' (12). There were pageant devices en route, from Fenchurch to Temple Bar, dramatic interludes on specially erected scaffolds, each taking place as the Queen reached them, who then proceeded further once each (interconnecting) interlude came to an end. These theatrical performances took the form of various allegorical representations of the Queen and her perceived functions:

> Elizabeth's descent was illustrated in a vast rose tree of the houses of York and Lancaster, there was a pageant in the form of Virtues defeating Vices, another celebrated the Queen's devotion to the biblical beatitudes, another showed a withered and a flourishing landscape to typify a good and bad commonwealth and, finally, there was a vision of Elizabeth as Deborah, consulting with her estates for the good of her realm.[14]

These shows were no doubt colourful and impressive, as well as propagandist. There was music, bells pealing, cannons intermittently firing, and the streets were lined with the Queen's 'most loving People',[15] cheering without pause. These were the streets that constituted and traversed the heart of the city of London, the arterial link between the Tower and Westminster, through the commercial centre of the nation.

The procession itself, both in terms of content and form, was the responsibility of the Office of the Revels, and more specifically of Sir Thomas Cawarden, the Master of the Revels at the time of Elizabeth's coronation. This office was responsible for all aspects of court entertainment, including masques and tilts. It had been established in the previous century, and by the time of Elizabeth's Recognition March was well practised in the organisation of such massive spectacles. It was charged not merely to summon all of the participants of the procession, but also to prepare all of the costumes, horses, and necessary finery. The Office was answerable to the sovereign, and made sure that all of her wishes were carried out. It would ensure that the formation of the procession was correct, this being to a great extent hierarchically formalised by the time of Elizabeth, and guarantee that the suitable note was struck in terms of the procession's effects. This formal hierarchy is clearly evident in the 1588 inventory, building gradually as it does to its climax, the Queen surrounded by her bodyguards.

Adding to the splendour of the actual pre-coronation procession itself were five pageant devices specifically written for the occasion and acted out upon specially constructed stages. Along the streets streamers and banners hung and, in specially railed-off enclosures the members of the various City companies stood, dressed in their official uniforms:

> well apparelled with many riche furres, and their livery whodes uppon their shoulders, in comely and semely maner, having before them sondry persones well apparelled in silkes and chaines of golde, as wyflers and garders of the sayd companies, beside a number of riche hanginges, as well of tapistrie, arras, clothes of golde, silver, velvet, damaske, sattin, and other silkes, plentifullye hanged all the way as the Quenes Highnes passed from the Towre through the Citie.[16]

That these members of the City companies should have such pride of place is not surprising, as they were responsible for financing the celebratory devices through which the procession passed. Furthermore, these men formed what was effectively the government of the City at the time and ran civic matters with a great deal of independence from the Crown. Twenty-six Aldermen, each elected by the various Trade Guilds (for life), were charged with the management of a ward of the city, and they in turn annually elected one of their number to be the new Lord Mayor. These individuals represented a merchant oligarchy, and in the name of the Trade Guilds exercised a controlling influence upon the commercial life of the City. As the highest power in the City, these Guilds, collectively known as the London Corporation, made the arrangements for such celebrations, financing the construction of the pageant stages and the decoration of the streets, as well as paying actors to participate in each of the pageant devices. For this particular procession they also paid for the streets to be gravelled.[17] The Aldermen formed part of the leading section of the procession, and the Lord Mayor proceeded in close proximity to the Queen, demonstrating his position as first citizen, possessing power both in connection with and independent of the sovereign. This relationship between civic and royal authority was emphasised when, during the Recognition March Ralph Cholmley, the Recorder of the City, presented the Queen with 1000 marks in gold on behalf of the Trade Guilds.

The cultural and ideological textures of a pre-coronation procession and that of a victory procession are naturally and importantly different, not least in the fact that the latter is less contrived and therefore need not seek to transmit its message in as allegorical a fashion as the former. In the pre-coronation procession, the nation addresses and is addressed by the impending monarch, a dialectic that negotiates and monitors notions of sovereign worthiness, suitability and competence, as well as those of subjectification. A victory procession, on the other hand, witnesses a monarch who has already shown themself to be worthy, suitable and competent, and who can furthermore be represented as the nation's saviour. This latter position is naturally less ambiguous and uncertain than the former, and does not require the extent of mythologising in order to convince the nation/populace of the appropriate nature of their taking a subject position.[18] Such a reality is underlined by the fact that the pre-coronation procession saw the production of five elaborate pageant devices, whereas the Victory procession merely proceeded along the streets to St Paul's, where thanks were given to God.

This difference between the two types of royal entry is underlined by the fact that no celebratory pamphlet was commissioned by the City in order to commemorate Elizabeth's procession through London in 1588, suggesting that the praise offered to the Queen was self-evidently deserved. The material procession was every bit as elaborate and spectacular as that which progressed through the City in 1558 however, evidenced by both the previously mentioned inventory of participants and in a letter sent by the new Lord Mayor of London, Sir Martin Calthorpe to the various Livery companies, ordering them to prepare for the Queen's procession.[19] As well as ordering the companies to 'be in readynesse against the said tyme, with theire liverye hoodes, attyred in their best apparel', he required the 'standinges to be stronge, and well rayled; the fore-rayle to be covered with a faire blewe clothe'.[20] Documents existent in the Court books of the Company of Stationers[21] itemise some of the costs incurred, including those for the 'standers and streamers to be set up as shall best beseeme the place' ordered by the Mayor.[22] A description of the procession emphasises its spectacular nature, where along with the great number of participants, the Queen came 'in a chariot-throne made with foure pillars behind to have a canopie, on the toppe whereof was made a crowne imperiall, and two lower pillars before, whereon stood a lyon and a dragon, supporters of the armes of England, drawne by two white horses ...'.[23] As in the pre-coronation procession a gift was presented to the Queen as 'Edward Schets Corvinus, an officer of her Privie Chamber, gave her Majestie a jewell, contayning a crapon or toade-stone set in golde ...'.[24] The Queen was again met by the Mayor and some of the Aldermen who then accompanied her to the service at St Paul's. In their display of grandeur and affluence, therefore, both the pre-coronation and Victory processions could be considered 'total' events as, despite their differences, they represent a material demonstration of dissymmetry, and form spectacular material centres. Just such a material entity is marked in the rural processional displays that the Queen and Court annually produced, the Royal progresses.

Like the royal entries and pageants, summer progresses were not an Elizabethan innovation but rather had their roots in the Middle Ages. Elizabeth herself was an enthusiastic visitor who, Alison Plowden informs us, 'covered a lot of ground and actually slept in 241 different recorded places',[25] and, according to Mary Hill Cole visited 'over 400 individual and civic hosts' during her reign.[26] With the exception of the years when there were graver than usual fears for her safety, Elizabeth and her Court left the city in order to enjoy the country air. One of the major reasons for these royal tours was to escape the very real danger of the city, rank with the threat of the Plague. This was no idle threat, as Paul Slack points out in his detailed study of Plague epidemics; in 1563, for example, 24 per cent of London's population died because of the disease.[27] The death rate was particularly high in the capital, and concentrated also in the summer months. Another practical reason for going on progress was the Queen's ability for shifting a part of the enormous cost of keeping her Court onto one of her nobles, thus alleviating the burden on her own coffers. This too was no small matter as Elizabeth observed the depletion of her treasury year by year, not least because of the continuing conflict with the Spanish. Some of the costs for the entertainment and lodging of the Queen and her Court were borne by the host, and he would additionally be expected to present the sovereign with a symbol of his affection, usually in the form of expensive jewellery.

The overriding function of the progresses, however, was a political one, as it was for the royal entries. The parade that left London and wound its way through the countryside would not, in spectacular terms, be very different from that outlined in the Victory procession, and might indeed have been more impressive considering the sheer length of a procession which contained up to 400 carts and some 2400 pack-horses.[28] The entire Court and all of its belongings often accompanied the Queen, forming a congregation that radiated affluence and power. A plan produced by Lord Burleigh in 1583 for his entertainment of Elizabeth at Theobalds describes a guest inventory, and indicates the scale of the task of having the Queen and her Court visit (see Appendix 2).[29] Jean Wilson writes in the context of this inventory: 'What Burleigh had to cater for was not just Elizabeth and her Court, but that Court's servants, the servants' servants, the Queen's private kitchen staff, and the administrative staff that was necessary even when she was away from London ...'.[30]

While it is probable that Burleigh was anything but impressed by such a logistical and financial task, Elizabeth was aware of the propagandist rewards that were to be reaped from such a display of affluence and power, rewards founded in the effects that this perceived accessibility produced. En route to the various stately homes of the nobles and gentry to be visited she was visible to the common people, and indeed made herself so visible as this was a primary function of the progress. Not only was the Queen tying the bonds of loyalty between herself and various nobles, such as the Earl of Leicester (Kenilworth), Lord Norris (Rycote), Lord Montague (Cowdray), and the Earl of Hertford (Elevetham) among others, she was cementing them between herself and the people who were in the service of those same nobles. Thus while, as Chambers says, the 'give and take of gracious courtesies' took place within the house of a particular noble and confirmed 'the bonds of personal affection and loyalty upon which much ... of Elizabeth's domestic statecraft so securely rested' (1:107), these same bonds between Elizabeth and the majority of her rural subjects were seen to be tied both by this honourable exchange in aristocratic surroundings and by her presence on the path or highway. The splendour of the sovereign in this rural place can be regarded as a major underlying mode of spectacular representation that was seen to be effective in terms of subjecting those at whom the display was aimed.

In these rural processions, civic authority is not as important as in their urban equivalent, and although all areas had some form of this authority, it did not play the determining role it did in London. One consequence of this was that, to a great extent, the space through which the procession was to pass was not prepared, other than having the royal Waymaker study the roads earlier in the year, having the area checked for cases of plague, and having the itinerary confirmed with the Queen's hosts. However, it is possible to perceive a positive propagandist effect created by the passing of the sovereign and the procession. As the progress made its way through the land – land which would, as they neared their destination, belong to the member of the aristocracy to be visited – it would invoke a process whereby it would contribute to the credibility of the prospective host and, simultaneously, siphon off a similar (local) legitimacy by its association with them. Just such a reality is apparent in the Ditchley Portrait of Elizabeth, painted in 1592 to commemorate the visit of the Queen to Sir Henry Lee, Master of the Armoury, at his stately home in Ditchley, Oxfordshire (see cover illustration).[31] Elizabeth stands with her feet squarely in the county of Oxfordshire, the very centre of Sir Henry Lee's land. She towers above England, which itself seems to stretch over the earth, setting Ditchley, by her presence, at the centre of the world. In this scenario, Ditchley/Sir Henry Lee and Elizabeth feed off each other in a constitution of reciprocal legitimation. This mutual exchange is further exemplified as the Queen 'symbolically banishes storms behind her and ushers in golden sunshine', bringing prosperity to that land where, in the entertainments that Sir Henry Lee provided, she symbolically 'dispelled enchantments and thus awoke her host from a magical slumber'.[32] Elizabeth's presence pulls Ditchley to the very centre where she 'stands as an empress on the globe of the world',[33] whilst Lee's land enables and supports such a global possibility.

Elizabeth and her Court visited many stately homes on their summer progresses and were entertained with pageant devices and masques on many of these visits.[34] Often the destination of the progress would be another city, such as Bristol, Norwich, Coventry, or Warwick, and in each the Queen would make a royal entry, though never on the scale of those which took place in London. These too had a foundation in propaganda, the Queen seeking the affection and thus loyalty of the inhabitants of these cities through the device of spectacle. However, in terms of such propaganda, whether in the city or in the country, on the streets or the highways, there is a cut-off point, a limit that is the interface of inclusion and exclusion. There is a defining limit of those who display and those at whom the display is aimed. The immediate population is pulled toward these official centres in order to underwrite them, but can instead reject them. Furthermore, this official desire for underwriting is based on an exclusion of certain groups that is a major defining element of the material centre. It is a process which is always a founding moment of the spectacular display itself, a condition of its very existence. It is a process discernible in contemporary documents dealing with these processions.

'To require the people to be silent'

Traditional readings of Elizabethan processions and entertainments, whether urban or rural, have taken their cue from the commissioned descriptions/pamphlets that appeared to coincide with the respective celebrations and, while initially admitting their propagandist nature, proceed to take them at face value as articulating a genuine exchange of mutual affection. That this practice is deeply conventional is evidenced by the fact that it is difficult to find any account of these texts that takes their ideological thrust seriously, and that consistently considers the implications that any reading of them must take into consideration. These conventional analyses are lacking in this respect, a defining repercussion of an evident slippage that occurs between the initial perception of propaganda and the final uncovering of an unproblematic dialectic of love between sovereign and subjects. A closer examination of this process with regard to the pre-coronation and Victory processions will demonstrate this lack, and will enable also the production of a plethora of information that constitutes this lack.

The founding and inspirational text for conventional readings of Elizabeth's pre-coronation procession is the pamphlet attributed to Richard Mulcaster, *The Passage Of Our Most Drad Soveraigne Lady Quene Elyzabeth Through The Citie Of London To Westminster The Daye Before Her Coronacion*,[35] commissioned by the London Corporation in order to celebrate the occasion as well as to disseminate the message of the spectacle enacted in the streets of the capital. The existent record of Mulcaster's payment for his commission is interesting in many ways, not least in the fact that it is made clear that the Queen herself received a copy of his pamphlet:

> Itm yt was orderyd and agreyd by the Court here this day that the Chamblyn shall geue vnto Rychard Mulcaster for his reward for makyng of the boke conteynynge and declaryng the historyes set furth in and by the Cyties pageaunte at the tyme of the Quenes highnes comyng thurrough the Cytye to her coronacon xls wch boke was geuyn vnto the Quenes grace.[36]

The pamphlet appeared nine days after the procession itself, and seems also to have been reprinted almost immediately, indicating its popularity.[37] In the next chapter this pamphlet will be subjected to a close textual reading, based around an investigation of the description of the pageant devices performed for Elizabeth. For now, I wish to examine the tone of this text, in terms of the emphasis that Mulcaster puts upon the adoration and love shown by the procession's audience for their Queen, and to note also that subsequent analyses of this procession have uncritically accepted and drawn upon this emphasis.

Mulcaster's opening sentence records the entrance of the Queen into the city, 'richely furnished', and 'most honourably accompanied' by the splendour of 'Gentlemen, Barons, and other the Nobilite of this Realme, as also with a notable trayne of goodly and beawtifull Ladies, richly appoynted' (38). This immediately communicates the spectacular nature of the event, a reality that Mulcaster demonstrates by his recording of the audience's response to the procession's entrance in his next sentence:

> And entryng the Citie was of the People received marveylous entirely, as appeared by the assemblie, prayers, wishes, welcomminges, cryes, tender woordes, and all other signes, which argue a wonderfull earnest love of most obedient subjectes towarde theyr soveraigne (38).

Mulcaster makes it clear that this is not a love that travels in one direction, but insists on its mutual nature, the Queen demonstrating her love for the people 'so that on eyther syde there was nothing but gladnes, nothing but prayer, nothing but comfort' (38). He continues in the same manner, perceiving the circulation of this mutual adoration:

> The Quenes Majestie rejoysed marveilously to see that so exceadingly shewed towarde her Grace, which all good Princes have ever desyred. I meane so earnest love of subjectes, so evidently declared even to her Grace's owne person, being carried in the middest of them. The People again were wonderfully rauished with the louing answers and gestures of theyr Princesse, like to the which they had before tryed at her first comming to the Towre from Hatfield. This her Grace's loving behaviour preconceived in the People's heades upon these considerations was then throughly confirmed, and indede emplanted a wonderfull hope in them touchyng her woorthy Governement in the reste of her Reygne. For in all her passage, she did not only shew her most gracious love toward the people in generall, but also privately, if the baser personages had offered her Grace any flowers or such like as a signification of their good wyll, or moved to her any sute, she most gently, to the common rejoysing of all lookers on, and private comfort of the partie, staid her chariot, and heard theyr requestes. So that if a man shoulde say well, he could not better tearme the Citie of London that time, than a stage wherein was shewed the wonderfull spectacle, of a noble hearted Princesse toward her most loving People, and the People's exceding comfort in beholding so worthy a Soveraigne, and hearing so Prince like a voice ... could not but enflame her naturall, obedient, and most loving People ... . Thus therefore the Quenes Majestie passed from the Towre till she came to Fanchurche, the People on eche side joyously beholdyng the viewe of so gracious a Ladye theyr Quene ... (38–9).

This account of an exchange of reciprocal love has been reproduced at some length in order to show how Mulcaster delineates for the reader an occasion characterised by its unproblematic and implicit acknowledgment of degree, indeed its effusive celebration of hierarchy. In this account, the Queen has already been successful in gaining the support and love of her subjects, has already won them over, has already become the fulfilment of their desire to be justly and nobly ruled. While this excerpt articulates both the skill with which Elizabeth presented herself publicly, and the sense in which this presentation took place in a 'theatrical' setting,[38] it is Mulcaster's construction of the nature of the audience that I wish to focus upon. The importance of such a study cannot be overstressed, as his delineation of this audience and its responses to the sovereign's presence has been transmitted throughout history, being endlessly reproduced in a manner characterised by a focusing upon the dominant and dominating figure of Elizabeth herself and ignoring to a great extent the complexity of the procession's possible contemporary audience.

This conventional reading of the procession began almost immediately, as is demonstrated by its coverage in Holinshed's *Chronicles*, where it is evident that Mulcaster's pamphlet has simply been reproduced word for word.[39] It begins:

> At hir entring the citie, she was of the people receiued maruellous intierlie, as appeared by the assemblies, praiers, wishes, welcommings, cries, tender words, and all other signes which argued a wonderfull earnest love of most obedient subiects towards their souereigne (159).

The text continues in this manner, mutual love obviously once more the overriding theme. Holinshed commissioned his *Chronicle* in 1570, finally appeared in 1577, and was for many years regarded as historically accurate and not as a work of propaganda. The propagandist nature of this work is underlined, however, by the fact that it merely reproduces Mulcaster's report. But it is important also in the way that, through this reproduction, it initiates the construction of a credibility around the truth-value of the events as produced by Mulcaster. An incremental integrity is apparent in the casting as 'truth' of the initial 'truth' of an earlier text, a reality that is visible in the further transmission of those 'truths' to our own day. In his influential study of *The Reign of Elizabeth 1558–1603*, a part of 'The Oxford History of England' series, J. B. Black demonstrates precisely this process of transmission, whereby assumed knowledge is passed off as fact. Regarding the pre-coronation procession he writes: 'From the first day of her arrival in the capital ... the young queen revelled in the enthusiastic loyalty of her subjects, feasting their eyes with equipages ... . The popular rejoicing reached a climax on the eve of the coronation ...'.[40] This is typical of the sort of statement regarding the nature of the audience that has traditionally appeared in historical writings, as is clear from the influential works of J. B. Neale, E. C. Wilson, Frances Yates, and Roy Strong. This is further evidenced by that most highly regarded examination of processions to date, David Bergeron's *English Civic Pageantry: 1558–1642* where, despite the disclaimer that Mulcaster's pamphlet is indeed 'a marvellous piece of propaganda' in which 'Elizabeth is seen in an extremely favourable light' (13), he writes that from 'Fenchurch to Temple Bar the sovereign has moved through the city amid the shouts and acclamations of London's citizens' (22). This demonstrates 'a give-

and-take ... an intimacy of reaction', so that one 'is impressed with how the elements of actor, audience, and honoured guest fuse into a single compound of entertainment ...' (15). Thus Bergeron perceives the dominant theme of the event to have been one of unity, and he perceives with what success this has been achieved.

Naturally enough, this kind of admiration reaches its peak in the more hagiographic, popularising studies of Elizabeth such as that previously looked at, Alison Plowden's *Elizabethan England: Life in an Age of Adventure*. Here there is an attempt to bring the occasion to life, filling it with pathos and melodrama: 'It was a cold January day, with flurries of snow in the air and muddy underfoot, but no discomforts of cold or wet feet could dampen the enthusiasm of the Londoners as they waited to greet their Queen ...' (13). Plowden grounds her observations in a historical context by then quoting from a 'contemporary account', the author of which (Mulcaster) she does not name, nor indicates had written this account on a commission. She continues: 'Bells pealed, musicians played and everywhere the crowds cheered in ecstasy as they caught their first glimpse of the slim, red-headed young woman in her sumptuous robes ...' (13). Much of the contemporary account is further referred to until the procession comes to an end: 'And so, as the winter dusk closed in, borne along on a great warm emotional wave-crest of love and joy, England's Elizabeth came home ...' (17). As previously stated, Plowden's study happens to be one of the most pervasive accounts of the pre-coronation procession, and is certainly one of the most accessible. It would indeed be possible to suggest that its status as popular history disqualifies its being taken seriously, and that its methodology and its aims do not require the attention to bibliographical detail more scholarly studies do. The desire behind its use in this current study is, however, an attempt to outline the wide range that this conventional knowledge covers, the success which typifies the transmission of this field of evidence. And, with regard to Plowden's absences, it is interesting to note that Stephen Greenblatt, when quoting from the very same source in an attempt to support his theory of Elizabeth as successful actress and processions as successful sites for the subjectification of the population, informs us that it was written by 'one observer'.[41] There is no mention in Greenblatt's analysis, one of the most important modern academic studies of the period, of who this observer was, nor indeed of the status of his contemporary account.

The failure of Greenblatt and Plowden to state the ideological positioning of their source material is important in terms of a further, similar lack that is discernible. For while those scholars who acknowledge their use of Mulcaster further agree that they are drawing upon a text characterised by its function as propaganda, they immediately allow a slippage that enables them to accept much, if not all, of what it says as fact. Thus we can read Bergeron's disclaimer about the pamphlet being 'a marvellous piece of propaganda', and then, within the same sentence, that it is 'in addition ... a record of the events ...'. This is perhaps acceptable in the sense that there is little documentation of the event itself, and every record that exists needs to be read carefully. However, it is necessary to take it seriously not just as a record of events, but as propaganda also. For, despite the fact that evidence regarding the procession is scarce, there are two other eyewitness accounts of the event (one of which is extensive and highly detailed) that could be said to be more disinterested than Mulcaster's in their observation of events. The authors of these accounts may have been somewhat disadvantaged in comparison to Mulcaster in that they were perhaps not privy to certain information and so their observations are not as full as the official author's. Whatever they consist of or lack, however, they do need to be taken seriously.

It would be unfair to deny the fact that scholars do indeed draw upon these other eyewitness accounts in their analysis of the pre-coronation procession. Bergeron, for example, quotes liberally from the text of Il Schifanoya, the Venetian Ambassador who wrote a long report concerning the procession to the Castellan of Mantua, one that Bergeron quite rightly states is the 'chief contemporary account in addition to the specially prepared quarto' attributed to Mulcaster.[42] Alison Plowden and Clifford Geertz peruse it also and extract certain details regarding both the size and the splendour of the occasion,[43] a move that typifies many studies of the procession. Particularly important for all of these studies is the Venetian Ambassador's estimation of the number of horses in the procession (and thus by extension the number of humans present), as well as his description of the splendid and rich appearance of the Queen. Important too is his description of the decoration of the streets, and of the positioning of the members of the Guilds in specially constructed wooden enclosures. This information is reproduced in most descriptions of the procession, and tends to confirm the spectacular nature of the whole event, particularly when immersed in an analysis that uses the Mulcaster text descriptively. Occasionally, the third existent eyewitness account of the procession is used, though because it is rather brief (a mere two pages), and because much of what it reports is contained in the Venetian despatch, the relevant excerpt from Henry Machyn's *Diary* is often ignored.[44]

The use of these two eyewitness accounts, in conjunction with Mulcaster's, brings us to an important point. For, these texts tend to be read in a parallel manner, that is to say, additionally. They are rarely read against each other, rarely set at odds, in terms that perceive them to be texts of differing status. They are read as though they are interchangeable, and Mulcaster's text is seldom read sceptically in comparison, seldom read as propaganda. On the one occasion where this does happen, in Sandra Logan's important study 'Making History: The Rhetorical and Historical Occasion of Elizabeth Tudor's Coronation Entry',[45] the conflict between the various accounts is seen in religious terms alone. Logan writes that Mulcaster's text represents a Protestant interpretation of the event, while those of Henry Machyn and Il Schifanoya, both of whom were Catholics, are essentially Catholic interpretations. While Logan's reading is important for this current study in the sense that it questions the 'truth-value' of Mulcaster's text, at no point does she ponder the way in which Mulcaster attempts to achieve his aims by representing the audience of the procession in certain ways. This being the case, Logan's essay stands as an example of the type of processional analysis that has appeared since the high point of New Historicism. She questions the transmission of conventional knowledge but, in contrast to this current study, sees the conflict as one between various dominant groups rather than considering those other, less powerful groups at whom the spectacular display was aimed. The importance of such a perception and methodology becomes clear with regard to the nature of the common people/audience and their response to the coming of the Queen when it is realised that of the three accounts it is only Mulcaster who mentions the crowd at all. In both the Venetian account, and that of Machyn, there is not a single mention of the presence that defines the content and tone of Mulcaster's report and that, in many ways, constitutes the ideological thrust of his whole project.[46] For Mulcaster, this presence is a determining one, emphasising both the mutual love that circulated between population and sovereign and the acceptance of a Foucauldian dissymmetry by the former. It defines for us a unified population, content in its certainty of a rigid, secure and natural hierarchy. And of course, as demonstrated, this presence fills the pages of analyses of this procession from Holinshed onwards, through the likes of Bergeron and Plowden, into the modern readings of the New Historicism and beyond. The presence of these 'most obedient subjects' has in turn become a constitutive element in studies of the nature of Elizabeth, of Elizabethan processions and, further, of Elizabethan society itself.

The absence articulated by these two eyewitness accounts obviously needs to be considered and must be negotiated. What they fail to record is not proof that the audience described by Mulcaster was in fact absent. Perhaps they suggest rather something similar to what Glynne Wickham has observed with regard to medieval processions:

> The starting point – of a ruler's claim to rule – was the physical manifestation of the ruler's person to the subjects assembled within the capital city. This could most conveniently be achieved by a procession through the streets which were lined for the occasion with beholders. *I say 'lined' rather than 'thronged' because the fullest discipline that medieval civic administration could achieve was enforced on these occasions* (emphasis added).[47]

The early modern period had a much more sophisticated system of communication (and coercion), but Wickham's observation is relevant. It should be remembered (though in the majority of studies it is not) that the decoration and gravelling of the streets, as well as the actual presence of the members of the Guilds, had been ordered by the Lord Mayor. Thus the 'City was at very great charge to express their love and joy',[48] an order that the Guilds were careful to adhere to for, as contemporary evidence demonstrates, their failure to do so would have consequences: 'Not failinge hereof, as you will answere the contraire at your perill'.[49] As stated, most studies use the information concerning the presence of the Guilds, yet do so as a way of adding to the implicit agreement of all sections of Elizabethan London to play their part in the event, and also to help conjure up the sense of spontaneous celebration that characterised the procession. There is very rarely mention of the Guilds being ordered to follow certain instructions.

Returning to the theme of the common people as audience, perhaps they are absent in Machyn's and Il Schifanoya's accounts because they were, in fact, rather quiet, rather un-celebratory, as the crowd had apparently been in 1533 for the entry of Anne Boleyn.[50] Or perhaps because these recorders of the event, members of the higher orders of society, viewed the procession in such a way as to remain blind to the presence of the mob. If so, perhaps the crowds of 'adoring subjects' were simply not seen, or not recorded, because it was felt that they were not important. Whatever we wish to surmise regarding this absence, the reading of these documents in this way asks certain questions of Mulcaster's text, and contributes to a desire to read it sceptically. It adds to the need to read it as a propagandist text, especially in terms of what it actually makes out of the status of the audience. This is important in the further terms of what has been made out of that presence which Mulcaster represents in such an emphatic manner. This is particularly apparent in certain sections of the procession where Elizabeth continually has difficulty in hearing and requests the crowd to be silent to enable her to hear what is being said (to her) at the pageant devices. Much has been made of this, not least in terms of how interested Elizabeth was in hearing the normative lessons that were being enacted, thus giving the impression of being a good and obedient sovereign, one who takes the views of her subjects into account. Her ability as an effective actress has also been stressed in this context, as has her skill in manipulating the crowd. Finally, the fact that there was so much cheering has been interpreted as an indication of the love felt for her by her subjects. However, not only are the crowds absent in the other accounts of the procession, there is also no mention of the Queen having to halt and quieten anybody, or having to send a messenger forward to request silence at each pageant device as she approached, as it appears in Mulcaster (and many subsequent studies): 'And ere the Quenes Majestie came wythin hearing of thys Pageaunt, she sent certaine, as also at all the other Pageauntes, to require the People to be silent. For her Majestie was disposed to heare all that shoulde be sayde unto her' (44).

The final section of Mulcaster's pamphlet is particularly interesting in this context, and reveals in its textual form the constructed nature of his undertaking. This section takes the form of an addendum or an appendix and is entitled 'Certain notes of the Queenes Majesties great mercie, clemencie, and wisdom, used in this passage' (58). This appendix contains a number of examples of the Queen's interchanges with certain members of the crowd during the procession, and lists her responses to certain situations and comments she had overheard. Among other things, she cheers up a crying man, smiles at the mention of the name of her own father and confirms the authority of the city. These various examples attempt to personalise the Queen, to underline her caring nature, and to instil a sense of her integrity through communicating the nobility of her thought even when expressed spontaneously. The fact that they are tacked on to the end of the record of the procession invokes the possibility that they were in fact invented events. They appear almost as an afterthought, as though her humanity and approachability had not been made apparent enough in the main body of the text. These examples of the Queen's humanity/integrity have often been repeated, and much has also been made of them. Yet again, however, none of these events are present in the other eyewitness accounts of the procession, neither in the main texts nor in the form of appendices. This is another example of that absence noted above, but now with an added dimension. For stress should be laid upon the fact that the report of Il Schifanoya is a very full description of the procession and the pageants performed for the Queen. As such, it is relevant that, within the context of such a full description, certain defining moments and events (for Mulcaster) are absent. These moments and events are defining in the history of analysis of this procession and of this society, and need to be seen to have arisen from a document that has been 'scratched over and recopied many times'.

Traditional analysis has relied upon Mulcaster's pamphlet to initiate the construction of a defining relationship between sovereign and subjects that has developed into a greater delineation of the power relations of Elizabethan society as a whole. Spectacular display/ritual is regarded as the touchstone of the representation of the dissymmetrical nature of these power relations, the population being subjected by their contemplation of the arbitrary potency of the monarch. Foucault writes (with regard to public executions which, as stated earlier, he equates with such practices as royal entries) that in 'the ceremonies of the public execution, the main character was the people, whose real and immediate presence was required for the performance'.[51] If it is therefore accepted that such rituals as royal entries did seek to interpellate/hail the population – their 'main character' – then this main character would obviously need to be present in order to receive their lesson. The above discussion of the main character at the entry for Elizabeth suggests that their presence was not perhaps what it has traditionally been made out to be. There is the possibility that they were in fact, to a large extent, absent. Conversely, there is the possibility that this main character was indeed present, but not in the way outlined by Mulcaster. There are other potential perspectives from which this presence can be observed to suggest a more realistic setting than that defined for us by those conventional readings of the relationship between Elizabeth and her subjects. If a crowd of common people was present at Elizabeth's pre-coronation procession, it is possible that they would not have received and celebrated the Queen in the manner claimed by Mulcaster, but in a much more sporadic, reluctant, attenuated way. Given the harsh and arbitrary social conditions in which many people lived in London at that time, is it convincing to perceive the common response to a spectacular display of affluence as one of monolithic adoration? It is worth examining the evidence that exists with regard to these social conditions in order to try to determine what this reaction is likely to have been, to see whether the common presence was in fact a reluctant and sceptical one.

'The insolence of the mob is extreme'

The social stability of the population in early modern London is the site of an ongoing and controversial debate within the subject area of historical studies, a conflict that has witnessed the emergence of two major conceptions of the population that divide into camps which claim the ruling factor to be one of stability or, alternatively, instability. The camp which tends towards the perception of a guiding principle of stability is characterised by the studies of V. Pearl and Steve Rappaport, who take as their overarching historical proof the fact that London did not witness any kind of major uprising in the Elizabethan period, demonstrating the reality of a well-governed City with each level of society accepting its hierarchical position and collectively working towards the greater good.[52] These studies are characterised by their depiction of a city ruled by consensus, and continually set themselves up against prior studies that recognised a certain level of instability in the capital at the time. Such are the findings of A. L. Beier, Paul Slack and Peter Clark, scholars who tend to suggest that London sometimes lurched towards a significant popular rebellion, particularly in the troublesome final decade of Elizabeth's rule.[53]

While it should be noted that Pearl and Rappaport tend to overstate their case against this latter group of historians, in the sense that they believe this group to be drawing conclusions much more extreme than in fact they actually are, rather than follow the logic of either of these courses it suits the purposes of this study to follow the trajectory set up by Ian Archer, in which he outlines a convincing case for the perception of *potential* instability by the governing classes of Elizabethan London, a perception that led them to attempt to counter subversive forces with a (confused) mixture of legislation and physical force.[54] Archer believes that the ruling elite came more and more to perceive a sense of crisis, and therefore felt the need to counter it. This accounts both for the apparent obsession of the authorities with regard to the passing of laws against such groups as vagrants, apprentices and disbanded soldiers and sailors during this period, and for the fact that the vast numbers of individuals who were disadvantaged by the social structure in the capital never joined in sufficient numbers to endanger that structure. Records for the latter part of Elizabeth's reign are much fuller than for the early part, and it is therefore important to acknowledge that to take an extreme position as to the reality of actual instability in this period would perhaps be foolhardy. A lack of evidence makes it impossible to generalise about such a matter. However, it is worth looking at the statistics that do exist in an attempt to both diversify and question the notion of the common people as having been successfully subjected in the way suggested by traditional criticism in the case of, for example, the pre-coronation procession. The aim of such a perusal is not to suggest that these individuals were forcibly held back at the procession in their attempt to harm the monarch. Rather it is to suggest that conceptions of their presence as uncritical consumers of successful spectacle is more to do with normative (re)constructions of the reality of an overriding principle of unity than with any notion of historical accuracy. A brief examination of the several material factors that would have impacted upon the lives of the common people is necessary in order to ascertain what their experience of such spectacles is likely to have been.

Perhaps the most remarkable aspect of London during this period was its vast growth in population. According to statistics reproduced by Beier and Finlay, London 'grew from a middling city of 120,000 in 1550, to 200,000 in 1600 (a 67% increase), 375,000 in 1650 (an 88% increase)',[55] a process that naturally caused problems regarding housing, employment, disease and crime. Much of this growth was the direct result of the enclosure of land, as well as harvest failures and the laying-off of retainers, soldiers and sailors.[56] This being the case, the vast majority of migrants into London through the course of this period were poor, single males who were often completely destitute. These groups added to the burgeoning population of urban poor, subject to the vagaries of London's economic life, particularly the insecurity of its centralised cloth trade.[57] The suburbs especially witnessed a soaring rise in population, thus the emergence of pervasive poverty and vagrancy occurred amongst a population very much at the mercy of the plague.

The early years of Elizabeth's reign witnessed a plague epidemic that seriously affected London's population. In 1563, for example, Paul Slack notes that nearly a quarter of the capital's populace was wiped out. Slack goes on to state that there was also a high recovery rate for plague – somewhere in the region of 40 per cent – and that therefore in 1563, particularly in the summer months, perhaps as much as 40 per cent of London's population was incapacitated.[58] It should be noted that 1563 also seems to have been one of the worst years for plague in Elizabeth's reign. However, even if we accept that perhaps only half of the figure quoted for population incapacitation could be applied to the year of the pre-coronation procession, it still presents us with the probability of there being a real crisis in terms of disease. And further, this possibility is emphasised if we also take into account the fact that, at the very moment of Elizabeth's coronation – the height of winter – England was in the middle of its worst ever influenza epidemic. Again according to Slack, this epidemic 'produced the greatest mortality crisis of the whole period [1485–1665] between 1557 and 1559, when 11 per cent of the population of England may have died',[59] a fact that witnessed 'the worst demographic disaster in the country's history in the whole period covered by parish registers'.[60] Needless to say, much like the plague, there was also no doubt a high recovery rate for influenza, the recorded death rate therefore not reflecting the true impact of the disease, nor indeed its pervasiveness. While it is certain that the impact of this epidemic, which was at its height at the time of Elizabeth's entry into London in January 1558, was felt by the poorer classes to a much greater extent than by those better off, it should be stressed that this epidemic did not respect class and in 'its later stages ... [it] seems to have affected the prosperous classes at least as much as the poor, as the will statistics suggest ...'.[61]

That London's social structure came under great pressure with this combination of migration and disease is borne out by a plethora of evidence demonstrating the rise of poverty and vagrancy during Elizabeth's reign. A. L. Beier and Roger Finlay point out, for example, that between 1550 and 1598, censuses showed a 3-fold rise in the number of houses in need when the population rose by only a quarter, and show also that vagrancy increased '12-fold from 1560 to 1625, a period in which metropolitan population only quadrupled'.[62] Although problems were greater in the 1590s, much of the legislation passed in the early years of Elizabeth's reign demonstrates an attempt by the authorities to deal with this problem of vagrancy. This included proposals to Parliament in 1559 which 'contained swingeing attacks upon social mobility',[63] a process that was to eventually lead to the so-called 'whipping campaign' of 1569–72, whereby vagrants were encouraged to return to their home towns initially by the threat, and subsequently by the implementation of such a punishment. Beier is very probably overstating his case when he writes that there 'was something like a state of war between the City authorities and the suburban vagrant',[64] but contemporary evidence demonstrates the extent to which the authorities found it necessary to punish this social group.[65]

It is possible, given this scenario, to imagine a large section of the audience (vagrants tended to spend winter in the cities) for the pre-coronation procession as consisting of individuals who were not constituted by their circumstances as 'most loving People'. A significant number of people, whether migrant or indigenous, subject to hunger, poverty, bad housing, overcrowding, plague, influenza, and finding themselves criminalised because of this, would have typified the Londoners present as Elizabeth passed. A mass of poor individuals, often forced into criminal activity, for whom no laws existed that could alleviate their condition, but rather laws that could and would punish them for it, probably stood and witnessed the procession of absolute affluence and absolute inequality pass through the streets, and (we are told) were joyously overcome by the splendour of it all.

While no records exist that relate to any sort of disruption or disorder during Elizabeth's progress through the city, official processions were not always trouble free. Such an occasion is that recorded in the *Calendar of State Papers (Venetian)*, with regard to the 1617 Lord Mayor's Show, *The Triumphs of Honour and Industry*, written by Thomas Middleton.[66] In his despatch, Orazio Busino describes a scene of disorder:

> the insolence of the mob is extreme. They cling behind the coaches and should the coachman use his whip, they jump down and pelt him with mud. In this way we saw them bedaub the smart livery of one coachman, who was obliged to put up with it. In these great uproars no sword is ever unsheathed, everything ends in kicks, fisty cuffs and muddy faces.[67]

While this scene demonstrates the unruliness of the crowd at a spectacular procession, it would be unwise to make too much of it in the terms of this current study. Not only is it anecdotal, it took place some sixty years after the pre-coronation procession, and is also different in the fact that it is a civic rather than a royal entry. However, placed into the context of what has already been said regarding this common presence, it contributes to the problematisation of what has traditionally been held to characterise that presence. This is particularly the case given the specific hardships – plague and influenza – under which the audience for the 1558 procession suffered.

The problematisation of the success of this spectacular event in terms of its ideological aims is further emphasised when certain important allegorical figures present in the pre-coronation procession are examined. The final pageant device, for example, saw the Queen reach Temple Bar, 'which was dressed fynelye with the two ymages of Gotmagot the Albione, and Corineus the Briton, two gyantes bigge in stature, furnished accordingly; which held in their handes, even above the gate, a table, wherin was written ... theffect of all the Pageantes which the Citie before had erected ...'.[68] The sheer size and appearance of these two figures of London mythical history contributed, it was believed, to the spectacular nature of the procession, indeed of every procession in London, belonging as they did to the

Guildhall and representing both the authority and grandeur of the City government.[69] Lawrence Manley clarifies this idea:

> The discursive exchange in the later Tudor entries was reinforced by the strange reappearance of the ancient City palladia at the very limit of the City's jurisdiction at Temple Bar. Both Philip II and then Elizabeth were confronted at the Bar by twin giants – identified in Elizabeth's entry as 'Gotmagot' and 'Corineus' – the city palladia who had stood in apotropaic defiance at the initial entry of many earlier monarchs. Because these figures manifested the City's might and defiant spirit, their new role at Temple Bar was especially significant ... . It is as if in moving their position the City had found ... a new meaning in the strength of its giant representatives. As elsewhere in Europe, where the giant effigies of towns came to symbolise 'the imposition of culture and authority', the power of Gotmagot and Corineus now rested not so much in being 'grym of sight' as in drawing and inscribing powerful conclusions.[70]

In terms of the pre-coronation procession, it can be surmised that these 'powerful conclusions' would be drawn and that the audience would be subjected by the sight of these mythological giants. Not according to George Puttenham however, who in *The Arte Of English Poesie* (1589), referring to the presence of the giants in the Lord Mayor's Show, determines quite the opposite effect:

> But generally the high stile is disgraced and made foolish and ridiculous by all wordes affected, counterfait, and puffed vp ... and can not be better resembled than to these midsommer pageants in London, where, *to make the people wonder*, are set forth great and vglie Gyants marching as if they were aliue, and armed at all points, but within they are stuffed full of browne paper and tow, *which the shrewd boyes vnderpeering do guilefully discouer and turne to a great derision* ... (emphasis added).[71]

What Puttenham is articulating here is the failure of an intended effect, an example of unsuccessful hailing, that both evokes the existence in this ideological desire of its opposite effect and demonstrates the presence of scepticism on the part of the 'shrewd boyes'.[72] It shows the manifestation of a carnival spirit, an opposition to a central authority in terms of physicality and meaning, an antagonism that, if the likes of Dekker and Greene are to be believed in their insistence upon the fact that the Lord Mayor's Show was the natural site for the operation of pickpockets and other criminals, is both defining and uncontroversial.[73] Most of all, it contributes to the construction of an alternative presence constituting the audience of the pre-coronation procession.

This reading of the pre-coronation procession, then, questions the conceptualisation of the crowd both in terms of whether it was there at all and, if it was, what form it took. This general 'hermeneutics of suspicion'[74] produces a number of connecting difficulties with the result that, apart from the general problem of the crowd, a number of local problems also arise. These local difficulties could be said, both individually and collectively, to tarnish the aura of the procession as a successful spectacle. And these local difficulties adhere themselves to a central and general problem that forms a dynamic which places in jeopardy received notions of what the pre-coronation procession has been made to mean.

One striking example emphasises the constructed nature of the procession's meaning and its contemporary setting in a society that was not monolithic but was rather divided in terms of social positionings/groupings. Whilst passing between two of the major pageant devices, Mulcaster informs us that the Queen 'came againste the Great Conduite in Cheape, which was bewtified with pictures and sentences accordinglye against her Graces coming thether' (46). David Bergeron reproduces Mulcaster's observation exactly, and informs us that in the *Repertories* of the Corporation of London there is a record that shows 'payments to painters for decorating the Conduit in Cheapside ...'.[75] However, if we return to the precise record he quotes (*Repertory* XIV: fol.103b), we find that he has missed something. For the record in fact reads as follows: 'Itm for as much as the painters of this City *did utterly refuse* to new paint and trim the Great Conduit in Cheapside ... for the Queen Majesty's coming to her Coronation for the sum of 20 marks ...' (emphasis added).[76] This return to the original records is reminiscent of that in the previous examination of a royal progress and its reproduction in conventional studies such as that by Alison Plowden. A wide-ranging search through the various accounts of the pre-coronation procession has brought to light only one acknowledgement of this refusal by the painters, and that occurs in R. R. Sharpe's *London and the Kingdom*, which is effectively a history of the City read precisely from these original *Repertories* (and thus would be difficult to ignore). Even here, it is recorded as the 'curious instance of a strike among painters',[77] and no reason is given as to why the painters decided to strike, or why Sharpe claims it to be curious. However, the painters' strike meant that:

> the surveyors of the city were instructed to cause the same to be covered with cloth of Arras having escutcheons of the queen's Arms finely made and set therein and the wardens of the Painters' Company were called upon to render assistance with advice and men for reasonable remuneration.[78]

This final 'reasonable remuneration' suggests the reason for the painters' refusal, and the wardens being called in shows that the Painters' Company was no doubt held responsible for the problem. The important point here, however, is that Bergeron's failure to register this refusal, in a record to which he directly refers, is both troubling and confusing. This curious instance, of both the reality of the strike and its subsequent disappearance from contemporary accounts of the work of the painters themselves (let us not forget that Bergeron informs us that the records state that the painters were paid and thus there is no suspicion of strike/refusal – that is, of non-payment), is a real and determining example of the carefully protected identities that Foucault's genealogical methodology attempts to scratch away at. Furthermore, there is a similar problem with Mulcaster's description of the relevant pageant being 'bewtified with pictures'. If the instructions in the *Repertories* are to be believed, the pageant stage was 'covered with cloth of

Arras', rather than pictures, although such cloth could possibly have been decorated with pictures of some sort. The question arises, however, whether Mulcaster was in fact referring to painted pictures that he expected the Conduit to display, as was the case with other pageants in the procession that had been prepared according to the original plan. Thus the Conduit in Fleet Street, the 'fifte and last Pageaunt erected', was, Mulcaster writes, 'bewtified with painting' (53). If this is the case, the suspicion arises that Mulcaster in fact did not witness the earlier pageant device, took no account of the problem caused by the painters' strike, and reported the event according to prior instructions he had received and which detailed what the stage should have looked like. Mulcaster's account is therefore undermined in this instance. And if it is the case that he did not see this particular pageant device, it is possible that he did not see some or all of the others. It is also possible that, whether he saw them or not, he did not report them accurately. Essentially, his possible misreporting of this particular instance could be regarded as undermining his total endeavour. If nothing else, it arouses the suspicion of any modern reader as to the truth-value of Mulcaster's observations. And, however the stage finally appeared, it can be certain that the striking painters themselves, if they were present at the procession at all, certainly would not have been won over by it, and would not have been cheering the spectacle produced by the sovereign and the City.

Another potential local problem could have been caused by the Revels Office carrying out an express order of the Queen herself. This related to the fact that Elizabeth desired that her Gentlemen Pensioners should wear crimson silk for the procession, no doubt in an attempt to make the most impressive kind of show. This led the Privy Council to pass a specific act:

> A letter to the Customers of London to staye all sylkes of the coulour of crymosyn as shall arryve within that Porte untyll the Quenes Majestie shall first have had her choyse towardes the furnyture of her Coronacion, and to geve warning if any suche shall arryve there to the Lordes of the Counsell, and to kepe this matter secrete, etc.[79]

This was an instruction that would have caused silk traders problems, and represents an instance of the Crown's unpopular policy of purveyance whereby goods and services were requisitioned at the will of the crown, and for a price it determined itself. While there are no records (to my knowledge) of complaint with regard to this particular instance, this policy of purveyance was the source of much annoyance among many levels of society. Here, this example merely adds to the possibility of a less than universal welcoming of the fact of the procession and its requirements, most resonant in the Privy Council's final instruction that this was a secret matter. Though perhaps not present at the procession, one can imagine that there were a number of disgruntled silk traders somewhere in England at the time.

This event also brings up the question of Elizabeth's spontaneity with regard to certain reported actions and responses during the procession, and certainly questions the notion of her as an 'unscheduled actor'.[80] This notion has now been seriously compromised, not least by the sort of evidence provided by this act of purveyance. This specific case led Bergeron, for example, to drop the idea of Elizabeth as this unscheduled actor, and to suggest rather that, as part-patron, she was 'no mere passive spectator or grateful recipient of the event'.[81] Helen Hackett believes that Elizabeth's responses at the pageant devices demonstrate that 'she knew what was coming, either because she had been briefed in advance, or possibly even because she had had some influence in the content of the pageants'.[82] Needless to say, studies such as Alison Plowden's (written after Bergeron's new evidence) have failed to register such developments, and continue to (re)produce a reading of the behaviour of the Queen in a way reminiscent of Mulcaster. However, the revelation that Elizabeth was in fact a part-patron of the pageant devices compromises the Mulcaster pamphlet and its insistence on the Queen's spontaneity in terms of its reporting of actual events. For, as Hackett goes on to say, 'the performance of the love between the Queen and her people was less spontaneous than the pamphleteer pretended', was more 'an act of propaganda' (48), and less than a reliable source of historical accuracy. And, although she says it in reference to Mulcaster, Hackett could just as well be talking of Plowden when she writes that in 'its very purporting to be merely a record of a spontaneous up-welling of love between the Queen and her subjects, the pamphlet performs a political function' (48). One wonders to what extent this political function was served by Mulcaster, and whether it extended, as was earlier suggested, to inventing an audience of common people, or at least constructing one whose actual presence was very different to that which finally appears in his pamphlet. If nothing else, it is possible that he misrepresents them.

By examining the ways in which Elizabeth's pre-coronation procession has been transmitted through history to the present day it is possible to see that our understanding of it is still very rooted in the text attributed to Mulcaster, written on a commission from the organisers of the procession. That it should be propagandist is, given this status, no surprise. What is surprising, however, is precisely the fact that our present understanding of this event relies so heavily on an uncritical reproduction of this commissioned text. In many ways the process by which this knowledge has been transmitted is the apotheosis of Walter Benjamin's conceptualisation of the triumphal procession. Much the same can be said for the second major London procession undertaken by Elizabeth, that to celebrate victory over the Spanish Armada on 24 November 1588.

The human inventory for the Victory procession has been referred to previously in terms of its perceived spectacular nature, its sheer size and affluence demonstrating Foucauldian dissymmetry, initiating awe and a process of subjectification in onlookers, particularly those at the base of the social hierarchy. In many ways this procession is constituted by the same ideological elements as the pre-coronation procession in the sense that it is the material centre demonstrating its power in the form of display. As stated earlier, a procession commemorating the victory over a foreign enemy has less allegorical work to do in the sense that any audience would be patriotically moved to celebrate the passing of those regarded as having been responsible for such a victory, particularly the commander-in-chief, the Queen. Such a reality is perhaps best demonstrated by the fact that no pageant devices took place during the procession, as this kind of display was not deemed necessary. Furthermore, this reality is emphasised in the sense that very little has been written about this procession of 1588, a revealing fact when compared to the amount of material available on the procession of 1558. This suggests a perceived lack of potential ambiguity surrounding the Victory procession, allowing for little in the way of interpretation by historians or literary critics. If a broader context is considered in the way it was for the pre-coronation procession, however, it becomes clear that this is not necessarily the case.

Understandably, upon news that the Spanish Armada had been defeated, 'the kingdom was filled with joy, and a sense of gratitude to God'.[83] In London, the site of St Paul's became the central location for the acknowledgement of the victory, the 20 August witnessing the first public celebration, 'when Dr Nowel, Dean of St Paul's, preached at the Cross a Sermon of Thanksgiving, the Lord Maior and Aldermen present, and the Companies in their best liveries'.[84] This was followed by another official day of thanksgiving on 8 September, when 'the Preacher at St Paul's Cross moved the people to give God thanks for the late wonderful overthrow of their enemies, the Spaniards'.[85] Preparations were subsequently made for a victory procession, to culminate in a service at St Paul's, organised by the livery companies through their chief representative, the Lord Mayor. In a letter dated 8 November, Sir Martin Calthorpe, the Mayor, instructed the livery companies to prepare both themselves and the streets for this procession. These preparations included the setting up of railed standings along the side of the road as well as the employment of 'Wiffelers in coates of velvet and chaynes, tenn at the leaste'.[86] As in the pre-coronation procession, the Lord Mayor ends his letter with the following warning: 'requiringe you not to faile hereof, as you will answere the contrarye at your peril'.[87] This procession was due to take place on 17 November to coincide with the celebration of Elizabeth's accession to the throne, but was postponed until the following Sunday as the Queen, for unknown reasons, was unable to attend. Major celebrations took place at St Paul's on 17 November despite Elizabeth's absence, as they did on 19 November, again at St Paul's. Finally, on the 24 November the Victory procession took place, the Queen and other participants progressing through the streets from Somerset House to St Paul's (see Appendix 1).

As well as her Privy Council, various nobles, foreign ambassadors and the civic authorities of London participating in the procession, it is noted that Elizabeth progressed in a 'chariot-throne' with 'her footemen and pensioners about her', and 'the guarde on foote in their rich coats, and halbards in their hands'.[88] As in the pre-coronation procession, the Queen was surrounded by armed guards, protected against any possible attack by a potential foreign or domestic enemy. Furthermore, as in the earlier procession, the Mayor, after a number of speeches, took pride of place alongside Elizabeth and the 'Companies of the Cittie in their liveries stoode in their rayles of tymber, covered with blue cloth, all of them saluting her Highnesse as she proceeded ...'.[89] At St Paul's the Queen was met by the 'Bishop of London, the Deane of Paul's, and other of the Clergie, to the number of more than fiftie, all in rich coapes',[90] and then entered to hear a sermon by the Bishop of Salisbury before going to the Bishop's palace to dine.

It is clear from this description of events, in combination with the human inventory previously mentioned, that the Victory procession is a classic example of an early modern 'total event', and that it would be seen to work in the same way ideologically as the pre-coronation procession: as a triumphal procession. However, with the mention of the guards surrounding Elizabeth as she progressed through the city there is the potential for a different kind of reading, one which questions the effectiveness of this event as propaganda, one which again considers it from the perspective of its targeted subject, the common people. In this particular case, an examination of the contemporary lot of a specific section of the common people sheds a different light upon the fact that Elizabeth was so heavily guarded and, in the process, destabilises the propagandist desire of the entire procession.

In the thirty years that separated the pre-coronation and Victory processions little had changed in the lives of the common people of London. Plague was still a constant threat, and life generally was still ruled by the fact of the continuing rapid increase in the population and the resultant problems concerning housing, employment, disease and crime. No epidemic of influenza is recorded for this year as it was in 1558, but conditions for the common population were, with this exception, effectively the same. Indeed, the enclosure of land by the gentry had increased as Elizabeth's reign progressed, and more and more poor, single males found themselves in the capital, often as beggars and, in turn, criminals. A growing problem for the authorities in London, particularly through the 1580s, was the number of disbanded soldiers and sailors who tended to head for the capital city and who, records show us, were willing to demonstrate their unhappy lot in the streets of the city. This is particularly true of the soldiers and sailors disbanded around the time of the Victory procession.

According to C. G. Cruickshank, the common soldier's lot in the army of Elizabeth I was an almost intolerable one, these young men finding that 'wars held only hardship and misery', and that they were 'powerless to alleviate their suffering'.[91] Cruickshank details the various hardships under which the soldiers suffered, corruption of the upper ranks and the consequent non-payment of wages being chief among them. This resentment felt between the common soldier and his commander-in-chief is recorded in a letter preserved in the *Calendar of State Papers (Foreign)*, where Captain Peter Crips reports on an event that occurred during the Netherlands campaign, in the army camp in Utrecht, on 28 March 1586. Captain Crips' explanation of the origins of a mutiny by the soldiers is worth reproducing here at length:

> The Earl of Leicester going to Count Maurice to dinner, there came certain soldiers of Capt. Thomas Poole's company, and one A. T. in behalf of the rest, demanded their pay. His Excellency conferred with Sir John Norreys, who commanded me, Peter Crips, then marshal, to take and hang the said A. T., whom I carried to prison. Then all the soldiers in the town 'grew into arms', broke open the prison, carried away the said A. T. and offered to shoot at me and my men, staying me by force while the prisoner was carried away.

At that instant, two companies of 'Welshmen' came into the town, by whose aid the prisoner was again committed to prison, with nine of the chief mutineers. Sir John then ordered every company to march severally to camp, and when they were ready, came to his own company, and finding one using mutinous words, struck him and hurt him in the arm and sent him to the marshal; and another being not ready, cut him on the head, 'who are both living without danger of death, except they be hanged [...] but the report was that they were both dead'.

The companies then marched towards the camp, and being out of the town, those in the Marshalsea accused one Roger Greene of being 'one of the principal that brake up the prison'. Whereupon Sir John sent Captain Roper to fetch him. Being sent back, I carried him and the rest before his Excellency, who gave order that Doctor Clarke and I should examine them; who giving information to his Excellency he gave me commission for the [hangin]g of three of them in the presence of the other seven [...].[92]

The contempt in which the ordinary soldiers were held by their military superiors, apparent in this example, characterised the long-running Irish campaign particularly, as is demonstrated by the following report held in the *Calendar of State Papers (Ireland)*, for December 1596:

> Of all the captains in Ireland, Sir Thomas North hath from the beginning kept a most miserable, unfurnished, naked, and hunger-starven band. Many of his soldiers died wretchedly and woefully at Dublin; some whose feet and legs rotted off for want of shoes [...].[93]

This is a typical example of the condition of the ordinary soldiers in Ireland, and one of many that reports the possibility of their mutiny.[94] Along with Peter Crips' letter from 1586, this is one of many reports describing the desperate circumstances serving soldiers endured around this period and which led to serious outbreaks of dissatisfaction among English soldiers.

The conditions in which the soldiers found themselves when pressed were indeed harsh and led to many cases of desertion in the later decades of Elizabeth's reign. Many cases have been documented, such as those individuals that deserted from Drake in April 1587[95] and in London in June a case is reported whereby, due to lack of pay a company of ordinary soldiers 'levied in the city for service in the Low Countries ... mutinied against Captain Sampson ...'.[96] The soldiers responsible, when captured, were 'tied to carts and flogged through Cheapside to Tower Hill, then ... set upon a pillory, and each [had] ... one ear cut off'.[97] Indeed, desertion was a common reality at the very height of the Armada campaign as is recorded in a letter from the Earl of Leicester to Francis Walsingham.[98]

Given the ways in which the common men were forced into fighting, and the conditions they faced once part of the army, it is perhaps no surprise that most military campaigns during this period witnessed cases of mass desertion. Important cases occurred in France in 1562,[99] in the Netherlands in 1585,[100] at Ostend in 1588,[101] in Cambridge in 1591[102] and in France again in 1592.[103] A series of reports in the *Acts of the Privy Council* for 1599 and 1600 demonstrate the readiness of the troops to desert, as well as the help that they received from the local population in doing so successfully. On 5 March 1599, for example, the Mayor of Bristol received a letter from the Privy Council concerning troops gathered in his city for dispatch to Ireland. The letter tells of the 'notable disorders of a great number of the soldiers, both in running awaye and in making violent resistance againste their comanders'.[104] The Council also informed Edward Gorges and Samuel Norton, the local Justices of the Peace, 'to have speciall care to prevent the disorders and running awaie of soldiers', and assumed 'somme fault of slacknes and negligence, without the which it were impossible for so many to escape thoroughout the countrie ...' (139–40). Earlier in the year the great number of soldiers deserting from Ireland became a cause for concern, not least because 'divers of theis souldiers do give forthe very sclaunderous speeches to discourage others ...'(56). The authorities in this case were instructed that 'in the meane season you shall see them imprested anewe and detayned...'(56). Another series of letters relate the tale of a troop ship bound for Ireland from Bristol that, due to bad weather, docked in Wales. This enabled many of the troops to desert and lose themselves in the Welsh countryside.[105] Another event of significance occurred in Hampshire in 1600 when in a march from the town where they had been levied to another town, 'more than a hundred men had escaped'.[106] It was reported, however, that not a single deserter was captured, because 'Villagers had given the escaped men sanctuary in their homes, and had helped to smuggle away both them and their equipment'.[107] The fact that the common soldiers were aided by the common people in their criminal activity demonstrates a general rejection of what was considered an oppressive practice, the seriousness of which is underlined by the fact that the deserters would have proceeded to sell their weapons, a capital offence in itself.[108] What all of these records demonstrate is the internal conflict that was apparent in Elizabeth's army through the latter decades of her reign, a conflict that often came home from abroad and manifested itself in the streets of London. Such is the case in the months around the time of the Victory procession, an event that called for the celebration of, among others, those same armed forces. In this case, it is the dire straits in which these suffering soldiers found themselves when they were disbanded that caused problems for the authorities and which throws the spectacular nature of the procession into sharp relief.

The defeat of the Spanish Armada is seen as one of the great military events in English history and is often regarded as Elizabeth's crowning moment. At the time, according to Helen Hackett, the victory over the Armada was generally received as proof that 'God was an Englishman' (134). The visit made by the Queen to Tilbury and the speech that she gave to English soldiers there in the lead up to the victory are regarded as indicative of her universal popularity as well as an example of her ability to strategically identify herself with both her soldiers and England as a national entity. Studies of the speech generally relate how she rode through the camp 'like some Amazonian empress', that she gave the troops 'a rousing speech', and that there 'were incredible expressions of loyalty to her'.[109] However, in her article 'The Myth of Elizabeth I at Tilbury', Susan Frye informs us that, in contrast to how most studies report this event, Elizabeth made her way to Tilbury *after* news of the defeat of the Armada.[110] Furthermore, Frye informs us, there are no records of eyewitness accounts of the speech and no record of Elizabeth either saying it or writing it down. Indeed, the speech did not appear in print until 1654, almost seventy years after it is supposed to have taken place. This being the case, this account, written by Dr Leonel Sharp, could be considered the starting point of a Benjaminian 'triumphal procession' in which this document becomes knowledge transmitted through history until it reaches us as conventional truth.[111]

While the ambivalent status of the text of the speech is interesting in itself, in her article Frye proceeds to comment on the audience of common soldiers for whom Elizabeth (we are told) made the speech and who she roused to a united and patriotic fervour. Frye writes:

> To those alive in 1588, England must have seemed anything but united, just as Elizabeth's Tilbury visit may have only provided ineffectual pageantry: for she performed before unpaid and ill-equipped and even hungry soldiers, many of whom, we know by royal proclamation, tried to sell their armour the moment they were disbanded (114).

The proclamation to which Frye refers, dated 25 August and sent to the Mayor and Sheriffs of London, names these very soldiers. It reads:

> The Queen's Majesty, being given to understand that divers soldiers, upon the dissolving of the camp at Tilbury in the county of Essex, have in their way homeward sold divers their armors and weapons which have been delivered unto them by the officers of those counties where they have been levied and set out, and besides the sale of their said armor and weapons have most falsely and slanderously given out that they were compelled to make sale of them for that they received no pay, which is most untruly reported.[112]

These are the same troops that Elizabeth addressed as her 'loving people' just days before (we are told), thrust from one state of poverty and hardship into another. For, despite the final claim that the troops were spreading lies regarding non-payment of wages, the *Acts of the Privy Council*, on the very same day, passed an order to 'examin certain matters of abuse complained of in the Captains for not paying the soldiours haveing received their full paie heere'.[113] The disbanded soldiers made their way to London, to the very streets where, three months later, the Victory procession took place, relating tales of disease, corruption and the non-payment of wages. In November, it is claimed, these same disgruntled individuals celebrated the passing of their commander-in-chief and her fellow officers. The fact that a substantial pressing campaign began again in London in October, shortly before the procession, lends to the perception that adulation and celebration were perhaps not the reactions of a large section of the common people, both soldiers and civilians, when the procession passed through the streets of the capital in November.

According to Curtis C. Breight, the period surrounding the Victory procession was one that was especially hard for common soldiers and for a particular reason. He writes that between 'mid-1588 and the end of 1589 thousands of Englishmen had been slaughtered in the Armada campaign, the Portugal affair, and Lord Willoughby's French expedition. These men were killed largely by the brutal conditions of service, not in battle'.[114] That these soldiers would be both desperate and angry at the conditions under which they suffered is understandable, as is demonstrated by the action required by the Crown detailed above. However, the problem remained and indeed became much worse when the soldiers pressed in October 1588, many of whom had already suffered in the Armada campaign, were released after the Portugal campaign. Their level of discontent is recorded in reports collected in the *Acts of the Privy Council* and the *Journals* and *Repertories* of the Corporation of London. These records state that disbanded soldiers and sailors, who had been pressed for action in Portugal, converged on London and caused disturbances at the Royal Exchange on 20 July 1589.[115] The 'disorderlie proceeding' of these 'marryners and other lewd fellowes' saw them attempting to sell their armour and weapons because, during their service, they claimed they had received little or no pay.[116] As stated earlier, the Corporation of London denied these claims. The soldiers and sailors proceeded to cause a good deal of trouble both in London and at their point of disembarkation in Maidstone, Kent.[117] Indeed, their behaviour got so out of hand that the authorities demanded that something be done, the Lord Mayor being instructed that they were to be 'apprehended and ... laied by the heeles...'.[118] This deterrent was unsuccessful however, and the Privy Council reported that the 'maryners and soldyers ... do remayn about the Cytye', indulging in 'contemptuous behavyour'.[119] The authorities decided therefore that these 'souldiours and mariners which do resorte in great numbers to the said Cyttie', were to be treated like 'masterles men and vagrant persons', and sent 'home to their cuntries'.[120] Despite these orders, the 16 August witnessed 'great disorders comitted by the souldyours' in Maidstone, as well as the suppression of rioting mariners at the Royal Exchange.[121] On 20 August 1589, day and night watches were set up in order to discourage the soldiers from assembling, not least 'bycause their Lordships are informed that some of the souldiers have of late offered violence to persons they have mett withall on the highe waye, and have taken money from them by force ...'.[122] A Royal Proclamation was passed stating that they were to be sent back to the county in which they were pressed in order to receive any payment owed to them.[123]

Despite the severity of all of these measures, it is clear from existent records that they did not work. In November 1589 Elizabeth ordered the appointment of a provost-marshall for every county in order to deal with the growing problems 'daily committed by soldiers, mariners, and others that pretend to have served as soldiers upon her highness' good and loving subjects'.[124] This proclamation, dated 13 November, reiterated the order for all of the above to return to their place of birth and to remain there. These 'soldiers, mariners, masterless men and other vagrant persons'[125] were instructed to go to the nearest justice of the peace in order to receive a passport declaring their place of birth, and then onto that place. At precisely this time, pressing for Ireland began in earnest and the problem of dealing with the conditions of these individuals became transferred once more to the army authorities.

The purpose of outlining this continuing problem of unrest and disorder in London itself is to put the Victory procession into some kind of realistic context. As already stated, it is quite understandable that the common civilian population would, for the duration of the procession (or for the entire period of celebration) put aside the problems, suffering and anger caused by the conditions in which they lived. Indeed, historically speaking, one could expect this to be the case, the population as a whole demonstrating its thanks to God and, by extension, its sovereign for delivering them from the hated enemy. In this sense, the common audience for the Victory procession would indeed have been potentially very different to that which may have witnessed the pre-coronation procession. However, it is clear from the records that many of the common soldiers, disbanded and present in the streets of London both on the day of the procession and generally around the time of celebration, would not have been able to put aside their anger and hunger. Every attempt they made to alleviate their situation, such as selling their armour or weapons, became criminalised activity and, if caught, they were severely punished. And their number was not few. Furthermore, drawn as they were from the common population it is quite possible that they would have found many of the ordinary people sympathetic to their discontent. The Victory procession needs to be seen in the light of these facts.

According to J. B. Neale, in the aftermath of the defeat of the Spanish 'England the nation exulted and thanked God'.[126] This thanks manifested itself as 'the Queen came in procession to St Paul's, such another spectacle as at her Coronation' (282). While this can be said to be generally the case, if the general disorder surrounding the ritual of November 1588 is taken into consideration, then certain problems with this view are apparent. For, whatever its effect on the population in general, it is clear that the Victory procession was an unsuccessful spectacular ritual as far as the common soldiers, mariners and, if the records are correct, masterless men and vagrants were concerned. A significant proportion of the common people can be said to have remained unimpressed. At worst, for conventional readings of the pre-coronation and Victory processions an enormous common audience simply was not present to be subjected by their propagandist desire. At best, this common audience was possibly rowdy, troublesome and unimpressed.[127] Both of these possibilities are born from the wretched conditions suffered by much of the urban population, both civilian and military in this period. The rural population of common people also suffered under conditions of poverty and disease at the time, a pertinent factor when considering Elizabeth's rural progresses.

'A King may go a progress through the guts of a beggar'

Many of the entertainments produced and performed in honour of Elizabeth during her summer progresses have been preserved, though they differ from the type of text attributed to Richard Mulcaster for the pre-coronation procession in the sense that they are literary rather than descriptive, the audience rarely therefore being mentioned. The presence of the common people on the actual estate of the Queen's host, in the form of servants or retainers is not described, or is only acknowledged in their participation in the entertainment itself, acting the parts of certain mythological or pastoral figures. Their presence outside of the entertainment, and thus outside of the estate is not described, and it is therefore difficult to form a consistent picture of them (possibly) lining the country road or lane as the procession passed. The few references that do mention this presence in rural processions generally appear in the State Records, such as that of the Spanish Ambassador discussed in the Introduction. The pervasiveness of this particular record in analyses of Elizabeth and Elizabethan processions testifies to the lack of descriptive evidence regarding the common audience at progresses, and the normative desire of the various analyses is evident in their refusal to admit to this record's ambiguous detailing of the Queen/crowd relationship. Despite this lack of evidence, however, progresses have traditionally been regarded as further examples of effective propaganda, as successful regulatory rituals. This success, as well as Elizabeth's deliberate propagation of such a policy of propaganda, is outlined by John Nichols, writing in 1823: 'The plan of popularity which Elizabeth laid down from the beginning of her Reign is marked by no trait so strongly as her practice of making Progresses about her dominions'.[128] This is echoed by Christopher Haigh when he writes that progresses 'were major public relations exercises, with careful preparations for maximum impact',[129] a chance, as David Bergeron says, 'to see and be seen', and 'for winning additional loyalty and support'.[130] While it was held for many years (and still is in a number of studies) that these propagandist efforts were directed at cementing relations between Elizabeth and her (powerful) nobles, modern scholars such as Haigh and Neville Williams believe that these progresses were in fact aimed at a much wider public. Williams, for example, writes that 'Nothing did so much to strengthen the average subject's bonds of affection to his sovereign as catching sight of her as she rode by with her train of followers, and Elizabeth's progresses became legendary'.[131] That these bonds of affection were strengthened by this public display of the monarch to her subjects in general is accepted unquestioningly where the progresses are regarded as 'one of the Queen's major – and successful – policies',[132] aimed at the people, who were suitably subjected in the process.[133] According to these readings (all of which are importantly based upon the despatch written by the Spanish Ambassador discussed earlier, and all of which fail, as Alison Plowden does, to refer to the first two sentences of that report), the rural audience of Elizabethan processions constituted a presence that replicates precisely that produced by Mulcaster for the pre-coronation procession, and which has been subsequently endlessly reproduced by generations of scholars. Here, once again, Elizabethan spectacular propaganda is always successful.

Because of the difficulties that exist in examining the real presence of the common people at Elizabethan progresses, it is again necessary to return to those records that have been preserved and that do indirectly refer to the possible presence that an audience of common people may have constituted. It is worth examining events and experiences in and around progresses that may have affected the lives of the ordinary people, and thus have coloured their consumption of such a cultural/spectacular occurrence. Before proceeding to do so, it would also be interesting to briefly review aristocratic reactions/responses to the news that the Queen and (often) her entire court were to visit, in an attempt to discern whether the notion that the Queen was perhaps not as welcome a visitor as we have often been led to believe holds any truth.

As discussed in the Introduction, the reality of the Queen and her court coming to visit was a prospect that many of her nobles considered with a good deal of trepidation. The exorbitant costs and enormous demands put upon any prospective host caused a certain amount of panic and discontent, summed up by Bishop Hurd in his *Dialogues Moral and Political*, where he states that it 'has been objected that these visits ... were calculated only to impoverish her wealthiest and best subjects, under colour of her high favours'.[134] While this is probably overstating the case, evidence collected together by E. K. Chambers in the form of letters that passed between prospective hosts and the officials of the Lord Chamberlain's office charged with arranging progresses demonstrate the anxiety felt by the hosts.[135] As well as fears about the costs of entertaining the Queen, these letters show the use of a number of ploys to discourage her coming; overestimation of the current prevalence of plague in the vicinity of their estate, for example. The Marquis of Winchester was perhaps one of the most honest prospective hosts when he wrote bluntly that 'the Queen's stay would make "more charge than the constitution of Basing [his country estate] may well bear"'.[136] It lends credibility to Bishop Hurd's feelings when it is realised that the Queen was not put off and, subsequently, as Nichols informs us, the 'Marquis of Winchester was nearly ruined by the last Royal Visit at Basing ...'.[137] Indeed, Lord Burleigh himself, builder of Theobalds, 'always shuddered at the costs of a royal visit',[138] and hosts as varied as the Sir Henry Lee, Sir William Clark and Thomas Arundell, among many others, expressed their displeasure at the proposed visit of the Queen.[139] According to Lawrence Stone, Henry Clinton, Earl of Lincoln on hearing of the Queen's intention to visit him bolted his doors against her before fleeing.[140]

The plethora of evidence collected by Chambers and, for example, H. Ellis, suggests that the attitude of the nobility themselves to the Queen's progresses was often at best ambivalent, and at worst, if they were to be visited, oppositional.[141] Stone may also be guilty of overstating the case, but it is possible that many of the Queen's hosts, victims of having their estates denuded of deer and their houses plundered for crockery and cutlery, viewed these visits in the following manner:

> Erratic and destructive as a hurricane, summer after summer Elizabeth wandered about the English countryside bringing ruin in her train, while apprehensive noblemen abandoned their homes and fled at the mere rumour of her approach. As early as the 1570s the Earl of Bedford tried to divert Her Majesty from Chenies, and at the end of the reign we find Sir Henry Lee prophesying ruin on hearing that 'Her Majesty threatens a progress and her coming to my houses'.[142]

If the nobility could be said to have been somewhat reluctant to allow the Queen and the court to use their hospitality and their property, it is possible to say that the common people felt the same way about certain abuses of their own property. This is clear with regard to both Elizabeth's and her administration's widespread practice of purveyance, an example of which was the aforementioned requisitioning of crimson silk for use in the pre-coronation procession. Purveyance was a pervasive practice with regard to the summer progresses, the Queen's representatives using the system to compulsorily purchase provisions at low prices, and to rent carts at similarly cheap rates. It is important not to underestimate the amount of goods and materials needed for some progresses as, occasionally, as many as 350 people could travel with the Queen. The Public Record Office records one such example with 300 people comprising servants alone.[143] Naturally enough, this system of purveyance 'was liable to cause considerable hardship and was extremely unpopular'.[144] Chambers refers to this practice as 'the abuses of purveyance',[145] which he says included 'the impressment of vehicles by the royal cart-takers ...'.[146] Lawrence Stone characteristically puts it even more bluntly, stating that the '400 to 600 carts' needed for the transport of the Court's belongings on progress were 'forcibly impressed from a reluctant peasantry' (451). Nichols refers to this unhappy state of affairs also:

> The abuses of the Purveyors of the Royal Household, in procuring, amongst other things, carriages for removing goods, provisions, and other things, which they took at their own prices, which were less than the real value, and sometimes even that money not paid, occasioned frequent complaints ... .[147]

Nichols does in fact reproduce extracts from 'an old book (kept in the chest) in the Church of Chalk', which testify to this kind of non-payment for carriages in the year 1591, one Robert Rowswell failing to receive payment for his services on two occasions.[148] The Middlesex County Records for 1583 contain a petition from George Ashby, a Justice of the Peace, protesting at the frequency with which the people of Middlesex were subjected to purveyance and the supplying of carts for the Queen's household in progress.[149] And while this compulsory taking of goods and carts was difficult enough for the peasantry to bear, the carts being required in order to collect the harvest, there is a further hardship that had to be borne and which was also the cause for much complaint. This was perhaps even more serious than the actual impressment of goods and vehicles, as the 'household officers were accused of blackmailing owners of carts to avoid impressment', as well as of 'requisitioning superfluous provisions and reselling them at a profit'.[150] The reality of this practice as a source of disquiet is attested to in a letter drafted by the Privy Council and dated 12 August 1565:

> A letter to Sir Thomas Throckmorton and Sir Nicholas Pointz of thankes for theyr diligence used in serching owt of the disordres committed in that countrie by the servauntes of Thomas Russell, one of the Queen's Majesties Purveyours, which matter the Lordes think very necessarie shall be reformed and the offendours punisshed to thexample of other ... .[151]

Henry Machyn records such abuse in his *Diary* whereby a purveyor was pilloried with a collar of smelt for purchasing smelt in the name of the Queen and then selling it on for a profit (189). In the various *Assize Records* compiled by Cockburn, many such cases are shown, punishment ranging from a small fine to execution by hanging.[152] Irrespective of the punishment or indeed the seriousness of the offence, however, common unhappiness arose from the extra hardships that were endured when carts were taken away, from the additional problem of the Queen's representatives demanding money from the peasants in order for them to keep their own carts at such an important time of year, and from the obvious corruption of the entire practice.

The point being raised here, of course, is one regarding the possible attitudes of the common people/peasants to the Court on progress, given the practical effects its presence had on their everyday existence. This could mean that their carts were forcibly requisitioned and they received payment, or they were requisitioned without payment. It could mean that they could indeed keep their carts but to do so they had been blackmailed, or had been forced to sell their goods for low prices which were then possibly sold on for private profit. Whichever it was, it is certain that a great number of the rural population would either have experienced or have heard of these injustices carried out by the Crown. As Mary Hill Cole writes, 'the continued abuses were generating much local anger', a feeling which could indeed 'extend to the court itself' (49). Given these circumstances, it is questionable at least whether the rural population, direct victims of both official and unofficial Crown policy, would have had their bonds of affection strengthened as the sovereign, the embodiment of these injustices, passed along and they (perhaps unwillingly) lined the route. Here the policy that sought to 'establish and maintain her personal popularity among her people',[153] could have conversely given rise to a good deal of disaffection, and could possibly have been unsuccessful.

Such behaviour by the Crown's representatives caused the rural population with whom they came into contact great hardship therefore, with their livelihoods threatened, and hunger a very real possible consequence. The passing of the Queen would have done little to alleviate such a possibility, and indeed her entourage brought with it another cause for anxiety, one that could be said to demonstrate anything but the glory and majesty of such a procession, and one very rarely noted by historians. Most procession analyses stress that one of the major reasons for Elizabeth and her court leaving the city and embarking upon a progress in the summer months was to escape the dangers of the plague, rife in the city at that time of year. However, the local population through which any progress passed, whether urban or rural, would probably have been aware of the fact that the individuals that comprised the spectacular procession could (and did) actually bring the plague with them. This is corroborated by the fact that in 1578, for example, both Bury St Edmunds and Norwich suffered their most severe outbreaks of plague after the Court (in progress) had left them. Indeed, the epidemic that Norwich witnessed wiped out almost one third of its population. Whether this was indeed the fault of the London-based Court or not, in Norfolk itself the outbreak was blamed on the progress.[154] Once again, the suggestion is that, at least from this date, and at least in this area, the coming of the Queen and her entourage was, for the common people, perhaps not predominantly an encounter that strengthened the bonds of affection, but was rather an encounter with disease and death. The passing of the Queen prompted fear perhaps, rather than admiration and loyalty.

The possible lack of affection is apparent in a number of recorded instances between the Queen and her common subjects, where the latter's presence is not characterised by their loud cheering and ecstatic welcoming. John Nichols, for example, records an incident (unreferenced) that occurred in 1581 as Elizabeth rode out one evening towards Islington (then a country town), where she was 'invironed with a number of begging rouges ... which gave the Queen much disturbance'.[155] While she came to no harm, the following day saw complaints made to both the Lord Mayor of London and to Fleetwood, the Recorder, which resulted in the arrest 'that day [of] seventy-four rogues, whereof some were blind, and yet great usurers, and very rich. They were sent to Bridewell, and punished'.[156] Whether those arrested were the guilty parties is not mentioned, but as previously shown, being a beggar was, in itself, a punishable crime. The point being made here, however, is one with regard to the nature of the relationship between the Queen and these subjects of hers. Her presence does not seem to have induced feelings of awe and celebration in these beggars, and she does not seem to revel in their common presence. Rather than mutual love, this meeting at least is characterised by reciprocal suspicion and menace. The basis for the beggars' punishment was simply their encountering the Queen, their happening to be on the route chosen for her outing from Charterhouse. Such incidents no doubt prompted the royal proclamation produced in 1601 in preparation for a progress by the Queen. This proclamation, dated 5 August, made it clear that 'all masterless men, boys, vagabonds, rogues and unauthorised women were to avoid the court' en route.[157]

A similar tone of mutual suspicion, perhaps even dislike, is recorded in the Spanish Ambassador's report to Madrid whilst accompanying the Queen on the progress/entry through Norwich in 1578. Discussions of the Norwich visit usually end with Holinshed's description of Elizabeth's parting words from the city, which saw her claim that she would 'never forget Norwich', and bid it farewell 'with the water standing in hir eies'.[158] The Ambassador, however, records something rather different: 'When she entered Norwich the large crowds of people came out to receive her, and one company of children knelt as she passed and said, as usual, "God save the Queen". She turned to them and said, "Speak up; I know you do not love me here"'.[159] While this report needs to be treated with the same kind of scepticism as that discussed earlier with regard to the Spanish Ambassador's despatch of 1568 (in terms of religious and political opposition), it might once again suggest a failure in policy, and an evident distance and difficulty in the relationship between Elizabeth and the crowd. Like the incident near Islington, it conjures up a weakening rather than a strengthening of bonds between sovereign and subjects, an articulation of deeply problematic divisions. The tension evident in these examples in the relationship between the Queen and the people, and the latter's failure to be successfully interpellated by her spectacular presence, is further corroborated by an incident at the Osterley home of Sir Thomas Gresham, where this relationship evidently breaks down completely.

In order to entertain the Queen during her stay at his residence in May 1576, Gresham commissioned Thomas Churchyard to compose a play and pageant device, neither of which, with the exception of the title of the pageant, are any longer in existence.[160] The importance of the occasion is clear in Gresham's commissioning of Churchyard, one of the leading pageant writers of his day.[161] *The Acts of the Privy Council* for that year record a rather different event which took place during the visit, however, noting the following:

> Certaine persons are committed to the Marshalsey, whose names are Johan Ayre, Mary Harris, George Lenton and George Bennet, for burninge Sir Thomas Gressham's parke pale at that time when the Quenes Majestie was there, wherewith her Highnes was very much offendid, and commaundid that thoffendours should be serched out and punished acording to their offence ... .[162]

The record proceeds to instruct 'Mr. Justice Southcote and Mr. Recorder of London' to set aside 'some tyme and place to have the prisoners brought before them', and then 'to examine them and to induce them by all meanes they can to open the trouthe' (126). In order for the full weight of justice to be administered, 'for their better instuctions ... Sir Thomas Gressham will instructe them ...' (126). Unfortunately, the full record of the result of these investigations seems to have been lost, but the Middlesex County Records fill in some of the details of both the incident and its outcome:

> Indictment of Joan Eyer and Mary Harrys, both of Heston, who pleaded guilty to breaking into the park at Osterley, while the Queen and many members of the Privy Council were in residence as guests of Sir Thomas Gresham.
>
> They 'with force and arms and with spades, shovels, staves and hatchets then and there maliciously, diabolically and illegally tore up, pulled out and threw down and laid on the ground four rods of posts and pales of the same Thomas Gresham ... on the seventh day of May ... about the hour of two and three early in the morning ... the aforesaid Joan and Mary maliciously, diabolically and wickedly burnt and consumed with fire ... not only to the great disquiet and disturbance of the said lady the Queen ... but indeed in manifest contempt of the same lady the Queen and her laws, and to the no small damage of the same Thomas Gresham'.[163]

On one level this event no doubt describes the popular discontentment with the fact that in 1565 Gresham received a royal licence to enclose 600 acres of his land, and that 'the villagers may have used the Queen's visit as an occasion to make known their discontent'.[164] Indeed, on 19 July 1576 'it is recorded that complaints were laid against Gresham by sundry poor men, for having enclosed certain common ground'.[165] Burgon states that 'Gresham's enclosure of the park surrounding Osterely-House was a very unpopular act; and probably led to the outrage in question' (449). However, what it also outlines, in the terms of this current study, and in combination with the previously described examples (of which it is the most extreme case), is the problematisation of the effectiveness of so-called spectacular rituals/presences, whereby all of those components that would constitute successful interpellation of the subject(s) seem to have failed to register. The extremity of the actions of Joan Eyer and Mary Harrys (as well as George Lenton and George Bennet, though both their role and punishment is unclear) undoubtedly articulate desperation and discontent, a radical protest against enclosure, as well as one directed at the Queen. It is a protest that uses the Queen's presence in order to make an oppositional statement rather than a supportive one. Above all, the actions of the two women describe a lack of subjection. Such a lack was to have its most serious articulation in Oxfordshire twenty years later.

As discussed earlier, in 1592, as part of her long summer progress in Oxfordshire, Elizabeth visited Lord and Lady Norris on their estate at Rycote, where she was greeted with a short, unelaborated welcoming performance which saw her receive a number of expensive gifts from her hosts. As part of the same progress she visited Sir Henry Lee on one of his estates, Ditchley, the scene of a lengthier, more complex allegorical entertainment. These entertainments are typically pastoral, and are characterised by their portrayal of Elizabeth as the romantic object of desire, as the righter of all wrongs, and as being the embodiment of constancy in a universe defined by its opposite. Both of these houses were obvious destinations for Elizabeth on progress, the former being that of 'her closest and most trustworthy friends',[166] whilst the latter was the home of her former Champion (retired in 1590), and organiser of her Accession Day Tilts. While it would be interesting to closely examine the precise nature of the relationships that existed between the Queen and these nobles, the interest of this present discussion lies elsewhere. For it is the impression made upon the servants and other employees of the Norrises and Lee by the presence of the Queen and her court in progress that I wish to investigate.

Jean Wilson, concerning herself with the (political) aims of progresses in general states that:

> Elizabeth's visits to great houses ... reinforced the power of the local magnate, enhancing his prestige in the eyes of his neighbours and dependants, and ensuring that should they be called upon to follow him on her service, they would do so more willingly for their belief that their master was high in the Queen's favour, and might be in a position to prefer his adherents (40).

Within this group of dependants Wilson includes not only 'the household servants, but the tenants ... and locals who wished to retain the favour of the land-owner' (40). According to this reading the Queen's visit would impress these dependants through their desire to remain loyal to their master, whose central position in terms of his relation to the Queen would ensure this loyalty. This view echoes a widely held assumption regarding a similar normative dynamic apparent in royal entries whereby such spectacles 'helped increase in onlookers a sense of the wealth, power and glory of the monarch – providing a focus of national unity among Englishmen ...'.[167] These readings must naturally dismiss the previously discussed Osterley incident, or must regard it as an exception, the deed of vagabonds and criminals. Whatever status the incident is given, however, it must be accepted that the individuals involved were not impressed in the ways suggested by Wilson (and traditional procession analysis), a reality that undermines this governing idea of the 'loyalty through majesty' that she professes. This idea is further compromised by a closer look at the Rycote/Ditchley example.

A brief glance once again at the Ditchley Portrait (cover illustration) clarifies the content and purpose of the progress visits of 1592, and demonstrates the negotiation of power relations between sovereign and noble suggested by Wilson. The Queen brings in fair weather and banishes storms, her feet planted firmly on Sir Henry Lee's land, brought to the centre of the world by Elizabeth's presence. This picture can perhaps be regarded as interior propaganda, hanging as it did in the house of the pictured noble, consumed daily by servants and dependants. [168] These type of paintings can perhaps be said to have fulfilled, on a more constant and permanent basis, what the progresses themselves attempted to achieve temporarily: an interpellative effect. This effect does not always seem to have worked, however.

In 1596, four years after the Queen's progress visit, a number of Lord Norris' dependants and servants, led by Bartholomew Steere, a carpenter at Rycote, combined to lead what has been called both an uprising[169] and a rebellion,[170] and who, according to the *Calendar of State Papers*, proposed a quite different progress to that of Elizabeth: 'Steere said that when they were up ... they would murder Mr Power, as also Mr Berry and his daughter, and spoil Rabone, the yeoman, Geo. Whilton, Sir Hen. Lee, Sir Wm. Spencer, Mr Frere, and Lord Norris, and then go to London ...'.[171] This proposed progress was set off by the third consecutive harvest failure, the blame for which was laid upon the likes of Sir Henry Lee and Lord Norris, two of Oxfordshire's most aggressive enclosers. It seems that in the autumn of 1596, forty to sixty men went to Rycote to see Lord Norris and 'petitioned [him] for some corn to relieve their distress, and for the putting down [of] enclosures' (343). Despite much remonstration Norris failed to respond, and thus Steere began to plot his uprising. It is important to note that Steere 'began to organise the conspiracy while still in Lord Norris's employ',[172] and under examination admitted that he 'meant to have risen to help his poor friends, and other poor people who lived in misery' (*CSP* 343). He believed 'that the servants of Lord Norris and other Oxfordshire gentry could be persuaded to join a rising because "they were kept like dogges"'.[173] Steere seems to have been right in his judgement, as 'he subverted several of Lord Norris's servants and those of other gentry who visited Rycote'.[174]

Although this disorder took a material form, the uprising failed without any action being taken on the part of the rebels, and they were subsequently arrested and punished, a consequence that will be dealt with at length in the next chapter in terms of allegory. For now, I want to stress that the uprising, consisting as it did almost exclusively of the employees of Norris and other nobles, contradicts those notions expounded by traditional progress analysis (such as that by Jean Wilson above) with regard to the successful interpellation of these common people by the spectacular nurturing of loyalty to their master. These individuals were not captured in this way, were not impressed or subjected, but rather displayed a lack of loyalty and hatred for their masters and the social structure that ensured their continued hardship and poverty. Indeed, as recorded in the *Calendar of State Papers*, they were 'ready to cut their master's throats' (344). Furthermore, not only were they not hailed in this manner, they were punished by death for presuming to demonstrate the fact that they were not. Two of the participants, Richard Bradshaw and Robert Burton, were hanged on Enslow Hill, convicted and sentenced by a number of landholders in Oxfordshire itself. The fate of the leader, Bartholomew Steere, is worth considering in greater detail.

Lord Norris 'could not comprehend that Bartholomew Steere had begun planning the rebellion under his own roof',[175] and both he and Sir Henry Lee were no doubt surprised and alarmed to learn that they were two of the rebels' main targets. The rebels had determined to deal with Lee at Ditchley, where he had become 'notorious as a "great sheep-master" and the man who had profited from selling villeins their freedom',[176] and Rycote was to witness their final act before they marched to London. Norris' reaction to his disbelief seems to have been a desire for revenge, and he took charge of the interrogation of Steere and his fellow rebels. Unable to extract any names from the prisoners, however, Norris recommended that the rebels be tortured in order to extract information. The prisoners were then taken to various prisons in London by Sir Henry Norris, Lord Norris' son and heir, and 'were tortured and examined at Bridewell Prison by attorney-general Coke, solicitor-general Francis Bacon, and the recorder of London'.[177] By the second week of January, Coke had extracted a full confession from Steere, who he regarded as the ringleader. And it is here, as demonstrated in the extended records of this entire process, existent in the *Calendar of State Papers*, with this mention of the lengthy period of torture, that the name of Bartholomew Steere, servant and carpenter to Lord Norris, almost certainly present at the progress of 1592 which should have ensured his loyalty to both Master and Sovereign, simply disappears.[178] He was not executed on Enslow Hill (as Richard Wilson incorrectly claims), nor was he freed.[179] It is evident rather that he was simply tortured to death in the Bridewell, far from the Oxfordshire countryside, far from the lanes along which the progress of 1592 passed, allowing the Queen to show herself to ordinary people, including Steere. It seems that he was not subjected, was not hailed, and was tortured to death for not being so. He is a marginal figure in the story of royal progresses, one that has simply been written out of history.

The figure of Bartholomew Steere is important in any discussion of the spectacular effects of such rituals as royal progresses because he and his accomplices (along with the two women from Osterley) articulate both the ideological aims of these rituals, and their limitations. By remaining unimpressed, these individuals demonstrate both the urge to subject them, and the limits that any such process contains when manifested merely as ritual. Steere was effectively subjected to death, in the sense that the failure of the ritual of 1592 necessitated his total physical punishment. His painful, secret death clarifies the fact that ritual alone was not enough, and that the process of material exclusion from the social and political centre required material practices that were more extreme than mere processions. For the margin to remain marginal, the centre needed to do more than simply display its magnificence. It needed to demonstrate its physical power. In these instances, the sovereign had, as Hamlet observes, to 'go a progress through the guts of a beggar'.[180]

That the common audiences for Elizabethan processions in general have been constructed as a monolithic, most loving Subject, effectively awe-struck by her presence in terms of its spectacular (that is, normative) nature, and by processions themselves as allegories for (God-given) order, is perhaps not surprising given the fact that these royal and civic rituals have traditionally been viewed from the perspective of those in authority. Jean Wilson's prestige-effect in relation to progresses is just one example of this. This being the case, when uncertainty regarding the effectiveness of such display is expressed, or when propagandist elements are admitted to, these take the form of discourses between authorities, conflicts between the ruler and the powerful ruled. This has recently been apparent in the plethora of (important) accounts of the problem of Elizabeth as an incoming Protestant, female monarch, as a woman being both head of state and head of the church.[181] A rudimentary examination of the pageants performed for her pre-coronation procession confirms a negotiation of these uncertainties, and demonstrates the attempt to found and make credible a particular iconography for the new Queen. Indeed, the discernment of disunity in the rituals of Elizabethan progresses and processions can be regarded as the principle dynamic of critical studies in recent years. However, it is essential to realise that, without exception, this disunity is examined as a manifestation of the desires of various powerful groups and individuals – both religious and political – and not from the perspective of the powerless. Thus recent studies underline the tensions between figures of authority in terms of powerful critiques of female monarchy, of the Protestant faith, and of Elizabeth's tenuous claim to the throne. The common people, powerless as they were, continue to be constructed as uniformly and successfully subjected. Similarly, the literary texts of these events have been consumed in a manner that regards only those same figures of authority. In the following chapter, I want to suggest that those same texts can be read in the way that the material events themselves have been read in this chapter, with the common people very much in mind.

Notes

1. Wickham lists a number of different types of processions characterised by this triumphal function: 'the visit of a distinguished foreigner (the Emperor Otho in 1207), a royal wedding (Henry III to Eleanor of Provence in 1236), a coronation (Edward I in 1274) and a major military victory (Edward I's defeat of the Scots at Falkirk in 1298)' (1:53).
2. Strong, *Splendour at Court* 21.
3. Wickham notes that the procession celebrating Edward I's defeat of the Scots in 1298 was the first that contained 'theatrical attributes', but it was not until later that royal processions became defined by these attributes. The celebration of the birth of Edward III in 1313 prompted the building of a theatrical 'gaily decorated' ship, and the

coronation of Richard II in 1377 saw the building of a stage which supported speaking actors (1:50–54).

4. Roy Strong has traced the development of the royal entry in Renaissance Europe through the entries which took place in Italy in the fourteenth and fifteenth centuries to those in France such as Anne of Brittany's entry into Paris in 1486 to celebrate her marriage to Charles VIII, that of Charles V into Bruges in 1515, Henry II into Rouen in 1550, and that of Elizabeth of Valois into Toledo in 1560. He also traces the development in England, from the entry of Anne Boleyn on her marriage to Henry VIII in 1533, through Elizabeth's pre-coronation procession of 1558, to that of James I (*Splendour at Court* 19–77). For a more detailed examination of the entry of James I, see Bergeron, *English Civic Pageantry* 65–89, and Goldberg *James* 33–54.

5. Strong, *Splendour at Court* 23. Jean Wilson makes the same point: 'Her coronation procession was unchanged in manner and general content from previous royal entries, consisting of allusions to the queen's illustrious ancestors, and demonstrations of the nature of the political regime expected of Elizabeth' (*Entertainments for Elizabeth I* 5).

6. This is not to deny the magnificence and presence of the numerous pageant devices. These no doubt gave the pre-coronation procession an additional spectacular quality. Here, it is important to note that I am discussing the human content of the procession itself, in order to attempt to perceive its spectacular presence.

7. *Records of the Lord Chamberlain and other Offices of the Royal Household, and the Clerk of the Recognizances*, Public Record Office, LC 2 4/3.

8. While this would be a more pertinent source to use for an examination of the pre-coronation procession than the 1588 inventory – in temporal terms as well as in the fact that many of those participating in the pre-coronation procession would also have attended the coronation – the Lord Chamberlain at no point articulates who actually formed the coronation procession, nor how many: he simply states who should attend. As such, this document, though useful in this present context, is inferior as a source to that of the list of participants for the 1588 procession.

9. L. E. Tanner, *The History of the Coronation* (London: Pitkin, 1952) 55.

10. Bergeron, *English Civic Pageantry* 12.

11. *The Passage Of Our Most Drad Soveraigne Lady Quene Elyzabeth Through The Citie Of London To Westminster The Daye Before Her Coronacion London 1558–9*: reproduced in full in Nichols, *Elizabeth* 1:38–60.

12. Bergeron, *English Civic Pageantry* 13.

13. *Calendar of State Papers (Venetian) (1558–80)* 12.

14. Strong, *Splendour at Court* 25. The precise content and form of these pageant devices will be discussed in detail in the next chapter.

15. They are described as such many times in Mulcaster's pamphlet.

16. Mulcaster 48. Michael Berlin has written of the (ideological) importance of such affluent display: 'The outward appearance of the citizenry, their behaviour and dress in both ceremonial and everyday life, was considered as a prime means of maintaining the social order' ('Civic Ceremony in Early Modern London', *Urban History Yearbook 1986* (Leicester: Leicester University Press, 1986) 3–30:23). The effects of such ceremonial display (as well as the effects of its everyday display) were therefore regarded as an essential part of any procession, and of the upholding of order itself.

17. This is perhaps too grand a term for what was actually done, as the Venetian Ambassador notes: 'Owing to the deep mud caused by the foul weather and by the multitude of people and of horses, everyone had made preparation, by placing sand and gravel in front of their houses' (*CSP (Ven) (1558–80)* 12).

18. Elizabeth made many other entries into cities during her reign, but only these two in London, the capital, can be regarded as national in the sense that the sovereign was

addressing herself to the whole of the nation. In the pre-coronation procession this address implied impending sovereignty (over the whole nation), and in the Victory procession it took the form of giving and taking thanks (to/from the whole nation) for victory over the Spanish. Other royal entries into such cities as Norwich, Coventry and Warwick were localised in nature, the desire being to induce local affection and loyalty. For a calendar of Elizabeth's entries, see Chambers, *The Elizabethan Stage* 4:75–130.

19. Reproduced from the Corporation of London Letter Book (220) in Nichols, *Elizabeth* 2:537–8.
20. Ibid., 537–8.
21. Ibid., 538.
22. Ibid., 538.
23. Ibid., 539.
24. Ibid., 539.
25. Plowden 51.
26. Cole, *The Portable Queen* 1.
27. Slack, *The Impact of The Plague* 151.
28. Plowden 51.
29. This list interestingly mirrors that of the Victory procession, though it must be read as a cross-section rather than viewed in a linear fashion. When looked at in this way, it too builds to a climax around the presence of the Queen: see Nichols, *Elizabeth* 2:400–404, and Jean Wilson 52–6.
30. Jean Wilson 56.
31. This portrait, which hangs in the National Portrait Gallery, is a pervasive image of Elizabeth and, like the Procession picture, appears in the vast majority of studies of the Queen and the age, and indeed appears on the covers of many works of Elizabethan literary criticism: see Leonard Tennenhouse's *Power on Display* and Frances Yates's *Astraea: The Imperial Theme in the Sixteenth Century*, for example.
32. Roy Strong and Julia T Oman 76.
33. Strong, *The Cult of Elizabeth* 154.
34. E. K. Chambers has collected together all of the visits and outings of the Queen, including her summer progresses and entries into cities (*The Elizabethan Stage* 4:75–130). The reference to the Ditchley progress appears in the same volume (107).
35. Nichols, *Elizabeth* 1:38–60.
36. Corporation of London, *Repertory (1558–60)* XIV: fol. 143.
37. It is worth detailing here the status of this text attributed to Mulcaster and which appears in Nichols *Elizabeth* 1:38–60. Nichols reproduces the publication details of his source text: *The Passage of our most drad Soueraigne Lady Quene Elyzabeth through the citie of London to westminster the daye before her coronacion. Anno 1558. Cum privilegio. Imprinted at London in flete strete within Temple barre, at the signe of the hand and starre, by Richard Tottull, the .xxiii. day of January.* The edition reproduced by Nichols and which is used in this book is that in the British Library. Another edition exists: *The Quenes Majesties Passage Through The Citie Of London To Westminster The Day Before Her Coronacion*, ed. James M. Osborn, introd. J. E. Neale (New Haven: Yale University Press, 1960). The Tottill text has traditionally been attributed to Richard Mulcaster, who, it is thought, was commissioned by the London Corporation to celebrate the occasion in print. As noted earlier, the existent record of Mulcaster's payment for his commission is the basis for it being attributed to him. It is uncertain whether Mulcaster was responsible for the entire text, or whether he was merely asked to provide the English and Latin verses. The possibility that he did not write the entire text originates from the fact that, among others, Richard Grafton was

charged with the overall responsibility of the pageant entertainments. In *Repertory* XIV, fol.99, dated 13 December 1558 (1557) the following is written: 'Item, this day Richarde and Francis Robynson grocers Richrd Hills merchant-taylor and Lionel Ducket mercer were assigned and apoynted by the Courte here to suruey the doings and deuyses of all the other coÿers of this Cytye which are already apoynted to make and deuyse suche pageauntes in sundry places of this Cytye agaynste the queens maiestie comynge to her coronacion as heretofore hathe byn accustomyd at the lyke tyme and to reforme alter or adde vnto the same as they with thadvyse of suche as they shall call vnto them shall think good and to make reporte here the nexte Courte day by a platte of all theire opynyons and doings therein and then to vnderstande here what some of money the city hathe in redynes towards the doynge thereof'. This is important as Richard Grafton (briefly) described the various pageants that were performed on the day in his *Abridgement of the Chronicles of England* (London, 1562) fol.167. It is, of course, possible that he merely reproduced Mulcaster's original. The text shall be referred to as Mulcaster's in this book, in the sense that it is attributed to him. However, for an examination of this question, see William Leahy,'Propaganda or a Record of Events? Richard Mulcaster's *The Passage Of Our Most Drad Soveraigne Lady Quene Elyzabeth Through The Citie Of London Westminster The Daye Before Her Coronacion*', *Early Modern Literary Studies* 9.1 (May 2003) 1–18.

38. This perception of Elizabeth as actress in this situation, as well as the essentially theatrical setting represented by her presence in the city streets, has been a favourite textual event of the New Historicism, for example in Greenblatt's 'To Fashion A Gentleman: Spenser And The Destruction Of The Bower Of Bliss', (*Renaissance Self Fashioning* 157–92). The sense in which Elizabeth acted perfectly in the pre-coronation procession itself is perhaps best summed up by Bergeron's definition of her as a (successful) 'unscheduled actor' (*English Civic Pageantry* 15).

39. Holinshed, *Chronicles of England, Scotland, and Ireland* 4:159–75.

40. J. B. Black, *The Reign of Elizabeth 1558-1603*, The Oxford History of England (Oxford: Clarendon Press, 1959) 5–6.

41. Greenblatt, *Renaissance Self-Fashioning* 168.

42. Bergeron, *English Civic Pageantry* 13. A translation of the despatch written by the Venetian Ambassador is reproduced in the *Calendar of State Papers (Venetian) (1558–80)* 12–16. It is worth stating that neither the positions of Mulcaster nor the Venetian Ambassador during the procession are indicated in their documents, and it is therefore difficult to give priority to either report on the grounds of superior accessibility to events.

43. Plowden does not acknowledge this use, though its use is apparent in her description of 'the splendid decoration of the streets' (15). Clifford Geertz does cite his Venetian source, and also that he found his information in the reproduction of some of the report in Bergeron (Geertz, 'Charisma', *Local Knowledge* 125–6).

44. Nichols, *The Diary of Henry Machyn* 186–7.

45. Sandra Logan, 'Making History' 251–92.

46. It is worth mentioning here a related debate concerning varying interpretations of the events of the following day, at the coronation ceremony itself. This debate takes place in the pages of the journal *English Historical Review*, vols 22–5, written in the years 1907–10. It concerns the conflicting accounts, one Spanish, one Italian, and one English regarding whether Elizabeth was present for the part of the coronation mass when the host was elevated (Protestants did not believe the bread to be the body of Christ – thus this was seen as a Catholic ritual), or whether she walked out at this point (returning only to be crowned). The debate is interesting in that it does precisely what has not been done with regard to the reports of the pre-coronation procession – that is,

the reading of the eyewitness accounts against each other. However, the underlying reasons for the debate come down to a dubious nationalism, scholars tending to side with the English account for no other apparent reason than the fact that it is English. This is perhaps due to the debate taking place in a jingoistic atmosphere in the years leading up to the First World War. Needless to say, this English report also happens to be the most sympathetic to Elizabeth herself.

47. Wickham 1:53.
48. Nichols, *Elizabeth* 1:35.
49. Corporation of London, *Repertory (1558–60)* XIV:fol.104. The instructions were clear: 'Item it was ordered that the Bachelors of the Mercers Company shall be permitted to stand at Conduit in Cheapside directly and against the Master of the same company on the furthest side of the street there at the Queen's coming to her Coronation'.
50. Smuts, 'Public Ceremony' 76.
51. He continues: 'An execution that was known to be taking place, but which did so in secret, would scarcely have had any meaning' (Foucault, *Discipline and Punish* 57–8).
52. See particularly V. Pearl, 'Change and Stability in Seventeenth Century London', *London Journal* 5:3–34, and 'Social Policy in Early Modern London', *History and Imagination: Essays in Honour of H. R. Trevor-Roper* 115–31; and Steve Rappaport, *Worlds Within Worlds*.
53. See Slack, *Poverty and Policy in Tudor And Stuart England*; Paul Clark and Paul Slack, introduction, *Crisis and Order in English Towns* 1–55 and *English Towns in Transition 1500–1700*; A. L. Beier, 'Vagrants and the Social Order in Elizabethan England', *Past And Present* 64:3–29 and *Masterless Men*; A. L. Beier and R. Finlay, eds, *London, 1500–1700*.
54. Ian W. Archer, *The Pursuit of Stability*.
55. Beier and Finlay, introduction, 'The Significance of the Metropolis', *London 1500–1700* 2. These figures are based upon the various surviving parish registers for London.
56. This last point is clarified by Martin Holmes in his *Elizabethan London*: 'there was no such thing, in Elizabeth's time, as a national standing army. Soldiers volunteered, or were pressed, for a specific enterprise and disbanded at the end of it, and not all of them had either the opportunity or the desire to go back to honest civilian occupations' (93). For contemporary documentation of the pressing of men, see John Stow, *Annales* (London: Thomas Adams, 1615) 1299, 1303, and 1308; *The Acts of the Privy Council (1597)* 290, *APC (1600–01)* 94–5, *APC (1592–93)* 43–4 and 585, and *APC (1601–04)* 27–8. For a broad discussion of the phenomenon, see C. G. Cruickshank, *Elizabeth's Army* (Oxford: Clarendon, 1966) and Lindsay Boynton, *The Elizabethan Militia 1558–1638* (London: Routledge & Kegan Paul, 1967).
57. See A. L. Beier, *Masterless Men* 20–27 and 91–2, and 'Engine of Manufacture: the Trades of London', *London: 1500–1700* 141–67. Beier bases his figures for the decline in the cloth trade upon the occupational titles existent in the surviving parish burial registers.
58. Slack, *London 1500–1700* 62. Slack provides a much more detailed analysis of the plague and its effects in *The Impact of the Plague in Tudor and Stuart England*, both with regard to London and the country as a whole. He actually shows figures for various years between 1563 and 1665, and clarifies that his statistics are based on records of burials and plague burials identified by the contemporary bills of mortality and collected by I. Sutherland in *A Summary Tabulation of Annual Totals of Burials, Plague Deaths and Christenings in London Prior to 1666*, a copy of which is in the Bodleian Library, Oxford.
59. Paul Slack, *Poverty and Policy in Tudor and Stuart England* 48–9.
60. Slack, *The Impact of the Plague* 71.

61. Ibid., 72.
62. Beier and Finlay, introduction, 'The Significance of the Metropolis', *London 1500–1700* 18.
63. Beier, *Masterless Men* 156.
64. Ibid., 43.
65. The most revealing sources in this context are the *Bridewell Hospital Court Books, 1559–1660*, in the Guildhall Library; J. C. Jeaffreson, ed., *Middlesex County Records I: Indictments, Coroners' Inquests, Post-Mortem and Recognizances from 3 Edward VI to the End of the Reign of Queen Elizabeth* (Middlesex: County Records Society, 1886); also, J. S. Cockburn, *Calendar of Assize Records: Home Circuit Indictments, Elizabeth I and James I* (London: HMSO, 1975–80).
66. *Calendar of State Papers (Venetian) (1617–19)* 60.
67. Ibid., 60.
68. Mulcaster 55.
69. See, for example, F. W. Fairholt, *Lord Mayors' Pageants* and *Gog and Magog: The Giants in Guildhall* (London: John Camden Hotten, 1859); J. G. Nichols, *London Pageants* (London: J. B. Nichols & Son, 1831); George Unwin, *The Gilds and Companies of London* (1908; London: Methuen, 1925); Shelia Williams, 'The Lord Mayor's Show in Tudor and Stuart Times', *The Guildhall Miscellany* 10 (London: The Malone Society, 1959).
70. Lawrence Manley, *Literature and Culture in Early Modern London* (Cambridge: Cambridge University Press, 1995) 251.
71. George Puttenham, *The Arte of English Poesie 1589*, 'Chapter VI: "Of the High, Low, and Meane Subiect"', in *Elizabethan Critical Essays*, ed Gregory Smith, 2 vols (Oxford: Clarendon Press, 1959) 1–193:159.
72. This is a point noted by Michael Bristol in *Carnival and Theatre*, where he writes of the ambivalent nature of the giants, that they were 'figures of awe but also figures of fun'(66). He places Puttenham's observation in a carnivalesque context: 'By "underpeering" and revealing the *other*sidedness of the giants imposing size and awe-inspiring power, the "shrewd boys" complete the relationships of travesty. The giant is only an oversized straw man; the ugly monster also has a funny and familiar side. In this gesture exposing the "browne paper and tow" underneath the imposture of the pageant giant, all social and cognitive distance is cancelled: the giant is able to "make the people wonder", but that wonder does not exclude "great derision" and homely familiarity' (66). It is also interesting to read in F. W. Fairholt's account of the history of the two Guildhall giants *Gog and Magog: The Giants in Guildhall*, what he has to say about Shirley's attitude to both the giants and the Lord Mayor's Shows in general: 'In Shirley's *Contention for Honour and Riches*, 1633 (afterwards in his *Honoria and Mammon*, 1652), he ridicules the annual Civic Pageants on Lord Mayor's Day, and the citizen's love of good cheer after them: "You march to Guildhall, with every man his spoon in his pocket, where you look upon the giants, and feed like Saracens"'(35).
73. Both of these are taken from Ann Jennalie Cook's *The Privileged Playgoers of Shakespeare's London* (Princeton, New Jersey: Princeton University Press, 1981) and refer to Dekker's and Greene's attitudes towards pickpockets: 'As Dekker pointed out, the cutpurse haunted the assemblies of the privileged – Paul's, Westminster, Chancery Lane in term time, London Bridge, suits at the Star Chamber, the Lord Mayor's oath taking ... . Greene agreed, saying "their chief walks in Paul's, Westminster, the Exchange, plays, beargarden, running at tilt, the Lord Mayor's day ..."' (205).
74. Toril Moi, *Sexual Textual Politics* 75.
75. Bergeron, *English Civic Pageantry* 12.
76. Corporation of London, *Repertory (1558–60)* XIV:fol.103b.

77. R. R. Sharpe, *London and the Kingdom*, 3 vols (London: Longman, Green and Co., 1894) 1:485.
78. Ibid., 1:485–6. Sharpe is merely reproducing the original record here.
79. *Acts of the Privy Council, (1558–70)* 10. The requisitioning of this cloth is referred to in the aforementioned inventory for the coronation (*Records of the Lord Chamberlain and other Offices of the Royal Household, and the Clerk of the Recognizances*, Public Record Office, LC 2 4/3).
80. Bergeron, *English Civic Pageantry* 15.
81. Bergeron, 'Elizabeth's Coronation Entry (1558): New Manuscript Evidence', *English Literary Renaissance* 8 (Winter 1978) 3–8:3.
82. Hackett, *Virgin Mother, Maiden Queen* 48.
83. Reproduced from the Corporation of London Letter Book (220) in Nichols, *Elizabeth* 2:537.
84. Ibid., 537.
85. Ibid., 537.
86. Reproduced from the Company of Stationers Court-Book in Ibid., 538.
87. Reproduced from the Corporation of London Letter Book (220) in Nichols, *Elizabeth* 2:539.
88. Ibid., 539.
89. Ibid., 539.
90. Ibid., 539.
91. Cruickshank 13. Also important in this context is Lindsay Boynton, *The Elizabethan Militia, 1558–1638*.
92. *CSP (Foreign) (Sept 1585–May 1586)* 495. For a more in-depth consideration of this report and its connection with Shakespeare's *Henry V*, see William Leahy, 'All would be Royal: The Effacement of Disunity in Shakespeare's *Henry V*', *Shakespeare Jahrbuch* 138 (2002) 89–98. For its further connection with *Henry VI*, see William Leahy '"Thy hunger-starved men": Shakespeare's *Henry* plays and the contemporary lot of the common soldier', *Parergon: Journal of the Australian and New Zealand Association for Medieval and Early Modern Studies* 20.2 (July 2003) 119–34.
93. *CSP (Ireland) (1596–97)* 195.
94. *CSP (Ireland) (1598–99)* 357.
95. *CSP (Dom) (1581–90)* 401.
96. Ibid., 415.
97. Ibid., 415.
98. Ibid., 513.
99. *CSP (Foreign) (Sept 1585–May 1586)* 219.
100. *CSP (Foreign) (June 1586–June 1588)* 2: 25. See also *APC (1590)* 189.
101. *APC (1588–9)* 387.
102. *CSP (Dom) (1591)* 141.
103. *APC (1592)* 309.
104. *APC (1599–1600)* 137.
105. Ibid., 726–7, 760–61 and 787–8.
106. Cruickshank 63.
107. Ibid., 63.
108. For the selling of weapons see *CSP (Ireland) (1598–99)* 138.
109. Neville Williams, *Elizabeth I* (London: Weidenfeld & Nicolson, 1972) 186. This reading is typical of traditional studies of this event and can be found the majority of studies about Elizabeth.
110. Susan Frye, 'The Myth of Elizabeth at Tilbury' 95–114.

111. The speech appeared in Sharp's *Cabala: Mysteries of State*, in the form of a fawning letter written to the Duke of Buckingham.

112. Corporation of London, *Journals (1585–90)* 22: fol.202b. See also *Tudor Royal Proclamations* eds. P.C. Hughes & J.F. Larkin, 3 vols (New Haven & London: Yale University Press, 1989) 3:25.

113. *APC (1588)* 249.

114. Curtis C. Breight, *Surveillance, Militarism and Drama in the Elizabethan Era* (London: Macmillan, 1996) 183. Breight also reproduces a number of letters written between commanders and authorities which relate the dire conditions of the soldiers and sailors in the lead up to the Armada campaign (176–80).

115. *APC (1588–89)* 416.

116. These events are related in detail in *APC (1588–89)* 416; 420–21; 453–4. See also *APC (1589–90)*, 47–8; 54–6.

117. *Journals (1585–90)* 22:fol.312.

118. *APC (1588–89)* 416.

119. Ibid., 420–21. Nichols describes an important event in this context under the heading 'Riot at Bartholomew Fair, 1589'. He writes: "'In 1589" says Stow, "certain of those furious undaunted spirits" (the Sailors and Soldiers who have been employed by Drake and Norris), "after they had performed many unrulie pranks, in divers shires, began to plot how they might atchieve some speciall act, to relieve their present want, and in the end concluded to surprise Bartholomew Fayre, and to that purpose five hundred of them were assembled about Westminster; the Lord Maior having knowledge thereof, upon the sudden raysed almost two thousand men very well appoynted, and about tenne a clocke at night they marched as farre as Temple Barre, to repulse that rowt; and then the Lord Treasurer sent word by the Chamberlaine of London, that the rabble was dispearst and gone, and then the Citizens returned"' (*Elizabeth* 3:31).

120. Ibid., 453–4.

121. *APC (1589–90)* 47–8.

122. Ibid., 54.

123. Ibid., 54–6.

124. *Tudor Royal Proclamations* 716:46.

125. Ibid., 46.

126. Neale, *Queen Elizabeth* 282.

127. Furthermore, as A. A. Bromham has shown, it was a section of the audience that, most probably, could not hear what was being said at the various instructive pageant devices. From their position far back from the central procession, it is doubtful that the words of the actors performing the pageants could be heard. See A. A. Bromham, 'Thomas Middleton's *The Triumphs of Truth*: City Politics in 1613', *The Seventeenth Century* X: 1 (Spring 1995) 1–25:4. This purely visual experience of the moral allegories performed would enable the production of differing and alternative interpretations of these normative lessons (which shall be dealt with in detail in the next chapter), a possibility that has led Susan Frye to suggest that each device was posted in English and Latin in an attempt to control and supervise interpretation itself. See Susan Frye, *Elizabeth 1: The Competition for Representation* 34.

128. Nichols, *Elizabeth* 1:xi.

129. Haigh, *Elizabeth I* 147.

130. Bergeron, *English Civic Pageantry* 9.

131. Williams, 'The Tudors', *The Courts of Europe* 164. Haigh believes that although progresses were indeed an opportunity for Elizabeth to garner support from her nobles, they 'were also occasions ... to show herself to ordinary people as she crossed the countryside at a sedate pace' (Haigh, *Elizabeth I* 147).

132. Dovey 1. It should be noted that Dovey uses the same despatch from the Spanish Ambassador as Alison Plowden, and in the same way (that is, minus the first two sentences) as evidence for this statement.

133. Neville Williams, again using the same despatch, and once again in the same way writes that 'country folk who came to gape and cheer as she went by knew they would be lucky if she passed their way again' ('The Tudors', *The Courts of Europe* 165). Roy Strong has written about the need for such a propagandist ritual (though he would not call it such): 'The Elizabethan monarchy did not only need powerful verbal and visual images to hold a divided people in loyalty; it also demanded the development of an elaborate ritual and ceremonial with which to frame and present the Queen to her subjects as the sacred virgin whose reign was ushering in a new golden age of peace and plenty. In order to achieve this, the apparatus of the formal progress through the countryside was deliberately developed' (*The Cult of Elizabeth* 114).

134. Bishop Hurd, *Dialogues Moral and Political* (1759) 193; quoted in Nichols, *Elizabeth* 1:xxiii–iv.

135. Chambers, *The Elizabethan Stage* 1:109–12.

136. Quoted in Williams, 'The Tudors', *The Courts of Europe* 165.

137. Nichols, *Elizabeth* 1:xxxi.

138. Williams, 'The Tudors', *The Courts of Europe* 164.

139. For an extended list of such hosts, see Mary Hill Cole, *The Portable Queen* 85–96.

140. Lawrence Stone, *The Crisis of the Aristocracy 1558–1641* (Oxford: Clarendon Press, 1965) 454.

141. H. Ellis, ed., *Original Letters Illustrative of English History*, 3 vols (London: Triphook & Lepard, 1824) 2:265–7.

142. Stone, *Crisis* 453–4. Chambers sums up in amusing fashion the dilemma of the Elizabethan noble: 'Contact with the great is not ordinarily, for the plain man, a bed of roses; and there is no reason to suppose that it was otherwise in the spacious times of Elizabeth. You probably got knighted, if you were not a knight already, which cost you some fees, and you received some sugared royal compliments on the excellence of your entertainment and the appropriateness of your "devices". But you had wrestled for a month with poulterers and with poets. You had "avoided" your house, and made yourself uncomfortable in a neighbouring lodge. You had seen your trim gardens and terraces encamped upon by a locust-swarm of all the tag-rag and bobtail that follows a court' (Chambers, *The Elizabethan Stage* 1:113).

143. PRO. LS. 13/168/368–71.

144. Middlesex Standing Joint Committee, *Middlesex in Shakespeare's Day: Exhibition of Records from the Middlesex County Record Office at the Middlesex Guildhall, Westminster* (London: The Committee, 1964) 9.

145. Chambers, *The Elizabethan Stage* 1:117.

146. Ibid., 1:117.

147. Nichols, *James* 1:43.

148. Nichols, *Elizabeth* 3:37. The records for James I's reign are much fuller, and in his first volume dealing with James, Nichols reproduces pages of complaints regarding the abuse of the Crown's purveyance policy: see Nichols, *James* 1:x–xvi.

149. *Middlesex County Records*, Microfilm. Acc. 312/565.

150. Chambers, *The Elizabethan Stage* 1:117. There is a record from 1605 of the Venetian Ambassador complaining at the behaviour of James I's servants in this respect (*Calendar of State Papers (Venetian) (1605)* 265 and 285). See also Allega Woodworth, 'Purveyance for the Royal Household in the Reign of Queen Elizabeth', *Transactions of the American Philosophical Society* 35 (1945) 1–89:34–8.

151. *APC (1558–70)* 241.

152. For more on the problems of purveyance, see Mary Hill Cole, *The Portable Queen* 46–52. For specific cases and the punishments delivered, see Cockburn, *Assize Records: Essex Indictments*, 389, 892, 1402, 1403, 2154 and 2253; *Kent Indictments*, 1483 and 2235; *Hertfordshire Indictments*, 400; *Surrey Indictments*, 1770.

153. Dovey 1.

154. Ibid., 87.

155. Nichols, *Elizabeth* 2:303.

156. Ibid., 2:303.

157. Cole 164. This relates to the record held in the National Archives, PRO 13/168/40, 14.

158. Holinshed 4:403.

159. *CSP (Spanish) (1568–79)* 611.

160. John William Burgon, *The Life and Times of Sir Thomas Gresham*, 2 vols (New York: Burt Franklin, 1964) 2:447–8. Churchyard named the pageant 'The Devise of Warre'.

161. Churchyard devised pageants for the Queen's at Bristol in 1574 and Norwich in 1578.

162. *APC 1575–77* 126.

163. *Middlesex County Records*, Micro. SR. 199/4.

164. Middlesex Standing Joint Committee 11.

165. Burgon, *Thomas Gresham*, 2:449(fn).

166. Jean Wilson 47. Wilson informs us that both 'Lord Norris and his wife were tied to Elizabeth by long acquaintance and family loyalties. His father had been one of the young men executed with Anne Boleyn as her "lovers"; hers, Lord Williams of Tame, had shown kindness to Elizabeth when, as a state prisoner under her sister, she had visited Rycote ... . They entertained Elizabeth there on at least five occasions ...' (51).

167. David Birt, *Elizabeth's England* (Harlow: Longman, 1981) 41.

168. My thanks to A. A. Bromham for this observation.

169. John Walter, 'A "Rising Of The People?"' 90–143.

170. Roger B. Manning, *Village Revolts* 220–29.

171. *CSP (Dom) (1595–97)* 345.

172. Manning, *Village Revolts* 221.

173. Ibid., 221.

174. Ibid., 221.

175. Ibid., 226. According to the records, this seems to have been the case with all of the parties threatened: 'Discovered all this to Mr Berry, examinate's landlord ... and he hardly believed it ...' *(CSP (Dom.) (1595–97)* 344).

176. Quoted in Manning 224.

177. Ibid., 227.

178. *CSP (Dom) (1595–97)* 316–18.

179. Wilson, *Will Power* 81.

180. William Shakespeare, *Hamlet*, IV. iii. 29–30.

181. See, for example, Carole Levin, *The Heart and Stomach of a King: Elizabeth I and the Politics of Sex and Power* 1–9, and Susan Frye, *Elizabeth I: The Competition for Representation* 22–55. For such critiques of the progresses, see Berry, *Of Chastity and Power* 83–110; Marie Axton, *The Queen's Two Bodies: Drama and the Elizabethan Succession* (London: Royal Historical Society, 1977) 61–72; Susan Doran, *Monarchy and Matrimony: The Courtships of Elizabeth I*.

Chapter 3

'Tyme hath brought me hether': Readings of Elizabeth on Procession

By drawing the critical gaze away from the centres of Elizabethan processions and concentrating instead upon their margins, it is possible to demonstrate the ambiguities and absences that are discernible in traditional conceptualisations of the constitution of early modern processional audiences. Further ambiguities can also be demonstrated regarding the same conceptualisations of the consciousness of these audiences in terms of their potential alliances. Consecutive readings of original documents have transmitted the notion of a monolithic audience response throughout history, such interpretations being based upon perceptibly partial readings. The historical transmission of the monolithic nature of the audience response has been achieved by taking these original documents at their word, despite the fact that they have been seen to be propagandist documents. Recognition of the propagandist nature of these documents, however, opens them up to readings of an alternative kind, readings which find an articulation of ambiguities and anxieties that have been traditionally ignored or overlooked.

These same original documents describe at length the pageant devices and shows performed for the Queen on procession, both in the city and in the country. These pageants and shows have traditionally been seen as unproblematic celebrations of the Queen in the same way as the descriptions of the audiences, and have indeed been regarded as key devices in the interpellation of these audiences. Traditional procession analysis has read these allegorical pageants and shows as impressing the audiences to the extent that they unquestioningly celebrate and support both the monarchy and the social hierarchy of which it is the pinnacle. Such analysis determines a process of successful normative display the splendour of which, much like the physical processions themselves, demonstrates dissymmetry and thus successfully hails the audience. The spectacular nature of these allegorical displays is regarded as contributing to this process of interpellation, and audiences have been monolithically construed as consumers of this successful normative moral lesson. It is an important argument of this book that such was not the case, however. Rather, I want to contend in the following that, just as in conceptions of the audience itself, a close examination of these original documents demonstrates many ambiguities. This close reading will show that traditional perceptions of the effects of these pageants and shows have been based upon readings which have likewise ignored and overlooked certain crucial details and events. Furthermore, I want to suggest that the sort of monolithic readings of the allegorical displays that procession analysis has traditionally produced are ill-founded due to the fact that allegory itself inherently produces multiple meanings.

In what follows I shall examine, in detail, the allegorical pageants and shows performed for Elizabeth at the London procession of 1558, the Kenilworth progress of 1575 and the Rycote/Ditchley progress of 1592 utilising many of the original documents examined in the previous chapter.[1] Before doing so, however, I want to explore Walter Benjamin's theories on the subject of allegory, and demonstrate the inability of this form of display to control the transmission of its desired meanings, rather beckoning alternative interpretations.[2] I will then subject the pageants and shows performed for the Queen in London in 1558, and some of those produced for her on the country estates of her courtiers to this conceptualisation of allegory. In this analysis I want to argue that real events undermined the meanings the producers of the pageants wished to transmit, and the same real events continue to undermine traditional readings based upon these original meanings. It will be shown that events closely related to the London procession and those at Kenilworth, Rycote and Ditchley compromise traditional concepts of the shows produced for the Queen due to the fact that, in these cases, 'Allegory is allegorised by reality'.[3]

In his *Apologie for Poetrie*, Sir Philip Sidney made the case for clarity through allegory, valorising its use in poetry, and in turn valuing poetry all the more for such a use. Susan Frye outlines this process of mutual valorisation, stating that 'his [Sidney's] entire ethical defence of poetry rests on poetry's ability to make clear through allegory a morality that philosophy teaches too abstractly and history, too particularly ...'.[4] Sidney in fact articulates allegory's paradoxical nature when he writes of poetry's 'dark conceits', a paradox that has continued to concern those who have wished to attribute the same characteristic of clarity to allegory as Sidney himself. In a number of extensive studies of medieval and Renaissance allegory, Rosamund Tuve, following Sidney, attempted to demonstrate the ways in which allegory (particularly written/spoken allegory) clarifies meaning as, she believes, words are less ambiguous than objects, and thus 'great allegories are usually the most concrete of all writings in texture'.[5] While this connects with Sidney in the sense that there is an apparent desire to reject the assumption that allegory inherently produces more than a single meaning, and at the same time gestures toward the fact that it does, Tuve's formulation of the stable nature of language has, in recent years particularly, become severely problematised. In fact, in 1928, almost forty years before Tuve wrote the above, Walter Benjamin had already taken the idea of the stability of language to task, writing in his *Ursprung des deutschen Trauerspiels* that the *word* itself, as part of the natural realm of objects, 'can be exploited for allegorical purposes'.[6] Indeed, this work by Benjamin can be regarded as the touchstone for the problematisation of traditional views of allegory with his dictum regarding allegorical representation: 'Any person, any object, any relationship can mean absolutely anything else'.[7]

The majority of modern critics would no doubt agree with Angus Fletcher that ambiguity is inherent in a form that in 'the simplest terms ... says one thing and means another'.[8] Fletcher directly challenges Rosamund Tuve's belief that 'allegorists finally wish "full comprehension"',[9] believing in contrast that allegory 'seems to aim at both clarity and obscurity together, each effect depending upon the other. Enigma, and not always decipherable enigma, appears to be allegory's most cherished function, and who will doubt that confusion in the symbolism will aid this function?'[10] While both Tuve and Fletcher are concerned, to a great extent, with the intentions of the allegory's creator, the former expresses doubts about the clarity of the form, and the latter at least hints at the inability of such a creator to control the meanings they intend. Benjamin, as shown above, goes much further, stating that clarity itself is impossible in allegory. He reiterates this by his reading of Hermann Cohen's *Ästhetik des reinen Gefühls*, where the latter states:

> The basic characteristic of allegory ... is ambiguity, multiplicity of meaning; allegory glor[ies] in richness of meaning. But the richness of this ambiguity is the richness of extravagance ... . Ambiguity is therefore always the opposite of clarity and unity of meaning.[11]

The instability inherent in allegorical representation as articulated by Cohen is apparent in a discussion by Helen Hackett that is pertinent to this current study. In her examination of the various allegorical images used in order to underwrite Elizabeth I's power in the 1590s, Hackett concentrates upon the ways in which lunar symbolism was associated with the Queen. Hackett shows how official allegory attempted to associate Elizabeth with the positive lunar powers of self-renewal, of immutability, and 'qualities of radiance, ethereality, mysticism and other-worldliness',[12] as well as providing a general symbol of female power. But the moon is quintessentially an ambiguous symbol, being also associated with 'the troubling changeability of the female body ... brain-sickness (that is, lunacy), strange behaviour in nature, darkness and night, the occult, sinister female powers, and female licentiousness'.[13]

These associations naturally undermine the ideological desire of official allegory, and Hackett goes on to show how lunar imagery was directly used to articulate female inferiority, quoting Richard Mulcaster who, 'in his educational treatise *Positions*, 1581, explained that girls' bodies were weaker, "as of a moonish influence"'.[14] The ambiguity evident in such examples is founded on the fact that allegories that could be classed as official (that is, those with a didactic aim), 'raise questions of value *directly*, by asserting certain propositions as good and others as bad'.[15] Naturally, in the above example, qualities such as self-renewal and immutability are being positively valued. However, though it is possible to attempt to direct the audience's perceptions of such valuation, it is impossible to control them: what is being allegorically cast as a virtue may well be viewed as a vice by certain members of the audience, or may indeed be given neither of these moral evaluations.

Walter Benjamin was of the opinion that 'Even great artists and exceptional theoreticians ... assume that allegory is a conventional relationship between an illustrative image and its abstract meaning'.[16] For Benjamin, allegory was not just 'a playful illustrative technique', but was rather 'a form of expression, just as speech is expression, and, indeed, just as writing is'.[17] This being the case, allegory

becomes as susceptible to the production of excess or surplus meanings as
language itself in a post-structuralist universe. This is a point taken up and
extended by modern critics influenced by Benjamin's ideas. Julian Roberts, in his
examination of Benjamin's theory, writes: 'The power of allegory, the play of
sense, lay in its ability to convert objects into signs. The natural world lay at its feet
as an inexhaustible store of signs which could be endlessly combined and related at
the whim of the allegorist'.[18] This mention of signs and their instability articulates
an essentially post-structural assessment of language, one which is outlined by
Susan Frye in her examination of the nature of allegory which, though cast in such
a post-structuralist vocabulary, is to a great extent a reiteration of Benjamin's
ideas.[19] Before examining the pre-coronation procession pageants with Benjamin's
thesis in mind, it is worth exploring his ideas further in order to seek a way out of a
dilemma that the formulation of the contingency of allegory seems to create. For if,
as Benjamin seems to believe, an allegorical image can mean absolutely anything,
is it not necessarily also true that such an image is characterised by total
indeterminacy of meaning? And, if the meaning of images is indeterminate, what
are the implications for allegory as a communicative mode of expression?

Benjamin's writings on the allegorical form stemmed from his study of
German Baroque Tragedy (*Trauerspiel*). His study of this genre led him to
recognise the inherent instability of allegory as a representational form, although it
is important to note that he stopped short of saying that all meanings produced by
allegory are contingent. For Benjamin believed that in allegory meanings were, in
effect, constrained by reality, or more specifically, by history. In that sense
Benjamin believed that though meaning was multiple, it was not limitless. In this
formulation of meaning constrained by reality, as in much else, Benjamin was
greatly influenced by Hegel's *Phänomenologie des Geistes*, the study which saw
the latter work out his idea of the dialectic.[20] Julian Roberts quotes Hegel and
demonstrates in what sense his work became important to Benjamin: '"The true
being of a man is his *deed*; for in it individuality is real"; and against the infinite
transferability of the allegorical sign the deed "*is* this, and its being is not *merely* a
sign, but the thing itself"'.[21] Thus Benjamin can say that any particular thing,
though it signifies, does not only signify, but is also that thing itself. Consequently,
he argues, it is reality itself that settles allegory's 'infinity of meanings within
which its superabundance of signification threatens to disappear',[22] the signs
themselves signifying their allegorisation of something real, and thus revealing 'the
limit set upon allegorical contemplation'.[23] The image that Benjamin uses to
demonstrate his idea is that of the grave or the place of execution, wherein the
'bleak confusion of Golgotha' is not 'just a symbol of the desolation of human
existence. In it transitoriness is not signified or allegorically represented, so much
as, in its own significance, displayed as allegory. As the allegory of resurrection'.[24]
There is a point then where the allegory 'turns in on itself',[25] where the site of
execution can represent an allegory of resurrection, and where the sign beckons a
reading constrained by history. This representation of history, whether of actual
historical characters, or mythological/moralistic ones, takes place in a reality that
essentially turns these images in upon themselves in a way in which 'Allegory is
allegorised by reality',[26] and what emerges is history. In the pre-coronation

procession and the various rural entertainments, there are examples of such a process of allegory allegorised by reality, examples which when examined can be seen to have a catastrophic effect upon the desired meanings of the pageant devices/entertainments, as well as upon subsequent readings of these spectacular events. I shall apply Benjamin's adage to the pageants of the pre-coronation procession in an attempt to scratch away at the surface of conventional interpretations of their meanings.

The pre-coronation procession

The overriding aim of the pre-coronation procession itself, as well as the pageants that structured it, was the introduction of an ascendant Elizabeth in ways that could be deemed suitable iconographically. The number of allegorical devices presented to the new Queen and audience were fundamentally part of a poetics of praise, as well as being attempts to link her with both historical and mythological figures in ways that would enhance her credibility as the new sovereign. This process was, to a great extent, defined by the fact that Elizabeth was a female head of Church and State, something that merely problematised her already rather tenuous claim to the throne.[27] Mulcaster's pamphlet describing the pre-coronation procession demonstrates this search for appropriate allegorical figures with which to connect Elizabeth, and shows the amount of care that was taken in this process. The first device which Elizabeth encountered as she entered the City was not an allegorical one however, consisting merely of a simple, welcoming oration. Mulcaster writes: 'Nere unto Fanchurch was erected a scaffolde richely furnished, wherein stode a noyes of instrumentes, and a chylde in costly apparell, whiche was appoynted to welcome the Quenes Majestie in the hole Cities behalfe' (39). Addressing Elizabeth, the child calls London 'thy Town', welcoming her with 'blessing tonges', which 'praise thee to the sky; / Which wish to thee long lyfe ...' (39). The four stanzas continue in their celebration of Elizabeth, whose person has 'all untruthe driven out' (40). Mulcaster immediately seizes the opportunity to underwrite the normative desire apparent in these verses when he observes: 'At which wordes of the last line the hole People gave a great shout, wishing with one assent, as the chylde had said' (40). The verses represent a conventional welcome to an entering monarch, and set the tone for the pageants that are to follow. Mulcaster himself sets exactly the same tone, in his own way, constructing as he does the monolithic reaction of the audience as being in accordance with the ideological desire of the child's verses.

The first thematic pageant of the procession followed this initial welcoming and, placed at the upper end of 'Gracious Streate' (40), had the underwriting of the legitimacy of Elizabeth's claim to the throne as its aim. Mulcaster again describes it in detail, saying that the stage 'extended from thone syde of the streate to thother', decorated with battlements 'conteining three portes, and over the middlemost was avaunced severall stages in degrees' (41). This pageant, entitled 'The uniting of the two Howses of Lancastre and Yorke' (42) presented, upon a lower stage, personages representing Henry VII and his wife Elizabeth. The former, from the House of Lancaster, was enclosed in a red rose, and the Queen, from the House of York, was enclosed in a white rose. Each of them was 'Royally crowned, and decently apparailled as apperteineth to Princes, with Sceptours in their hands, and one vawt surmounting their heades, wherein aptly were placed two tables, eche conteining the title of those two Princes' (41). This marking ensured that the audience was aware of who were being represented in this display, and the description of their appearance demonstrates the desire to present a realistic simulation of these two historical figures. Furthermore, these two figures joined hands over the 'ring of matrimonie', and 'Out of which two Roses sprang two branches gathered into one, which were directed upward to the second stage ...' (41). Upon this higher platform two actors representing King Henry VIII and his Queen, Anne Boleyn, were placed, who were likewise dressed and decorated, and who also wore a sign upon which their names were written. From their seat yet another branch extended upward to the third and highest stage, upon which a figure representing Queen Elizabeth herself sat, 'nowe our most dradde Soveraigne Ladie, crowned and apparalled as thother Prynces were' (41). A verbal explanation of the entire pageant was given as Elizabeth reached it, in verse form once more, again recited by a child. As well as this vocal explanation, from which only Elizabeth and those very close to the stages would have benefited, 'all emptie places ... were furnished with sentences concerning unitie', and to make the final ideological point, 'the hole Pageant [was] garnished with Redde Roses and White ...' (41).

The themes of unity and of legitimacy, both clearly negotiated in this pageant in terms of support for the idea of the Tudor myth view of history, are underlined by the desire to control possible meanings suggested by this genealogical allegory through the posting of messages describing the intentions of the pageant devisers. And this is further emphasised in Mulcaster's text itself, apparent in his emphatic concentration on its single meaning, betraying a desire to monitor and forbid the possibility of alternative meanings seeping through by a process of textual containment. Mulcaster represents a logical, rational progression when he writes:

> Thys Pageant was grounded upon the Quenes Majesties name. For like as the long warre betwene the two Houses of Yorke and Lancastre then ended, when Elizabeth doughter to Edward the Fourth matched in marriage with Henry the Seventhe, heyre to the Howse of Lancastre; so since that the Quenes Majesties name was Elizabeth, and forsomuch as she is the onelye heire of Henrye the Eighth ... it was devised, that like as Elizabeth was the first occasion of concorde, so she, another Elizabeth, myght maintaine the same among her subjectes, so that unitie was the ende whereat the whole devise shotte, as the Quenes Majesties names moved the first grounde (42).

The genealogical link being made, the accession of the Queen is legitimised, as though peace and unity are signified by the very name Elizabeth. It would seem that this legitimising link is made by Mulcaster himself by his reading of the symbols' connection between the two Elizabeths. As much as anything else, this pageant, through its valorisation of Elizabeth's father, Henry VIII, underlined the legitimacy of Protestantism as well as signalling an emerging nationalism centred on the Tudor dynasty.[28] Mulcaster's text registers these desired meanings when he notes that the verses explaining the pageant, in English and Latin, were again, 'drawen in voide places ... all tending to one ende, that quietness might be mainteyned, and all dissention displaced', and this by 'the Quenes Majestie, heire to agreement ...' (43).

Mulcaster describes the pageant of 'The uniting of the two Howses of Lancastre and Yorke' in much detail, informing us of the genealogical links made both between the two houses, and between Henry VII and Elizabeth, Henry VIII and Anne Boleyn, and Elizabeth herself. As already stated, the ideological desire of the pageant's creators is fairly clear, casting Elizabeth in terms of a legitimate heir to the throne, a throne that, from Henry VII through Henry VIII, represents national unity, peace and stability. At length Mulcaster valorises Henry VII's wife Elizabeth as having helped set this process in motion by joining the two warring houses of Lancaster and York together by marrying Henry, stating furthermore that the ascendant Queen Elizabeth would also maintain this as 'unitie was the ende whereat the whole devise shotte ...' (42). This process whereby the fate of the nation is regarded as being secure due to the fact that the new monarch happens to have the same name as a previous monarch who is conceived to have been very able seems to be a rather tenuous foundation upon which to build notions of a continuance of peace and national unity. However, it is significant, as it is a connection based in the occlusion of a more obvious link, one made clear by examining the verses recited in Elizabeth's presence as she reached this pageant device:

> The two Princes that sit under one cloth of state,
> The Man in the Redde Rose, the Woman in the White,
> Henry the VII. and Quene Elizabeth his Mate,
> By ring of marriage as Man and Wife unite.
>
> Both heires to both their bloodes, to Lancastre the Kyng,
> The Queene to Yorke, in one the two Howses did knit;
> Of whom as heire to both, Henry the Eighth did spring,
> In whose seat, his true heire, thou Quene Elisabeth doth sit.
>
> Therefore as civill warre, and fuede of blood did cease,
> When these two Houses were united into one,
> So now that jarrs shall stint, and quietnes encrease,
> We trust, O noble Quene, thou wilt be cause alone (42–3).

The absence is of course clear; of all those represented on the pageant stages, in the verses it is only the figure of Anne Boleyn, Elizabeth's mother, who is not mentioned. This is an absence noted by Susan Frye, who finds Mulcaster's document (and indeed all writing she describes as 'authoritative writing'), in its attempt at unity, in fact 'summons the very inconsistencies, anxieties, and doubts that it attempts to quash'.[29] For Frye, the staging of Anne Boleyn, coupled with her verbal absence, is an example of such inconsistency and anxiety, and demonstrates an enormous discomfort with having to include her representation at all. Boleyn is, in a sense, excluded in the same moment she is included. Her presence calls to mind that the event of 1558 was not in fact Elizabeth's first coronation procession, her mother having been six months pregnant with her on the occasion of her own coronation entry in 1533. Boleyn's allegorical presence at the 1558 procession could call to mind the fact that at her own entry she was celebrated, as Frye states, 'as Henry's fertile, chaste queen – and look what happened to her'.[30] Her own procession in 1533 witnessed a silent response from its audience,[31] her celebration as a chaste, Protestant heroine coinciding with her being heavily pregnant. This was further compounded by the fact that Henry's first wife was still living and the marriage between the two had not been sanctioned by the Pope. Here Anne Boleyn was lauded as the bringer of a golden age, as virtue personified, as virginal yet fruitful, precisely those (contradictory) properties for which Elizabeth was being celebrated in her own procession. And perhaps what this genealogical tableau articulated more than anything else was the precise opposite of its ideological desire – the very tenuousness of Elizabeth's claim to the throne. Henry VIII's will of 1546 had denied Elizabeth's legitimacy, as had the earlier Second Act of Succession of 1536. As this pageant demonstrated, her accession was built merely 'on the marital history of her progenitors'.[32] There is a sense that in fact this particular pageant could therefore have raised many doubts in the contemporary audience, not least ones regarding religion, peace, unity and stability. For whatever the pageant creators wanted the message to be, and whatever Mulcaster wanted his interpretation to mean, one thing is certain: the contemporary audience would have been aware of the real events surrounding Anne Boleyn, and would have been aware of her ambiguous status, both as an historical and an allegorical figure.[33] It is possible that many in the audience would have viewed the message of this present pageant with a good deal of scepticism. This scepticism would have been supported by the fact that ideas of a golden age embodied in a new monarch had been seen before, 25 years previously, in the same streets, and had been seen to be misplaced, not least because Anne did not last long as Queen in any case. This pageant's attempts to ensure that 'quietnes might be mainteyned, and all dissention displaced' (43), may have prompted a reading based in real (past and) current events that would have produced, conversely, divisive meanings. This allegorical representation of Anne Boleyn could indeed, in Benjaminian fashion, have been allegorised by the reality of her life and death, producing meanings very different from the official meanings desired.

From here the Queen proceeded to the next pageant device, at the Conduit in Cornhill, where she found a child 'representing her Majesties person, placed in a seate of Governement, supported by certyne vertues, which suppressed their contrarie vyces under their feete ...' (44). The Queen's name and title were displayed, as was the name of the pageant, 'The Seate of worthie Governance' (44). The figure representing Elizabeth sat in a chair that was held by four 'lively personages', each of whom in turn represented a virtue, and each having 'a table to expresse their effectes ...' (44). These virtues were named Pure Religion, Love of Subjects, Wisdom, and Justice, and they:

did treade their contrarie Vices under their feete; that is to witte, Pure Religion did treade upon Superstition and Ignoraunce; Love of Subjectes did treade upon Rebellion and Insolencie; Wisdome did treade upon Follie and Vaine Glorie; Justice did treade upon Adulacion and Bribery (44).

Each of these, according to Mulcaster, had their name clearly displayed, and were also 'aptly and properly apparelled', so as to 'expresse the same person that in title he represented' (45). Once again, every empty space was 'furnished with proper sentences', each 'commendyng the seate supported by Vertues, and defacing the Vices ...' (45). The verses spoken at this pageant cover the same ground generally, giving voice to the obvious allegorical meanings desired by the pageant devisers, to the effect that 'Vertues shall maintayn thy throne, / And Vyce be kept down still ...' (45). The ascendant Queen is seen as the embodiment of all of these virtues and thus the enemy to those vices. The use of these allegorical figures from the medieval morality plays also has an anti-Catholic effect here, vice being constructed as inherent in that confession, a further attempt to legitimise the Protestantism supplanting the Catholicism associated with Mary's reign.[34] While the drama of the pageant device, along with the spoken verses and the posted explanations clarify the ideological desire of this representation, Mulcaster ensures that the message is quite clear by informing us further:

> The ground of thys Pageant was, that like as by Vertues (whych does aboundantly appere in her Grace) the Quenes Majestie was established in the seate of Governement; so she should sette fast in the same so long as she embraced Vertue ... . For if Vice once gotte up the head, it would put the seate of Governement in peryll of falling (46).

Here various virtues, physically represented though, as the pageant explanation tells us, embodied in Elizabeth, are shown to tread upon and defeat opposing vices.

The work of Benjamin is again useful here, particularly in his use of Karl Giehlow's theories of Renaissance allegory. Giehlow writes that in such allegory, 'one and the same object can just as easily signify a virtue as a vice, and therefore more or less anything'.[35] While this does not state that a represented virtue can be read as a vice (or vice versa), it articulates the instability of such representations. When we read that 'Pure Religion did treade upon Superstition and Ignoraunce' (44), it is clear that the pageant creators and Mulcaster believe the virtue to be Protestantism and the vice Catholicism. However, in an atmosphere of religious ambiguity (Mary's reign had been rigidly Catholic), these directed readings are not the only possible ones. Indeed, in their valuation of one, and demonisation of the other, the pageant creators beckon ambiguous meanings. In the same way, members of an audience sceptical of the ways in which the elite represented both themselves and the naturalness of the social structure might well read that 'Wisdome did treade upon Follie and Vaine Glorie' (44) wryly, wondering whether the ascendant monarch and the Court itself could be conceived of as the personifications of the represented virtue rather than the vices. And again, where 'Justice did treade upon Adulacion and Bribery' (44), many would perhaps have regarded the Court as the embodiment of the represented vices rather than the virtue. The real, everyday experience of the common audience would possibly have allegorised these already unstable allegories, and produced meanings at variance with those desired and sanctioned by the centre.

Such a reality is again demonstrated with another look at the recording of the events of the pre-coronation procession by the Venetian Ambassador, Il Schifanoya. In a move that emphasises the instability of allegorical interpretation, the Venetian Ambassador reports that this particular pageant showed slightly different figures to those outlined by Mulcaster. According to the Ambassador, the vices presented were named 'Ignorance, Superstition, Hypocrisy, Vain Glory, Simulation, Rebellion and Idolatry', concluding that the general message of the pageant was 'that hitherto religion had been misunderstood and misdirected, and that now it will proceed on a better footing'.[36] This exclusively religious interpretation of the device differs from Mulcaster's political interpretation, thus concretely revealing allegory's plenitude in terms of meanings.[37] The Spanish Ambassador interprets the allegorical device in his own way and according to his own concerns. This is a point made by Sandra Logan in her study of Mulcaster's text, where she argues that these concerns, like those of the other eyewitness account of the entry, Henry Machyn's, are Catholic ones, leading to different interpretations of the pageant devices than those articulated by Mulcaster.[38] This plenitude of potential meanings and interpretations is demonstrated when it becomes clear that the Ambassador actually read the name of one of the vices, 'Hypocrisy', differently to Mulcaster.[39] Indeed, this fact has much wider implications for the notion of the instability of meanings produced by allegory. This becomes clear when the Ambassador's naming of 'Hypocrisy' is set in the context of the 'Truth/Tyme' pageant device which was performed later in the procession. For it is in this pageant that allegory is allegorised by reality to such an extent that all other pageants in the procession, and indeed the procession itself, become contaminated by meanings that official desire had no wish to produce, and that it rather sought to quash.

On her way to the 'Truth/Tyme' pageant, at the Great Conduit in Cheape, Elizabeth encountered eight children dressed to represent 'The eight Beautitudes expressed in the v chapter of the Gospel of St Matthew, applyed to our Soveraigne Lady Quene Elizabeth' (46), a title once again clearly displayed on the front of the pageant device. These were the eight Beatitudes of the Sermon on the Mount, and referred to Elizabeth thus:

> Thou hast been viii times blest, O Quene of worthy fame,
> By mekenes of thy spirite, when care did thee besette,
> By mourning in thy griefe, by mildnes in thy blame,
> By hunger and by thyrst, and justice couldst none gette.
>
> By mercy shewed, not felt, by cleanes of thyne harte,
> By seking peace alwayes, by persecucion wrong,
> Therefore trust thou in God, since he hath helpt thy smart,
> That as his promis is, so he will make thee strong (47).

Mulcaster notes that the message of the pageant was displayed upon every empty space near it and, once again, he interprets this message for us. He writes that, as applied to Elizabeth, the idea was that as she had always been virtuous 'these blessings might fall upon her', and that 'if her Grace did continue in her goodnes ... she shoulde hope for the fruit of these promises due unto them that doe exercise themselves in the blessings ...' (47).

From there Elizabeth proceeded to the Little Conduit in Cheape, to the 'Truth/Tyme' pageant which most analyses of the pre-coronation procession agree to be the most important. Jean Wilson calls it the 'crucial show',[40] David Bergeron the 'dramatic climax',[41] Sydney Anglo a 'critical juncture',[42] and Helen Hackett the pageant that generated the 'greatest excitement'.[43] The perceived importance of this particular pageant device is predominantly due to the fact that Elizabeth made what is for many critics a crucial interjection in the proceedings that demonstrated her ability both as an actress and a wily political manipulator. Those critics mentioned above would certainly subscribe to the idea of Elizabeth possessing both of these characteristics, and her awareness of and skill in representing herself has been a particularly fruitful area of exploration for New Historicist criticism.[44] The crucial moment which has so impressed critics throughout the ages actually occurred before the allegorical display had begun. Mulcaster writes that as Elizabeth reached the pageant stages, she inquired what the pageant was meant to signify. On being told that it represented 'Time', Elizabeth felt compelled to respond: "'Tyme?" quoth she, "and Tyme hath brought me hether"' (48). The importance of this interjection, where Elizabeth associates herself with Time, is fully realised when it becomes clear that in the action that then proceeded to unfold upon the pageant stage, an allegorical figure representing Time brings forth a further allegorical figure, the latter representing Truth. Thus Elizabeth clearly associates herself directly with the embodiment of truth itself. While this may indeed demonstrate (as most critics would now accept) Elizabeth's awareness of what would be contained in this particular performance,[45] for many of those same critics this represents a master-stroke in terms of self-representation. Thus Bergeron tells us that here 'the queen rises triumphantly to the dramatic occasion',[46] while Anglo believes she 'played her part to perfection', demonstrating that she 'was a true heir to her father in crowd-pleasing showmanship'.[47] However, these plaudits are not based on Elizabeth associating herself with Truth alone, but upon a further piece of showmanship that occurred later in the action of the performance.

The pageant device itself was made up of the representation of two hills or mountains, the one on the north side being 'cragged, barreyn, and stonye; in whiche was erected one tree, artificiallye made, all withered and deadde ...' (49). Under the tree sat a mourning figure in rags, over whose head was written his name, 'whiche was, "*Ruinosa Respublica*", "A decayed Commonweale"' (49). Upon the tree hung sentences 'expressing the causes of the decaye of a Common weale' (49). The southern hill in contrast was 'fayre, freshe, grene, and beawtifull, the grounde thereof full of flowers and beawtie', upon which stood a healthy tree, and under whom stood an 'uprighte' figure named "'*Respublica bene institute*", "A florishyng Commonweale"' (49–50). Between the two hills stood a cave out of which, as the Queen arrived, 'issued one personage, whose name was Tyme, apparaylled as an olde man, with a sythe in his hande ... leadinge a personage of lesser stature than himselfe', namely '"*Teemporis filia*", "The Daughter of Tyme"' (50). These two figures then proceeded to the flourishing southern hill, the latter figure with her true name, "*Veritas*" (Truth), written upon her breast. In her hand she carried a book upon which was written '"*Verbum Veritas*", "the Woorde of Trueth"' (50). A child standing upon the southern hill interpreted the pageant in verse, to the effect that the barren hill represented Mary's reign, and the flourishing hill, now that Father Time had brought forth his daughter Truth, that of Elizabeth. And furthermore, that this truth is embodied in the Word of Truth, the English Bible. This was then passed to Elizabeth, her reaction upon receiving it being that further example of her ability to be acutely politically manipulative. For, 'as soone as she had receyved the booke, [she] kissed it, and with both her handes held up the same, and so laid it upon her brest, with great thankes to the Citie therefore' (51). The dramatic nature of Elizabeth's behaviour here underlines this political astuteness, demonstrating a commitment to Protestantism, as well as to a general concept of legitimacy. And, in this moment, she links those commitments both to the institution of her monarchy, and to the powerful civic authorities.

The importance of this particular pageant, where the allegorical figure of Time brings forth his daughter Truth, who embodies a flourishing commonwealth, and whose presence dispels a decaying one, was indicated by Mulcaster as a dramatic climax. Bergeron writes that Mulcaster 'suggests that the meaning of this pageant is dependent on the previous ones, the queen having already been instructed about unity, the virtues which support the seat of government, and the blessings which accompany her'.[48] The message of the pageant is quite clear: Elizabeth, the personification of truth, brought forth by Time, relying on virtue and the word of truth (the English Bible), will oversee the return to a flourishing nation and the banishment of the decaying commonwealth representing Mary's rule. This is further underwritten by Elizabeth's identification of herself with the allegorical figure of Truth, and her dramatic clasping of the English Bible to her breast. Jean Wilson is correct in stating that by so doing Elizabeth 'was making a political statement', in the form of a response 'to London's invitation to be the Truth of Religion ... and transform the decayed Commonweal into a flourishing one'.[49] For David Bergeron, this pageant witnesses a key moment in Elizabethan representation, when he states: 'How striking and meaningful it must have been to the spectators to see Truth in visible union with their new sovereign ...'.[50] This was no doubt striking, but it should be remembered that the precise device of 'Truth, the Daughter of Time' was one already associated very closely with Mary. The portrait of Mary, painted by Frans Huys in (approximately) 1554, now in the British Library, has this actual motto '*Veritas Temporis Filia*' inscribed underneath it.[51] No doubt the idea of the pageant devisers was to replace the Catholic Mary's association with this motto with the Protestant Elizabeth's. And indeed, if as seems likely, given Elizabeth's performance at this pageant, she helped formulate it, or at least knew what was coming, her desire was the same. However, that is not to say that replacement or even displacement was successfully achieved. It is very possible that the most noticeable element for any contemporary audience was the attempt to re/displace, the manipulation of image involved in the effort for positive associations. The aspect of both the Queen's actions and the pageant device itself in this respect is, therefore, the demonstration of allegory as political expediency. And such expediency is likely to have been discernible to an audience familiar with Marian associations. For, in true Benjaminian fashion, the representation of Elizabeth as 'Truth' beckons the possibility of Mary as 'Truth'.[52]

The quintessentially climactic moment for most pageant analysts comes when the allegorical figure of Truth hands Elizabeth the English Bible, which she proceeds to use with dramatic aplomb. According to Mulcaster, a child who had recited verses explaining this pageant had had the Bible and 'reached his booke towardes the Quenes Majestie, whiche, a little before, Trueth had let downe unto him from the hill; which by Sir John Parrat was received, and delivered unto the Quene' (50). This is both an interesting and defining moment. In descriptions of the pre-coronation procession, the presence of 'Sir John Parrat' is frequently omitted, or he is referred to merely as an unnamed 'Gentleman' of the Queen.[53] When he is named, it is purely as a conduit between 'Truth' and Elizabeth, a mechanical agent allowing the pageant message to be successfully accomplished. In J. G. Nichols' study *London Pageants*, there is an interesting footnote in his (confused and misleading) description of this pageant. The footnote, appearing in connection with 'Sir John Perrott' in the main body of text, reads thus: 'Who is supposed to have been a *bastard brother* to the Queen; he was afterwards Viceroy of Ireland' (emphasis added).[54] That is to say then that the English Bible, 'the Woorde of Trueth',[55] was passed from Truth, an allegorical figure, to the ascendant sovereign, already both implicitly and explicitly identified with 'Truth' by the *real* figure of her bastard half-brother. At the very centre of this valorisation of truth personified therefore there is a troubling representation of 'Un-truth'.

The presence of the real in these allegorical circumstances is a defining moment, not least because it is not (only) a symbolic presence. Sir John Perrot was no doubt chosen to play a central role in this display because of the fact that he had sheltered Protestants during the reign of Mary, an act that had seen him spend a short time in prison. However, according to Hiram Morgan, 'Perrot is best known ... for who he may have been – the reputed son of Henry VIII ...'.[56] Morgan stresses that 'Perrot was popularly held to be his [Henry's] son, being large in frame, choleric in temper, tyrannical in government and a lady's man by inclination'.[57] As proof, Morgan quotes a number of records that show he was the son of Henry, and he even floats the idea (which he finally rejects) that Perrot's parentage (and thus claim on the throne) may well have been the reason for his execution towards the end of Elizabeth's reign.[58] Given his bastard status, his appearance in the pre-coronation procession could have cast a rather dim light on the tenuous nature of Elizabeth's claim to the throne, as she had been disinherited by her (and Sir John's) father. A contemporary audience would have been aware of Perrot's ambiguous position, both in terms of such claims to legitimacy, and as a bearer of Truth.

While the presence of Perrot thus compromises this particular dramatic climax and could be interpreted as producing an alternative message for a contemporary audience to that desired, in this allegorisation of allegory by reality the hypocrisy of the ruling elite would be an understandable and relevant reading. Furthermore, such a reading produced in this allegorical moment undermines the whole project of ideological desire apparent in the procession. If we recall that, according to the Venetian Ambassador, one of the vices that Elizabeth was to crush underfoot was indeed 'Hypocrisy', and that Mulcaster, in his official interpretation of the event did not delineate such a vice, there emerges a counter-force in terms of interpretation that undermines the official reading, indeed compromises it. Perrot's presence manifestly demonstrates the hypocrisy that the ruling elite in fact personified. In a Benjaminian sense, a vice summoned by official ideological desire in order that it could be enabled to identify itself against it and thus appear as personifying virtue cannot be held in place, cannot be stabilised or controlled, and in fact crosses over into the centre and contaminates it.

Following the above pageant, Elizabeth moved to St Paul's Churchyard, where she heard an oration in Latin that regarded her accession as the spur towards a new Golden Age, and then on to the Conduit in Fleet Street, where the last extravagant performance took place. Here, upon a stage, stood a tree 'beawtified with leaves as greene as arte could devise', and next to which sat, dressed in Parliament robes and crowned as a Queen, a figure representing 'Debora the judge and restorer of the house of Israel ...' (53). This figure was accompanied by other actors, 'two representing the Nobilitie, two the Clergie, and two the Comminaltye' (53). A child once again explained the pageant in verse, its meaning being, according to Mulcaster, that Elizabeth, 'might by this be put in remembrance to consult for the worthy government of her People', with the added realisation that 'God oftimes sent women nobly to rule among men; as Debora, whych governed Israell in peas the space of xl years ...' (54). Utilising the sanction of Scripture, this pageant attempts to associate Elizabeth with a successful female ruler and thereby attempts to underwrite the legitimacy of female rulership itself. The figure of Debora was a particularly useful one for the pageant devisers, as she had not been associated with the Catholic Mary, herself subject to similar iconographic associations.[59]

Finally, at Temple Bar, all of the meanings of the allegorical devices Elizabeth had witnessed during the procession were posted on tables held in the hands of the City giants Gotmagot and Corineus, and a final oration, underlining the need for the 'maintenaunce of Trueth and rooting out of Errour' (57), was performed. Elizabeth then passed on to the Tower, and the procession reached its end. Mulcaster completes his description with an effusive emphasis upon the mutual feelings of love and respect that had passed between the Queen and her subjects, the latter having been convinced of 'a sure hope for the rest of her gracious doinges hereafter' (58). However, the reality of Anne Boleyn and Sir John Perrot haunt these allegorical devices. When notions of a Golden Age and the promise of female leadership are articulated, the fate of both Anne Boleyn and indeed Mary are once more summoned. When both the 'maintenaunce of Trueth' and the 'rooting out of Errour' are articulated, the presence of Perrot is likewise summoned. Indeed, the reality of Sir John Perrot particularly clarifies, to a great extent, a process where allegory is allegorised, where what haunts the haunted work is exposed and, in this instance, from the common audience's perspective, may witness an 'episode of high political life ... decline inadvertently into self-travesty'.[60] In this example, an alternative message is possible, indeed is beckoned and, for the creators of the pre-coronation procession, for its participants, and for those critics/analysts who regard it as the pinnacle of the royal entry form, allegory becomes allegorised by undesired but unavoidable historical realities.

The principle upon which traditional readings of the allegorical devices performed for Elizabeth in the pre-coronation procession is founded is one that believes that these devices were successful in stating the evident meanings to which the allegories referred, as well as the fact that this meaning was both understood and accepted by the audience as a whole. This formulation in turn rests upon another assumption, being that allegory itself is unproblematic in its ability to declare and deliver its message clearly, or that this meaning can at least be controlled and directed in ways desired by its creators. Yet the problem for these readings, one signalled already in the fact that the pageant devices in the pre-coronation procession were marked by a plenitude of notices placed in public view, stating the unambiguous meaning of each allegory, is that allegory itself, as a form of representation, is inherently unstable in terms of its production of possible meanings. This is clear in the interpretations recorded by Il Schifanoya and Henry Machyn which reveal, as Sandra Logan states, 'the ideological ambiguity of the allegories and their invitation to multiple interpretations – or no interpretation'.[61] Furthermore, as she goes on to say these other interpretations emphasize 'the degree to which allegorical meaning was not inherent, fixed and unitary'.[62] As such, 'Mulcaster's attempts at unification and stabilisation represent his own interests and agenda as much as they reveal the meaning of the procession he describes'.[63] Allegory is thus characterised by the fact that it always produces more than one meaning, no matter how much a single meaning is desired and emphasised by the creator of the allegory. Such a reality can be seen in the allegorical entertainments performed for Elizabeth in many of her rural progresses such as those at Kenilworth in 1575 and at Rycote and Ditchley in 1592.

The Kenilworth entertainments

If the iconography negotiated and mobilised at the beginning of Elizabeth's reign, such as that produced for the pre-coronation procession, can be said to have witnessed the attempted constitution of a female, Protestant and national saviour, the iconography that typified such entertainments as that at Ditchley, which took place towards the end of Elizabeth's reign in 1592, demonstrates the concentration much more upon a mythical, spiritual and personal saviour. This transformation is clear when the iconography mobilised throughout her life as Queen is analysed, and is seen to be adapting to Elizabeth's changing personal and political status throughout the duration of her reign.[64] The imagery used in the pre-coronation procession is typical of its moment in that it underlines Elizabeth's marriageability and fertility, many of the verses recited emphasising the fact that she would (surely) soon marry wisely and beget a male heir. As her reign moved into its middle period, and uncertainty as to whether she would marry or not remained an important theme, an attempt at iconographic fusion of both virginity and fertility as positive necessities for good ruler-ship became more common, a reality that saw many panegyrists uncomfortably balancing these two opposing virtues.[65] To an extent, such a tension defines the allegorical representations produced for Elizabeth at Kenilworth in 1575. As her reign proceeded, the failure of the Anjou courtship in 1578 saw the probability of her marrying and thus begetting an heir as unlikely, and this iconography moved into its final stage. This stage was greatly influenced by Spenser's *Faerie Queene*, where Elizabeth came to be represented as a mythical figure, as the embodiment of the fusion of all oppositions and contradictions. It is in this period of her reign that she essentially becomes associated with such figures as the Moon, Cynthia and Astraea, where she becomes immutable, divine, the embodiment of ethereality and timelessness. It was during this final part of her reign that the Ditchley entertainment took place. Before examining this late entertainment, it is necessary to return to the middle years of her reign in order to take a closer look at the sorts of representations produced and iconography negotiated. It will therefore be productive to examine the lavish entertainments performed for Elizabeth on the Kenilworth estate of Robert Dudley, Earl of Leicester in 1575. Such an examination will clarify the nature of the relationship between Elizabeth and one of her closest courtiers, a relationship that contributed to making the Kenilworth entertainments both so lavish and unique. At the same time, concentration on certain events which occurred during Elizabeth's stay on the estate will open up the entertainments produced to alternative readings than those that have been provided to date.[66] More specifically, a closer look at the erotic nature of the pageant devices Elizabeth witnessed can be set in a more general context of the relationship between Dudley and the Queen, resulting in a Benjaminian process of allegorisation of allegory by reality.

The entertainments that took place on the Kenilworth estate of Robert Dudley in 1575 are generally regarded as the most lavish and spectacular of all of those produced for Elizabeth throughout her reign. Only the entertainments which took place on the Elevetham estate of the Earl of Hertford in 1591 are seen as a possible rival in terms of extravagance; however, the Queen spent eighteen days at Kenilworth as opposed to a mere four days at Elevetham. Indeed, it is believed that the Queen was due to stay even longer at Kenilworth but for reasons to which I shall return, she decided or was advised to leave earlier than planned. Despite this fact, there was still enough time for her to witness a number of mythological pageants in a grand entertainment that most scholars believe, in the words of Mary Hill Cole '[h]as come to signify all that was extravagant and ceremonial about the progresses'.[67] Susan Frye agrees with such a view: 'the Kenilworth entertainments were unprecedented. They were, moreover, of a length and expense never again attempted'.[68]

Scholars generally believe that the series of events which took place at Kenilworth represent the host, Robert Dudley, the Earl of Leicester making one final attempt at winning Elizabeth's hand in marriage. Marie Axton believes that the whole series of entertainments were centred upon 'Leicester's wooing',[69] Susan Doran that they were an elaborate 'proposal of marriage'[70] and Jean Wilson that they represented 'Leicester's final throw in the marriage-game which he had been playing for the first sixteen years of the reign'.[71] In many ways these entertainments have been read in this light not least because they have been felt to also represent Elizabeth's final opportunity to produce an heir and successor given the fact that she was forty-two years of age when they took place.[72] Furthermore, it is true to say that Dudley and Elizabeth had been very close throughout her reign, and many felt that they would eventually be married.[73] The pageants that were performed during her eighteen-day stay do, indeed, lend themselves to a reading founded in this romantic setting, as they construct debates between figures representing chastity and fertility, the latter winning many of these encounters. That said, certain scholars have questioned this conventional interpretation, Philippa Berry believing that such a reading is too simplistic and that any interpretation of the entertainment 'as a serious proposal of marriage seems doubtful'.[74] Helen Hackett makes a similar point, stating that although on the surface the entertainment 'looks like a last-ditch attempt by Leicester to advance his own suit as potential king consort', it would perhaps be wiser to consider the theme of marriage here as 'a metaphor for political favour'.[75] Whatever the case, it is worth examining the series of entertainments in greater detail in order to begin to perceive a fissure in the smooth surface of these interpretations, in the sense that a reading is possible that puts to one side these questions of marriage and underlines rather the jaundiced view of the common people regarding the relationship of Dudley and Elizabeth, particularly when the latter went on progress.

The events that took place on the estate of Kenilworth are among the best documented of all of Elizabeth's progress entertainments due to the fact that two separate and full records were published shortly afterwards. The first of these two texts was produced by the commissioned author of many of the verses and pageants that were performed, George Gascoigne. The second, in the form of an extended letter, is attributed to Robert Langham, about whom little is known but who has been the subject of much speculation.[76] Both texts outline at length the nature and content of the various pageant devices performed for Elizabeth as well as detailing the Queen's responses to these devices. Each also details the other activities undertaken by the Queen during her stay, such as hunting, dancing, feasting and bear-baiting. For the purposes of this study it is the allegorical content of the pageant devices that is of most interest.

The devices Elizabeth witnessed at Kenilworth consisted of relatively conventional allegorical representations of her ruler-ship at this point in her reign, balancing the two virtues of chastity and fertility, sometimes rather uncomfortably. This was already evident in the three short, Arthurian devices performed in her honour as she approached the estate on the evening of 9 July 1575. The first of these devices saw the appearance of a sibyl figure, dressed in white silk, who represented virginity and magical power and who recited verses praising the Queen for having brought peace to her realm: 'The rage of Warre, bound fast in chaines, shall never stirre ne move: / But peace shall governe all your daies, encreasing subjects love'.[77] The allegorical associations are clear in this first device; Elizabeth's effective ruler-ship is seen to be based in both her virginity and her Christ-like, supernatural powers.

Dudley's desire to represent himself as a suitable and marriageable partner for Elizabeth is evident in the very next device in which, by the use of a dumb-show, there is an attempt to display his ancient and noble pedigree. As Gascoigne writes, the dumb-show demonstrates 'that in the daies and reigne of King Arthure, men were of that stature; so that the Castle of Kenelworth should seeme still to be kept by Arthur's hieres ...'.[78] While it is to be expected that Dudley would indeed seek to eulogise himself and his ancestors in a mythological scenario set around the grounds of his own estate, allegorical representation becomes problematic at this very early stage in the proceedings, the difficulty lying in the precise fact that Dudley's attempt to provide himself with such a mythic pedigree cannot but set itself against the reality that both his father and grandfather had been executed for treason, a fate which he himself only narrowly avoided.[79] Indeed, this narrow escape took the form of imprisonment in the Tower of London where he first met, befriended and perhaps fell in love with the young Princess Elizabeth.[80] This particular device therefore represents an initial example of the allegorisation of allegory by reality, something that, as will be shown, can be regarded as defining the entertainment as a whole.

After being presented with the keys to Kenilworth by a porter, 'tall of parson, big of lim and stearn of coountinauns',[81] Elizabeth entered the estate to the sound of trumpets. The trumpeters were six in number, and each one was 'eight foot hy ... all in long garments of sylk sutabl, each with hiz sylvery Trumpet of a fyve foot long, foormed taperwyse ... yet so tempered by art, that ... they cast foorth no greater noyz ... then any oother common Trumpet ... '.[82] As this music continued, Elizabeth was met by the Lady of the Lake 'who came all over the Poole, being so conveyed, that it seemed shee had gone upon the water',[83] who officially welcomed the Queen to Dudley's estate. In verse she continued the eulogising of Dudley and his family and their ancient connection with Kenilworth. This, according to Langham, annoyed the Queen, who responded by reminding those present that the Kenilworth estate was in fact the property of the Crown: 'we had thought indeed the Lake had been oours, and doo you call it yourz noow?'[84] Despite this hitch, it is clear that in these uses of Arthurian chivalric figures, Dudley attempted to represent himself as an appropriate husband for Elizabeth by underlining both his ancient status and present power. At the same time, Elizabeth is represented as possessing both supernatural power and virtue associated with chastity.

The week that followed Elizabeth's arrival at Kenilworth was generally taken up with more everyday entertainments. Thus enormous firework displays were provided on the Sunday and later in the week. Sunday also witnessed much music and dancing, as did the following Wednesday. Another day saw an extended entertainment of bearbaiting and, in the evening, a performance by an Italian gymnast. Much hunting was also indulged in and, on returning from the hunt on the first Monday, Elizabeth was met by a Savage man 'with an Oken plant pluck up by the roots in hiz hande, him self forgrone all in moss and Ivy',[85] who claimed to be confused by all of the goings-on surrounding the Queen. He proceeded to call upon 'the Fawnz, the Satyrez, the Nymphs, the Dryades, and the Hamadriades', to explain all to him, but 'none making aunswer ... calld he aloowd at last after hiz olld freend Echo',[86] who clarified all for him. The appearance of the Savage is the first indication of Dudley's erotic agenda concerning Elizabeth, as this allegorical figure traditionally represented 'lustfulness' and an 'association with instinctual desires'.[87] This association was founded in his being a primitive creature, an inhabitant of the untamed forest, and being beyond or outside of the common law. He is thus a creature defined by passion rather than reason and can be said to represent the sexual element of courtly behaviour as manifested in progress entertainments.

This erotic theme was continued in the next major entertainment provided for Elizabeth, on the following Sunday, which saw many of the local, common people performing a carnivalesque mock-marriage between a groom and an 'ill-smellyng' bride, involving all of 'the lusty lads and bolld bachelarz of the parish', as well as 'prety puzels az bright az a brest of bacon'.[88] According to Langham's *Letter* the bride was 'a xxxv. yeer old, of cooler brounbay, not very beautifull indeed but ugly fooul ill favored ...'.[89] Susan Frye believes that this was a subtle attempt by Dudley to encourage Elizabeth to face the fact of her own age and condition in order to prompt her to realise that, as a last resort, she should take him as her husband.[90] Whether this is correct or not, it is clear that the theme of marriage was prominent, as was a general atmosphere of sensuality which, according to Langham 'woold have mooved sum man too a right meery mood, thoogh had it be toold him hiz wyfe lay a dying'.[91] The texts of the various pageant devices make it clear that the themes of marriage and sensuality were ones that Dudley wanted to continue to articulate. However, the next day saw a turning point in Elizabeth's stay, one which effectively halted Dudley's project.

As Elizabeth returned from hunting on Monday 18 July, the tenth day of her stay she witnessed Gascoigne's elaborate pageant device in which Triton, 'Neptune's blaster', swimming upon a construction resembling a mermaid, some eighteen feet long, entreated her to rescue the Lady of the Lake. Triton explained that the evil knight, Sir Bruse sans Pitie had imprisoned the Lady after having attempted to rape her:

> For looke, what Neptune doth command, of triton is obeyde:
> And now in charge I am guyde your poore distressed Mayde;
> Who, when your Highnesse hither came, dyd humbly yield her Lake;
> And to attend upon your Court, did loyall promise make.
> But parting hence, that yrefull knight Sir Bruce had hyr in chase;
> And sought by force her virgin's state full fowlie to deface (499).

Elizabeth took her place upon a bridge overlooking the lake, and then 'the lady by and by, with her too Nymphs, floting upon her moovabl Ilands (Triton on hiz Mermayd skimming by) approched toward her highness on the bridge: az well too declare that her Majestiez prezens hath so graciously thus wrought her deliverauns'.[92] Once again the presence of the theme of lust is important here, as is the fact that Elizabeth's mere presence frees the Lady from bondage. Interestingly, in the verses performed in this device the Lady is associated with the virgin, Diana, and is set up against the marriage goddess, Juno, who is said to be a helper of Sir Bruse. There is therefore another articulation of tension between lust and chastity, the latter, in this case, seeming to win the day. This is important, as it seems that this was the last device written by Gascoigne to be performed during the Queen's stay. Equally importantly, it seems that it was also not the intended scenario. Dudley had commissioned another elaborate device to be performed, in which the theme of marriage is once more the central point and in which, in this case, Juno, the goddess of marriage, is the victor. This device was never performed, however, as it was, it is widely believed, rejected by Elizabeth.

According to Gascoigne, this cancelled device 'never came to execution. The cause whereof I cannot attribute to any other thing than to lack of opportunity and seasonable weather'.[93] Many analyses of the Kenilworth entertainments take this view and accept Gascoigne's reason.[94] This interpretation is given greater credence by the fact that Gascoigne explains that he 'clad like unto Sylvanus, God of the woods', recited an edited version of the device riding alongside the Queen on horseback, on her day of departure.[95] Many scholars now reject this explanation, however, and believe rather that the Queen censored this device articulating Dudley's proposal of marriage for other reasons. Helen Cooper puts it succinctly: 'George Gascoigne … is being disingenuous: it was not rain that was the chief hazard. The Queen had had quite enough'.[96] Susan Frye believes that Elizabeth, in a demonstration of her power, forced both this device and another one promoting Dudley's cause to be cancelled.[97] Furthermore, she believes that Elizabeth had a hand in the device that turned out to be the final one, the freeing of the Lady of the Lake from the evil Sir Bruse sans Pitie.[98] This being the case, Elizabeth both rejected Dudley's proposal and, at the same time, reasserted her power over him. Many scholars now accept this version of events, as Matthew Woodcock writes: 'the queen refused to play the part of the fairy queen at Kenilworth, preferring instead a narrative that allowed her to unequivocally assert and display her sovereign power'.[99] Many others prefer to accept Gascoigne's explanation that time and weather would not allow the performance of these two devices. While this latter reasoning now seems rather suspect – the final device occurred eight days before the Queen's departure – there is another possibility that has not been considered to date. This reading begins with an examination of an event which occurred on the same day as the final device and which leads to a much greater questioning of the entire progress visit.

In the *Calendar of State Papers* for Spain for 18 July 1575 the following letter appears:

> The Queen who is now at a castle belonging to Lord Leicester, called Kenilworth, has been entertained with much rejoicing there, and it is said that whilst she was going hunting on one of the days, a traitor shot a cross-bow at her. He was immediately taken, although other people assert that the man was only shooting at the deer, and meant no harm. The bolt passed near the Queen but did her no harm, thank God![100]

It is important to note that this occurrence is not corroborated by any other evidence and is not recorded in any other source. As such, and coming from a Spanish individual, it must therefore be treated with a certain amount of scepticism. However, this report exists and needs to be taken seriously if not actually taken at its word. Indeed, the author of the letter, Antonio de Guarras, though Spanish, can be regarded as a respectable if not reliable source as he was both a merchant and, according to Conyers Read, 'a leading member of the Spanish community in London'.[101] Read goes on to outline a series of meetings held between de Guarras and Lord Burleigh in 1572, in which the Spanish merchant attempted to broker a deal for a lasting peace between England and Spain. Although nothing seems to have come of his efforts, both Lord Burleigh and Elizabeth were sympathetic to his efforts.[102] This piece of contextual evidence makes it a little less easy to dismiss de Guarras' letter out of hand, even with the knowledge that he is widely believed to have been a Spanish agent. Furthermore, the date of the letter does coincide with one of the days on which Elizabeth is known to have gone hunting at Kenilworth and, perhaps more importantly, the day on which the last device was performed for her. The importance of this lies in the fact that it was not the final, planned device; two more arranged for following days were cancelled. Thus there is perhaps a third possibility when considering the cancellation of these two pageant devices. It is indeed possible that it was, as Gascoigne claimed and as already stated, due to lack of time and poor weather. Alternatively, it was perhaps due, as so many analysts of the period believe, to Elizabeth calling a halt to Dudley's presumption and constant badgering of her to marry him. However, it could, if de Guarras is correct, be because Elizabeth's life was felt to be in danger and it was considered wise to initially stay indoors for the next week, and then to leave without undue ceremony.

De Guarras was not present at the festivities on Dudley's estate and thus it would be unwise to take his report at face value. This is particularly the case given that there is no supporting evidence. Possibly then, if it does not reflect the truth, it exists more within the realms of rumour. However, even if this is the case, as Susan Frye writes, 'the rumour itself suggests both the widespread fear of Elizabeth's death and a contemporary scepticism about the glories of Kenilworth'.[103] While the fear of assassination was indeed a constant and realistic worry, de Guarras' recording of a rumour, which indeed casts a shadow on the *Princely Pleasures* at Kenilworth, opens a new space in which to examine this progress visit. For rumour is something that characterised common perceptions of the relationship between Dudley and Elizabeth, particularly when the latter went on progress.

There is a certain irony in the fact that one of the major entertainments witnessed by Elizabeth at Kenilworth was the mock marriage performed for her by a large group of local, common people. The irony lies in the fact that this performance centred around the romantic and erotic coming together of groom and bride on the estate, in a reflection of, as common rumour at the time had it, the erotic coming together of Dudley and Elizabeth both at Kenilworth and on progress visits generally. Christopher Haigh lists a number of interesting rumours that spread through the English countryside regarding the true nature of Elizabeth's desire to go on progress, culminating in that which held that 'the Queen only went on summer progresses to have her babies away from London'.[104] More often than not, the person held responsible for making Elizabeth pregnant was Robert Dudley. Thus, as early as 1560 the *Calendar of State Papers* record the punishment of common individuals who are believed to have slandered the Queen in such a manner. An entry for 13 August reads: 'In closes examinations of certain persons of the shire of Essex, touching slanderous reports raised against the Queen. Have committed Anne Dowe, the principal offender, to gaol'. This is immediately followed by: 'Examinations of persons stating that Mother Dowe of Brentwood openly asserted that the Queen was with child by Robt. Duddeley'.[105] In 1563, the *Calendar of State Papers* record the following for 19 January: 'Edm. Baxter said that Lord Robert [Dudley] kept Her Majesty, and that she was a naughty woman … that several lords had told Lord Robert that he kept the Queen, and he gave them thanks. Was told by … wife of Baxter, that while Her Majesty was at Ipswich, she looked like one lately come out of child-bed'.[106] And, as Carole Levin informs us, in 1570 'a man named Marshame was condemned to lose both his ears or else pay a fine of a hundred pounds for saying that Elizabeth had two children by Robert Dudley'.[107] This kind of gossip and rumour-mongering was not restricted to the common people: the Spanish Ambassador, Antonio de Silva wrote on 4 February 1566 that 'the French Ambassador swore to me … that he had been assured by a person who was in a position to know that he (Leicester) had slept with the Queen on New Year's night'.[108]

To some extent it is to be expected that Elizabeth would be the target of such sexual slander given the fact that she was a powerful, single woman and due also to her parentage. As Carole Levin writes:

> Elizabeth was particularly vulnerable to such attacks, being not only a woman, and unmarried at that, but the daughter of Henry VIII, who went through six wives, and Anne Boleyn, whom people called whore and harlot, and who was executed for committing adultery with five men, one of whom was her own brother.[109]

However, as well as suffering the general types of slander that were typically aimed at women of the period, Elizabeth was the target of a very specific type of gossip that centred on her relationship with Robert Dudley. This could also be regarded as less than unexpected given both their close relationship and the suspicious circumstances surrounding the death of Dudley's wife in 1560, who had, it was said, accidentally fallen down some stairs and broken her neck. Resultant gossip had it that Dudley had murdered her in order to be free to wed Elizabeth. Whatever the truth of this incident, the damaging aspect of it for Elizabeth was precisely the gossip it generated. It should be remembered that similar rumours had helped to destroy the reputation of her mother barely thirty years earlier.[110]

The presence of Elizabeth on the estate of Robert Dudley in 1575 would naturally have added fuel to the fire of the gossip-mongerers. As previously stated, many argued that the actual reason for Elizabeth to go on progress in the first place was to hide her pregnancies and to bear (Dudley's) children. The strength of this belief cannot be underestimated, particularly as it was held by the common people, given the fact that such rumours continued long after Elizabeth had passed child-bearing age. Thus, in 1580, when Elizabeth was forty-seven years old Thomas Playfere, an Essex labourer, was indicted for treason, as he said 'that the Quene had two children by my Lord Robert (meaning the earl of Leicester) and that he did see them whene they were shipped at Rye in two of the best shippes the Quene hathe'.[111] 'The next year,' writes Carole Levin, 'Henry Hawkins explained Elizabeth's frequent progresses throughout the countryside as a way for her to leave court and have her illegitimate children by Dudley – he claimed that she had five. Hawkins said of Elizabeth, "She never goethe in progress but to be delivered"'.[112] The Essex Assize Indictments for July 1589 record that Thomas Wendon, a yeoman, was 'indicted for scandalous words. On 5 May 1589 at Colchester he publicly said, "Gods wounds, I will kepe yt no longer, Parson [John] Wylton spake openlie in the Churche ... that the Quenes majestie was an arrant whore." John Weste ... denied that Wylton had ever said this, whereupon Wendon retorted, "Whye, the Quene ys a dauncer and Wylton saithe all dauncers are whores"'.[113] In April 1590 the Essex Assize records detail the 'scandalous words' spoken by another two common people. Denise Deryck 'of Chipping Hill in Witham, widow ... publicly said that the queen "hath had alredye as manye childerne as I, and that too of them were yet alyve, thone beinge a man childe and thother a mayden childe. And further that the other were burned." And beinge demanded by whome she had them, she said by my Lord of Leycester who was father to them and wrapped them upp in the embers in the chimney which was in the Chamber wher they were borne.' The very next record states that Robert Gardner had 'publicly said, "that my lord of Leycester had foure childerne by the Queens Majestie, whereof thre of them were dawghters and alyve and the fourthe a sonne that was burnte"'.[114] As late as 1598 the *Calendar of State Papers* record that 'Edw. Fraunces, of Melbury Osmond, tried to win Elizabeth Baylie to lead an incontinent life with him, and upon her refusing, said that the best in England, i.e. the Queen, had done so, and had three bastards by noblemen of the Court, two sons and a daughter'.[115]

In the state and civic documents from the period under discussion there are all types of gossip recorded regarding Elizabeth and her government, from the corruption of her ministers to the death of the Queen herself. More specifically, there are many instances of rumours being spread and discussed by the common people, usually in the context of the punishment they received for such indiscretion. It is enlightening to learn that, to a great extent, such records represent the major body of common discourse that has been preserved and passed down to our own time. The kinds of comments made by these common people about the Queen range from the relatively harmless discussion of her unsuitability as a monarch (usually due to her gender) to the rather blunt opinions expressed by Jeremy Vanhill, a labourer, in 1585: 'Shyte uppon your Queene; I woulde to god shee were dead that I might shytt on her face'.[116] The seriousness with which the authorities viewed these kinds of comments are clear in that Vanhill was subsequently hanged. However, the number of records dealing with comments and rumours regarding the sexual relationship between Dudley and Elizabeth are noticeable by their frequency in comparison to rumours on other subjects and reflect what must have been a widely held belief at the time. These records only relate to those individuals who were caught and punished for making such comments. It is likely that many more common people would have related such tales and that many of them would have believed them at least in part, if not in their entirety.

For many common people, whether rightly or wrongly, the progresses Elizabeth undertook throughout her reign were mere excuses for her and her courtiers, most particularly Robert Dudley, to participate in sexual liaisons or, in turn, to deal with any potential offspring that resulted from such encounters. This would have remained the view of these common people whether allegorical pageant entertainments had been presented on the progresses or not. The fact that such allegories were performed, and more specifically that many of these entertainments were steeped in a symbolism characterised by its romantic and erotic nature, could only add to the common perception of illicit, sexual behaviour on the part of the Queen and her court. The further realisation that such erotic entertainment was provided by Robert Dudley, widely held to be both Elizabeth's lover and the father of any children she may have produced, on his private estate in 1575 would most certainly have reinforced such beliefs. Thus, when we consider the romantic and erotic symbolism of the entertainments provided for Elizabeth, even setting aside those highly erotic devices which were cancelled, it is important to ponder the potential view of the common population. This is particularly important in this case as, in the device of the mock marriage, Dudley effectively mobilised the local common population to help deliver his erotic message. Thus, when the common people, both local and national, came to consider the *Princely Pleasures* at Kenilworth, it is important to contemplate exactly what they felt these two words represented.

The entertainments provided for the Queen at Kenilworth have traditionally been seen as the highpoint of lavish panegyric and courtly desire. They have also been seen to represent the personal touch of Robert Dudley and an extravagant manifestation of his love and his ambition. No mention has been made of the common people involved, nor indeed of the possible ways in which this progress visit may have been viewed by the common people generally. The Kenilworth entertainments have, unlike many other progress entertainments in the past, been read with a critical eye. Many scholars have indeed regarded the visit as a romantic and political conflict between Elizabeth and the Earl of Leicester. Others have interpreted it as a struggle for Elizabeth to attempt to control the ways in which she could be represented. However, while such analyses are of crucial importance, they do not deal with the ways in which such progress visits and the entertainments provided entered the lives of the common people. Such is the case when other progress visits are considered, such as those to the Rycote and Ditchley estates in 1592.

The Rycote and Ditchley entertainments

The personal nature of the Ditchley entertainment when compared to, for example the pre-coronation procession, naturally has much to do with its form and location, as well as with the fact that it occurred at a late point in Elizabeth's reign. At Ditchley she is an unquestioned figure of authority and mythical strength, all-knowing and all-powerful, a presence to whom no advice is offered as it was in both the pre-coronation procession and at Kenilworth, and around whom there is no hint of religious, political or erotic anxiety. Precisely this kind of mythic presence is evident in the Ditchley Portrait (cover illustration), prompting Frances Yates to observe that the 'Queen stands fairy-like and majestic; light streams from her, defeating the dark clouds in the sky ...'.[117] Along with the entertainment, the painting induces David Bergeron to write that her 'charming power tames nature as well as men',[118] all of which, he continues, 'constitutes a grand compliment to the sovereign, no matter its overstatement'.[119] But, given certain evidence, it is questionable whether the population of Elizabethan Oxfordshire, the site of Ditchley, were charmed by these allegorical representations of the Queen. It is questionable that they believed in Elizabeth's positive influence and power over nature, that she would 'defeat the dark clouds', and that she would right all wrongs. Indeed, she did not right all wrongs for those individuals who, four years later came looking for Sir Henry Lee in order to 'spoil' him.[120] It is clear also that the actions of these individuals demonstrate that they were not convinced by what Roy Strong has called 'that extraordinary mythology which sustained the Elizabethan world ...'.[121] By considering the reality of certain events that impinge upon the meaning of the Rycote and Ditchley entertainments, much of what has been claimed for them can be seen to be problematic. Returning to certain documents enables a reading of these progress visits which throw up similar specific effects to those of Anne Boleyn and Sir John Perrot in the pre-coronation procession, of Dudley at Kenilworth and poses questions founded in the ways in which allegory is allegorised by reality.

The entertainment which took place on Sir Henry Lee's estate at Ditchley, Oxfordshire, formed part of the 1592 royal progress, which subsequently visited Lord Norris' estate at Rycote. This latter visit witnessed a personal and very simple performed greeting (it cannot be said to be an entertainment in the usual sense),[122] in which Lord Norris presented letters from his absent sons and brother, all of whom were serving soldiers, each of which emphasised their devotion to the Queen through the medium of panegyric and by presenting her with expensive jewellery. The letters tell of how, on hearing of the Queen's intended visit, the Norris sons and Sir Thomas, their uncle, wished that they could forgo their military duties in order to be present at Rycote. They all state that the ruling aspect of their lives was their affection for and duty towards her, and that they regard their lives as soldiers as being defined by inconstancy, the Queen's constancy enabling them to overcome the uncertainty this entailed which reassures them.

There is an irony apparent regarding the themes of constancy and affection in the letter supposedly sent by Lord Norris' brother, Sir Thomas Norris. For, at the very time of Elizabeth's visit, his nephew Sir John Norris was involved in a dispute with Robert Dudley, the Earl of Leicester, about the corruption of the commanders in the British forces. In this dispute, Dudley accused Sir Thomas of illegal activity. Harry H. Boyle delineates the nature of the dispute:

> Leicester charged the treasurer with 'fleecing ... poor soldiers' by paying them their
> wretched four-pence a-day in depreciated coin, so that for their 'naughty money they
> could get but naughty ware'; Norris ... came to the defense of his uncle and in a
> letter to Burghley begged the home government not to condemn the treasurer
> without a hearing.[123]

The involvement of Sir Thomas Norris in this scenario is interesting in the context
of what has already been said in this book regarding the tension that existed
between the common soldiers and their commanders. The further involvement of
Sir John Norris emphasises the problematic nature of this context.

The allegory of the triumph of constancy over inconstancy in this short,
personal greeting is couched in descriptions of the military duties of the Norris
sons abroad, most clearly articulated in a letter from Ostend:

> a skipper comming from Flaunders, delivered another letter, with a key of golde
> set with Diamonds with, this motto in dutch, 'I onlie open to you'.
>   My duety remembered, The enemy of late hath made many braveadoes, even to
> the gates of Ostend, but the succese was onely a florish. My selfe walking on the
> Ramparts, to over see the Sentenels, descryed a pink, of whom I enquired, where
> the Court was hee saide hee knew not, but that the 28 of September, her Majesty
> would be at Rycort. I was over-joyed, and in making haste, to remember my
> duety, I had almost forgot it, for I was shipping my selfe for England, with this
> Skipper, but to come without leave, might be to returne without welcome. To
> signifie that my hart is there, I most humbly entreat, that this key be presented; the
> Key of Ostende, and Ostend the Key of Flaunders, the wards are made of true
> harts, treachery cannot counterfeit the Key, nor treason her selfe picke the locke.
> None shal turne it, but whom her Majesty commands, none can. For my selfe, I
> can but wish, all happines to her highnes, and any occasion, that what my toung
> delivers, my bloud may seale, the end of my service, that in her service, my life
> may end.[124]

It is not certain which of the brothers is supposed to have written this letter, as
three of them, John, Henry and Maximilian, were all serving in the region at the
time.[125] As such, the letter can be regarded as being representative of the intentions
and the position of any one of them. However, it seems likely that the intended
author of the letter was either Sir John or Sir Henry Norris, a fact which sets an
interesting interpretive process in motion, similar to that witnessed by the presence
of Sir John Perrot at the pre-coronation procession.[126] For this letter from Ostend
beckons another received by Elizabeth from the same city a few years earlier in
1588.

In the previous chapter the condition of the common soldiers in this period of
Elizabeth's reign was shown to be a cause of great concern for the authorities.
Various outbreaks of disorder and rebellion were recorded by these same
authorities, culminating (though by no means ending) in the weeks of disorder in
London and Kent in the months before and following the Victory procession of
November 1588. The discontent of the common soldiers continued to plague the
authorities throughout the 1590s, and the condition of these soldiers in Ireland was
of particular concern. The Norris sons were directly involved in this experience,

each of them being soldiers and, more specifically, commanders. As was earlier demonstrated, one of the major grievances of the common soldiers was the corruption of their immediate superiors as well as the brutality shown to them by many of the men in command. In conjunction with the terrible provision made for them, particularly when abroad, this corruption and brutality led the soldiers to feel that they had no option open to them other than to resist their abusers. The reluctance with which they pursued such resistance is evident in the price that many of them had to pay when their commanders came to judge them.

A particularly pertinent case is that of troops in Ostend who in 1588 felt the need to write to the Queen personally due to their dire situation. In their letter they state that the 'soldiers ... humbly represent to her Majesty that they have long ... been in great penury', since they had been "lying upon straw, the better part scant that, much less fire, not so much as candle to answer the allarums ...'.[127] This situation led the soldiers to take the drastic action of both mutinying and writing to the Queen, and it is noted in the *Calendar of State Papers* for the latter half of 1588 that the Privy Council 'had been informed ... of their mutiny and the imprisonment of the Governor, captains, and officers ...'.[128] In November of that year Sir John Norris met no resistance when he entered the garrison with his forces, and arrested the mutineers. The report for 19 November states that 'the prisoners [were] brought forth, and one of every company was executed, being in number nine. And upon Tuesday next following there was executed four more ...'.[129] The reference to Sir John Norris is of great importance here, of course, as are the dates set for the execution of the common soldiers. It will be remembered that the official celebrations for the defeat of the Spanish, the Victory procession, took place on 24 November 1588. It was precisely around this time that Sir John Norris was executing thirteen soldiers of his own army, soldiers who were so poorly off that they felt they could pursue no other course but that of mutiny.

While this reference to the Victory procession is important and enables us to read this event differently, in the context of the Rycote progress it is the location from which both the Norris' and the common soldiers' letters were sent that is of greater interest. For with the knowledge of Sir John's instructions that the common soldiers who resisted be executed, we cannot help but read certain sections of the letter he or his brother supposedly sent to Elizabeth at Rycote differently. To return to the letter received by the Queen at Rycote is to begin to view the whole event differently. In the latter part of the letter the following appears:

> To signifie that my hart is there, I most humbly entreat, that this key be presented; the Key of Ostende, and Ostend the Key of Flaunders, the wards are made of true harts, treachery cannot counterfeit the Key, nor treason her selfe picke the locke. None shal turne it, but whom her Majesty commands, none can.[130]

These words beckon the Benjaminian process of the allegorisation of allegory by reality in the sense that the passage takes on a wholly ironic nature in the light of the events of November 1588 (and those occurring at the moment of its presentation) and the conditions of the common soldiers. For the 'wards' were not made of 'true harts' but rather empty stomachs, and the attempt to alleviate this state saw the common soldiers committing, in Norris' eyes, both 'treachery' and 'treason'. At the very moment the letter was sent and that at which Elizabeth heard it read out, a letter sent by a commander (whichever brother it was) to his ultimate commander-in-chief, a disorganised, hungry and dispirited army was suffering under a regime that encouraged a military system in which their own men 'were killed largely by the brutal conditions of service, not in battle'.[131] Interestingly, in 1596 Sir Henry Norris was to be involved in a similar round of executions as his brother John had conducted eight years earlier, but this time the executed were not soldiers, but various employees of his father and other nobles of the region. These executions of common men are closely connected to the entertainment which took place on his father's property at Rycote, as well as on that of Sir Henry Lee's Ditchley estate, Elizabeth's previous port of call.

Like the short entertainment that took place at Rycote, the theme of the triumph of constancy over inconstancy is the ruling element of the Ditchley entertainment, hosted by Sir Henry Lee and written, it is believed, by Richard Edes.[132] Lee had retired as the Queen's Champion of the Horse at the Accession Day Tilt of 1590, after experiencing a colourful career that saw him appointed Lieutenant of the Royal Manor at Woodstock in 1571, Master of the Leash in 1574, and Master of the Armoury in 1580. He is credited with originating the Accession Day Tilts at the start of Elizabeth's reign, and was certainly one of her favourites throughout her life.[133] Lee had entertained Elizabeth before on his estate at Woodstock, Oxfordshire, in 1575. This particular entertainment had followed that of the Earl of Leicester's at Kenilworth, as already shown, one of the most elaborate progress entertainments of Elizabeth's entire reign. Woodstock is interestingly regarded as articulating either a clear rejection of Leicester's amorous message to Elizabeth at the earlier Kenilworth or, conversely, as a continuation of Leicester's chivalric display.[134] Ditchley itself, like the earlier Woodstock, is very much cast as a chivalric romance, Lee representing himself as the knight-turned-hermit, evidence of his importance (along with the Accession Day Tilts) in a revival of the notion of English chivalry. The influential *Book of the Ordre of Chyvalry* by Ramon Lull, the medieval Catalan philosopher, translated and printed by William Caxton, had appeared in 1485, and was 'attributed ... to a hermit who was once a knight'.[135] The hermit is regarded as the ultimate chivalric figure in this context due to the fact that he represented a pastoral retreat from the vigorous actions of the knight in order to partake of an interior contemplation. His status as a chivalric persona is further valorised by the fact that he is also a figure from Arthurian romance, as personified by Sir Baudwin of Britayne in Malory's *Morte d'Arthur*, also printed by William Caxton in 1485. Thus, with this tradition to draw upon, as well as Lee's own inclination, it is no surprise that at Ditchley, 'Elizabeth found herself taking part in a chivalric romance'.[136]

   The romantic story to which Lee returned at Ditchley, having entertained Elizabeth with it at Woodstock seventeen years earlier, was one of two knights in conflict. Contarenus and Loricus are the knights in question, and at the earlier Woodstock entertainment had, according to Berry, represented Lee and Leicester.[137] Whereas at Woodstock a figure representing Hemetes the hermit had begged the Queen to intervene in order to resolve this conflict (which she does), Loricus himself (that is, Lee) is now, at Ditchley, the hermit. This hermit has fallen into a deep sleep, and Elizabeth as the 'Lady-Errant, the righter of wrongs and dispeller of enchantment',[138] is requested to awaken him. This action took place on the second day of the entertainment, and it is worth examining briefly the first day's entertainment in order to enable a more comprehensive analysis of the entire show.

As Elizabeth approached a grove on the estate, she was met by its guardian who informed her of the unhappiness she would meet if she were to enter. Enter she does, however, into the realm of 'Ladies' inconstant in their choice of lovers. These lovers are knights who are in the thrall of the ladies, tied to their inconstancy. There takes place a debate between allegorical figures representing 'Constancy' and 'Lightness' (that is, Inconstancy), a debate which remains unresolved. It is in fact the appearance of Elizabeth that resolves their differences, Lightness suddenly seeing in the Queen the overriding virtue of Constancy. Elizabeth has set the ladies free from Inconstancy (and thus the knights also) before this realisation, and has thus resolved all difficulties. Lightness' change of heart occurs when she sees Elizabeth as the embodiment of *Semper eadem* ('Always the same'), one of Elizabeth's favourite mottos, which Jean Wilson informs us was, 'referring to her virginity, her triumph over time, and her unchangeability' (169). The second day revolved around the awakening from a trance of the hermit Loricus (Lee), Elizabeth once more achieving this by her mere presence. Elizabeth is called 'his heavenlye Mistres' (137), and is thanked by a page for the 'suddaine recoverie of my distressed Maister', attributing to her supernatural powers whereby 'your Majestie hath don a miracle, & it can not be denied ...' (140). For such a miracle, 'Hereat Stellatus, his Chappelaine, besought him to blesse God onelie, for it was Gods spirite who recovered his spirites' (141). Loricus answers that, in a sense, Elizabeth is God when he says: 'whosoever blesseth her, blesseth God in her ...' (141). The entertainment ends with Loricus bequeathing to the Queen 'The Whole Mannor Of Love' (Ditchley) with its 'Groves of humble service, / Meddowes of green thoughtes, / Pastures of feeding fancies', and so on (141).

The influence of Spenser's *Faerie Queene* is apparent in this entertainment, both in its construction of Elizabeth as an immortal and divine mythical presence, and in its uses of certain imagery – the actual naming of the Fairy Queen herself, the sleeping knight in the bower, and the tree-form of certain knights and ladies.[139] Late in her reign, Elizabeth is represented as a kind of Christ-like figure, whose mere presence righted all wrongs, subdued and obliterated those lacking virtue, and who can raise the comatose. Helen Hackett believes that this 'quasi-religious veneration of Elizabeth was justified on the grounds that she was the instrument of God and the true earthly image of the divine purpose'.[140] This would certainly seem to be the case, though Philippa Berry goes even further, arguing that the 'figures of God and queen were implicitly fused'[141] in the chaplain's speech, evident in the emphasis upon Elizabeth's working of a miracle. However far this fusion is taken, it is clear that Elizabeth attains the level of some kind of divinity at least, embodied in her 'more than humane wisdome', in her existence as a 'Heavenlie Goddesse'.[142]

This reference to Spenser is appropriate at this point, as it enables the perception of a certain rupture in the smooth surface of the relationship thus far outlined between Lee and Elizabeth. This rupture is based in the ambiguous nature of the Queen herself, who according to George Steiner is 'the Janus-faced composite of tyrant and martyr ... who incarnates the mystery of absolute will and of its victim'.[143] Elizabeth represents a taboo figure, 'the unapproachable yet infinitely desirable object of courtly desire',[144] and for Lee the object both of fear and attraction. Angus Fletcher has written in detail upon this subject, saying that the hero of allegories has what he calls 'daemonic power', in that they exist between the human and divine worlds, and have superhuman power with which to resolve things.[145] This is an ambiguous position to occupy in the sense that feelings of fear are based in the realisation of the dissymmetry of power, fear of a powerful individual who is free of the usual moral restraints. Conversely, there is an attraction toward a figure of unadulterated power, toward a strong, charismatic individual. The implications of this tyrant/martyr dichotomy are particularly relevant to the Ditchley entertainment in its being influenced by Spenser's *Faerie Queene*, a work which, according to Fletcher, 'has a core of profound ambivalence'.[146] Indeed, the dichotomy is the determining foundation of meaning for Fletcher with regard to Spenser's poem: 'The taboo on Gloriana holds the poem together ... like a retreating glow of light around the deity, lambent in the distance, deadly when we approach it. While the taboo keeps the courtier from his actual Queen ... it ineluctably draws [him] ... into her embrace'.[147]

The ambiguity of this embrace is important for Sir Henry Lee: life-giving, but also, possibly, life-taking. This is evidenced in the entertainment itself, as well as in certain Latin inscriptions which appear on the picture painted to coincide with it, the Ditchley Portrait (cover illustration). Each of the three inscriptions underlines the idea of the Sovereign's duality. On the left of the picture is written (in Latin), 'She gives and does not expect'; on the bottom right (in Latin), 'In giving back she increases'; and, perhaps most potent of the three, on the top right is written (in Latin), 'She can but does not take revenge'. This stresses both the Queen's ability to use arbitrary power, while at the same time emphasising her wisdom and understanding. It also demonstrates that Sir Henry Lee, who commissioned the painting, felt that the Queen had a reason to take revenge, a point that enables real events to enter and destabilise desired allegorical readings by allegorising them.

In his brief look at Elizabethan progresses, Lawrence Stone shows that there are a number of records of the nobility's displeasure upon hearing of a proposed visit by Elizabeth, and says that 'at the end of the reign we find Sir Henry Lee prophesying ruin on hearing that "Her Majesty threatens a progress and her coming to my houses"'.[148] Lee was known to look unkindly upon progresses whether as a participant or as host, and his comment casts a different light upon the context of the chivalric romance that she witnessed upon her arrival at Ditchley.[149] For Lee's comment is neither chivalrous nor romantic. However, his chagrin at the Queen's visit could well have been founded in the fact that he was well aware of Elizabeth's displeasure at his having taken a mistress upon his wife's death in 1590, a woman who from that date onward lived with him on the site of the 1592 courtly romance at Ditchley. This point is referred to by the art historians at the National Portrait

Gallery, where the Ditchley Portrait hangs. They inform us that the theme of the painting itself is in fact forgiveness, due to Lee's taking of Anne Vavasour as his mistress, a theme articulated clearly in that Latin inscription, 'She can but does not take revenge'. Here, indeed, is that taboo figure, the subject of feelings of fear and attraction. References to this problematic situation (for Lee) also appear in the text of the entertainment itself, particularly in the section entitled 'The olde Knightes Tale', part of which reads:

> But loe unhappie I was overtaken,
> By fortune forst, a stranger ladies thrall,
> Whom when I sawe, all former care forsaken,
> To finde her out I lost my self and all,
> Through which neglect of dutie 'gan my fall ... .[150]

Lee seems to be repenting his sin here, albeit within the context of the 'Inconstancie of ladies', who lead knights (including Lee) astray. Thus he has fallen into 'a stranger ladies thrall', the consequences of which are clear:

> With this the just revengefull Fayrie Queene,
> As one that had conceaved anger deepe,
> And therefore ment to execute her teene,
> Resolved to caste mee in a deadlie sleepe ... .[151]

As in the painting, Lee seeks forgiveness, aware that he has aroused Elizabeth's anger.

The Queen often showed her displeasure at the relationships of her courtiers (Leicester and Essex are just two examples), and in this instance she would perhaps have been especially displeased given that Anne Vavasour's 'reputation was already tarnished when she became Lee's mistress',[152] due to the fact that in 1581, she had had an illegitimate son to the Earl of Oxford. The fact of this illegitimacy cannot help but remind us of the presence of Sir John Perrot in the pre-coronation procession, and here once again initiates a questioning of traditional readings of the Ditchley text. For given that Lee balked at the whole idea of Elizabeth visiting in the first place, and then cast his text as an apology to her for his taking of a mistress (one with a tarnished reputation at that), in what sense can this entertainment be defined as a chivalric romance? It is not simply, indeed not even chiefly, an articulation of courtly desire, and/or the valorisation of the qualities of a transcendent Queen. It is much more an attempt to escape displeasure and possible punishment by appeasing an angered monarch. Lee was not, like Loricus, awakened from the trance into which he had fallen (Vavasour), but indeed wished to remain in this 'stranger ladies thrall'. The Ditchley entertainment, like that at Elvetham the previous year, is primarily an attempt to placate Elizabeth's jealousy, and pre-empt any use of her power against an individual who had little desire for her attention in any respect.

This mention of Loricus' (Lee's) falling into a trance is an opportune entry into a final examination of the allegorisation of the Ditchley allegory in the light of an historical reading. On the first day of the entertainment, 20 September, the Queen was led into a grove by a warder knight. He warns her, however, that she should perhaps remain outside and not enter:

> presse not too far, unless you wish to see
> the dolefull case of them that live in woe
> & pittie wer it such a one as you
> shold se the sight wold make your hart to rew.[153]

The reason she should perhaps remain outside the grove and not have her eyes offended is, the knight explains, because it 'yealdes nothinge els but syghes & mornfull songes / of hopeless people by ther haples tryall ...'.[154] These 'hopeless people' who dwell in this 'more than most unhappie plase / the very seat of malcontentednes',[155] are the 'light harted' ladies and their 'heavy harted' knights, ruled by inconstancy and despair. The figures in this allegorical drama are the embodiments of a vice that the Queen, by her mere presence, shall (and does) dispel. The status of Anne Vavasour within this scenario, as such a 'light harted' lady and thus the personification of the vice which the Queen defeats, is interesting enough in terms of allegorisation by reality. However, more interesting is the fact that the words of the warder knight have a certain resonance in the context of the uprising that occurred in this vicinity four years later (an examination of which forms part of the previous chapter). For it is difficult, given the events of the uprising of 1596, not to regard these words as articulating the real inconstancy of the lives of the common people. The participants of the uprising were indeed 'hopeless people', full of 'syghes & mornfull songes' who actually lived 'in woe' and who wished to enter this very estate and 'spoil ... Sir Hen. Lee [that is, cut off his head] ...'.[156] Inconstancy ruled their lives due not to their inherent vice, but to the vicissitudes of life at the bottom of such a hierarchy. The hardship they encountered daily is apparent in the records of their interrogation at the hands of the authorities after the failure of their uprising.[157]

The very first sentence uttered in the 'Examination, in answer to interrogatories, of Bartholomew Steere' (342), demonstrates the uncomfortable status of Lee's allegorical offering to Elizabeth, as under torture in Bridewell, having been taken there by Sir Henry Norris, Steere's fellow conspirators describe the reasons for their uprising. The first to answer questions regarding the uprising, Jas. Bradshaw, states that they 'had threatened to pull down the hedges ... if they could not have remedy' (342–3). He then goes on to say that many people had indeed 'petitioned for some corn to relieve their distress, and for putting down enclosures ...' (343). The other conspirators echo these concerns, a baker named William (surname not given), stating that 'corn would not be cheaper until the hedges were thrown down ...' (344). John Ibill tells of how Steere said 'that there would be a rising of the people ... when they would pull down the enclosures, whereby the ways were stopped, and arable lands enclosed, and lay them open again ...' (345). The common people involved in this particular example of discontentment therefore clearly equated enclosure with both poverty and hunger. And there would seem to be a great deal of sense in their belief, as not only was much of the enclosure of land undertaken by Lee (and Norris) illegal, the village of Ditchley had itself become a deserted village by 1596 as a direct consequence of Lee's policy of enclosure of land in his possession.[158] The 'great sheep-master' Lee enclosed enormous areas of land around both Ditchley and Woodstock and effectively contributed to the depopulation of the entire area.[159] Norris was also 'loathed by the people',[160] not least because his policy of enclosure was also the reason for local depopulation. The opposition of Steere and his co-conspirators was not enclosure *per se*, however. Rather, it was, as far as the rural poor were concerned, the hunger and poverty which such enclosure produced and under which they had to suffer. Thus, Roger Symonds (under torture) reports Steere as telling of instances 'when he went to market, [and] he commonly heard the poor people say that they were ready to famish for want of corn', and stating that he knew of 'a farmer who had 80 quarters of corn, and that poor men could not have a bushel under 4s.2d., and their want of 2d. was often the occasion of their not having any …'.[161] Steere's observations seem to comply with contemporary evidence, both local and national, which shows 1596 to have been a particularly hard year for the rural poor, and particularly in this part of Oxfordshire.[162] The nature of this problem is perhaps best reflected in the rapidity of the government's response to the uprising. For in late January of 1597 proceedings against seven enclosers named by the conspirators under torture were initiated,[163] a process which eventually led to a much broader series of proceedings.[164]

Lee (and Norris) were surprised by the rebellion that took place in 1596, shocked at the level of discontentment existent among their own employees on their own estates. The Ditchley allegory sees Loricus awoken from his sleep, but the Oxford uprising sees Lee, some years later, still asleep, still in a trance regarding the condition of the common people in his area and employ. And the constant refrain 'Happie houre, happie daie, / That Eliza came this waie!'[165] recited at the end of the first day's entertainment seems restricted to a summary of Lee's attempt at appeasement and nothing else. Not only do these lines apparently contradict Lee's actual feelings about the presence of Elizabeth on his estate, the whole tenor of the allegory contradicts reality. For there is no evidence that Elizabeth righted wrongs in this instance, none that she embodied 'Justice', and none that, as is claimed in the Ditchley Portrait, she dispelled black clouds, brought in good weather and with it a Golden Age. As John Walter writes in this regard:

> Whatever the unresolved symbolism of the Ditchley portrait … depicting Elizabeth standing on a map of England dispelling heavenly storms, events in north Oxfordshire in 1596 were to suggest that Ditchley was not a happy spot upon which to place Astraea's feet.[166]

From 1592 onwards Lee continued to sleep, until the uprising of 1596 made him aware of the suffering caused by three consecutive failed harvests, the opposite of the claims of both the Ditchley Portrait and of the Ditchley entertainment. The 'syghes & mornfull songes' of the common people continued, but fell on the deaf ears of the sleeping Lee.

When Loricus is awoken by the Queen, he rewards her for resolving all of his troubles with the legacy of 'The Whole Mannor of Love'. This includes:

> Woodes of hie attemptes,
> Groves of humble service,
> Meddowes of greene thoughtes,
> Pastures of feeding fancies,
> Arable lande of large promisses,
> Rivers of ebbing & flowing favours,
> Gardens hedged about with private, for succorie, &
> bordered with tyme; of greene nothing but
> hartesease, drawen in the perfect forme of a true
> lovers knott.
> Orchards stored with the best fruit: Queene Apples,
> Pome Royalls, & Soveraigne Peare.[167]

And so on. Elizabeth is bequeathed all of the natural richness that Lee's estate can offer, including all of its plentiful foods. Yet the sleeping Loricus/Lee does not only fail to notice that the common population lack these same very basic needs, but that they lack them, in 1596, not only due to the bad weather that prevailed since Elizabeth's visit, but because of his systematic programme of enclosure. And the products of this programme (indeed the very programme itself) are offered as reward to the Queen. She is symbolically provided with that which Bartholomew Steere and his followers felt they had to fight, and for which they were subsequently killed.

The figure of the sleeping body of a fictional Loricus contrasts tellingly to the equally still but tortured and real body of Bartholomew Steere. The former is magically awoken by the powers of the Christ-like Queen, in a fantasy whereby he then recovers all of his faculties, including the ability to see clearly. The latter, in reality tortured to death by the real powers embodied in the Queen, has all of his faculties taken away including, of course, his sight. Blinded and anonymously buried, where it has remained, written out of the records, blind to history, the tortured body of Steere disappears from the official text and thus from official history. Yet by its corporeal reality and the reality of its textual disappearance, this body allegorises that official chivalric romance, that allegory of official culture and, by so doing, enters history at the edge of the grave, producing in that vision, an 'allegory of resurrection'. What is more, this body and all that it stands for undermines the traditional notion, articulated by Roy Strong, that a 'society is held together by the assumptions and images it carries in relation to the nature of power within its hierarchy'.[168] It is precisely this idea of the hierarchy's allegorical images of itself constituting that 'extraordinary mythology which sustained the Elizabethan world' that has contributed to the real occlusion of Bartholomew Steere's fate. Moreover, it has shown that such imagery cannot, in effect, sustain itself when immersed in the social realities surrounding it. It is clear, therefore, that the belief in the power of Elizabethan symbol which Strong describes and which 'held the hearts and minds of all its peoples',[169] has profound conceptual difficulties.

Notes

1. No pageant devices were produced for the Victory procession of 1588 and I will therefore concentrate solely on the lavish pageants performed for the Queen at the pre-coronation procession of 1558.
2. Benjamin, *The Origin of German Tragic Drama* 159–235.
3. Julian Roberts, *Walter Benjamin* (London: Macmillan, 1982) 150.
4. Frye, *Elizabeth I: The Competition for Representation* 162.
5. Rosamund Tuve, *Allegorical Imagery: Some Medieval Books and Their Posterity* (Princeton: Princeton University Press, 1966) 29. See also her *Elizabethan and Metaphysical Imagery: Renaissance Poetic and Twentieth-Century Critics* (Chicago: Chicago University Press, 1947).
6. Benjamin, *The Origin of German Tragic Drama* 207.
7. This is Osborne's translation in Benjamin's *The Origin of German Tragic Drama* 175. In his study of Benjamin's life and work, Julian Roberts has translated the same sentence thus: 'Every person, every thing, every relation can signify any other' (Roberts, *Walter Benjamin* 145). The main problem for the translators here is with the German adjective *jede* which is indeed more commonly translated as 'every'. For the present discussion, both translations are sufficient, though I would personally prefer that of Roberts.
8. Angus Fletcher, *Allegory: The Theory of a Symbolic Mode* (Ithaca, New York: Cornell University Press, 1964) 2.
9. Ibid., 72.
10. Ibid., 73.
11. Hermann Cohen, *Ästhetik des reinen Gefühls* II (Berlin: System der Philosophie 3, 1912) 305, quoted in Benjamin, *The Origin of German Tragic Drama* 177. Sarah Kofman is interesting in this context of ambiguity when she writes that 'While ambiguity, in an equivocal fashion, may equally well signal one meaning *or* another, ambivalence *simultaneously* asserts two opposed meanings, sense and non-sense; not love *or* death but love *and* death. The structure of ambivalence is the uncompromising structure of a two-faced Janus': quoted in Scott Wilson, *Cultural Materialism* 107.
12. Hackett, *Virgin Mother* 175.
13. Ibid., 182.
14. Ibid., 182.
15. Fletcher, *Allegory* 306.
16. Benjamin, *The Origin of German Tragic Drama* 162.
17. Ibid., 162.
18. Roberts, *Walter Benjamin* 145.
19. Frye, *Elizabeth I: The Competition for Representation* 16–19 and 33–6.
20. Georg Wilhelm Friedrich Hegel, *Phänomenologie des Geistes* (Frankfurt: Ullstein, 1973).
21. Roberts, *Walter Benjamin* 148.
22. Ibid., 150.
23. Benjamin, *The Origin of German Tragic Drama* 232.
24. Ibid., 232.
25. Roberts, *Walter Benjamin* 150.
26. Ibid., 150.
27. Recent studies, such as those by Susan Frye, Helen Hackett, Philippa Berry and Carole Levin have shown how gendered the pre-coronation procession was: see Frye, *Elizabeth I: The Competition for Representation* 22–55; Hackett, *Virgin Mother* 41–9;

Levin, *The Heart and Stomach of a King* 1–9; Philippa Berry, *Of Chastity and Power*, an examination of the gendering of Elizabeth in contemporary literature. Jean Wilson also demonstrates this gendering process, though to a lesser extent than the authors already mentioned (*Entertainments for Elizabeth I* 3–7).

28.	Sandra Logan makes the point that Mulcaster's interpretation was a quintessentially Protestant one, valorising religious stability over the economic stability valued by the producers of the pageants, the City fathers. See Logan, 'Making History' 256–7.

29.	Frye, *Elizabeth I: The Competition for Representation* 33.

30.	Ibid., 33. Helen Hackett also examines Anne Boleyn's procession in detail in *Virgin Mother* 29–34.

31.	See Smuts, 'Public Ceremony', in *The First Modern Society* 75–6.

32.	Frye, *Elizabeth I: The Competition for Representation* 33.

33.	For a detailed examination of the status of Anne Boleyn and her representation in both her own and Elizabeth's processions and in Shakespeare's *Henry VIII*, see William Leahy, '"You cannot show me": Two Tudor Coronation Processions, Shakespeare's *King Henry VIII* and the Staging of Anne Boleyn', *Renaissance Renegotiations*, eds William Leahy and Nina Taunton, *EnterText* (3:1 Spring 2003) 132–44.

34.	See Logan, 'Making History', 257–66.

35.	Karl Giehlow, *Die Hieroglyphenkunde des Humanismus in der Allegorie der Renaissance, besonders der Ehrenpforte Kaisers Maximilian I. Ein Versuch* (Vienna: Jahrbuch der kunsthistorischen Sammlungen des allerhösnsten Kaiserhauses, XXXII, 1, 1915) 36; quoted in Benjamin, *The Origin of German Tragic Drama* 174. Terry Eagleton quotes this section of Giehlow also in *Walter Benjamin: or Towards a Revolutionary Criticism* 20.

36.	*CSP (Ven) (1558–80)* 13.

37.	David Bergeron's reading of this pageant is conventional, although he does contrast the Venetian Ambassador's interpretation to that of Mulcaster. Having said that, the contrast set up is allowed to remain purely formal, in the sense that Bergeron states that the former's reading seems to be based more in recent English history. It does, however, admit to the possibility of different interpretations (Bergeron, *English Civic Pageantry* 18).

38.	Logan 'Making History' 251–82.

39.	There could no doubt be a problem with translation in this instance. However, what leads me to doubt this is that, of the vices named by Mulcaster, only 'Bribery' both comes close, and does not appear on the Ambassador's list. Moreover, that being the case, I believe that 'Bribery' does not translate as anything like 'Hypocrisy'. The two are simply not commensurate, but rather define very different vices.

40.	Wilson, *Entertainments for Elizabeth I* 6.

41.	Bergeron, *English Civic Pageantry* 21.

42.	Anglo, *Spectacle* 351.

43.	Helen Hackett, *Virgin Mother* 43.

44.	Stephen Greenblatt's *Renaissance Self-Fashioning* deals with this theme (particularly his chapter on Spenser), and more specifically on 165–9. Leonard Tennenhouse is also interested in Elizabeth as actress in his *Power on Display* 102–5. See also Louis Montrose's '"Eliza, Queene of shepheardes"', in *English Literary Renaissance* 153–82 and Jonathan Goldberg's observations in his *James I* 33–6.

45.	Bergeron, 'Elizabeth's Coronation Entry', *English Literary Renaissance* 3–8:8; Hackett, *Virgin Mother* 48.

46.	Bergeron, *English Civic Pageantry* 20.

47.	Anglo, *Spectacle* 351.

48.	Bergeron, *English Civic Pageantry* 21.

49. Wilson, *Entertainments for Elizabeth I* 6.
50. Bergeron, *English Civic Pageantry* 21.
51. The portrait with inscription is reproduced in Frye, *Elizabeth I: The Competition for Representation* 44.
52. Such is the drift of Logan's reading of the Spanish Ambassador's interpretation of this pageant device. She believes that Il Schifanoya interprets the decayed hill as the distant past and the flourishing one not as the future, but as the present state of the nation as inherited from the Catholic Mary (Logan 'Making History' 263–5).
53. Nichols and Bergeron mention him, Jean Wilson, Helen Hackett, Lawrence Manley, Alison Plowden and Clifford Geertz do not.
54. J. G. Nichols, *London Pageants* 56. At the time of the pre-coronation procession, Perrot held no particular office but was an important member of the (impending) Queen's household. For more on Perrot, see Simon Adams, 'The Patronage of the Crown in Elizabethan Politics: the 1590s in perspective', *The Reign of Elizabeth I: Court and Culture in the Last Decade*, ed. John Guy (Cambridge: Cambridge University Press, 1995) 20–45.
55. Mulcaster 50.
56. Hiram Morgan, 'The Fall of Sir John Perrot', *The Reign of Elizabeth I: Court and Culture in the Last Decade* 109–25:109.
57. Ibid., 109.
58. Ibid., 123. For contemporary statements regarding Perrot's parentage, see *MS State Papers* at the Public Record Office; SP 63/167: 6(1).
59. See particularly Hackett, *Virgin Mother* 38–52 and Frye, *Elizabeth I: The Competition for Representation* 22–55 for discussions of the necessity of such iconographic association.
60. Bristol, *Carnival and Theatre* 70.
61. Logan, 'Making History' 261.
62. Ibid., 266.
63. Ibid., 266.
64. Helen Hackett, *Virgin Mother*; Philippa Berry, *Of Chastity*.
65. The following represent some attempts at negotiating this paradox: Sir Philip Sidney, *The Lady of May*, *The Prose Works of Sir Philip Sidney*, ed. Albert Feuillert, 4 vols (Cambridge: Cambridge University Press, 1962) 2:208–17; Edmund Spenser, 'Aprill Ecologue', *The Shepheardes Calendar*, *The Works of Edmund Spenser*, ed. Rev. H. J. Todd, 8 vols (London: Rivington, Payne, Cadell, Davies & Evans, 1805) 1:60–76; John Lyly, *Euphues and his England*, *The Complete Works of John Lyly*, ed. R. W. Bond, 3 vols (Oxford: Oxford University Press, 1902) 2:208–12.
66. The reading offered in the following will be alternative in the sense that it differs from the traditional analyses of the entertainment and also from those readings, such as Susan Frye's, which view the entertainment sceptically (see *Elizabeth I: The Competition for Representation* 56–96).
67. Mary Hill Cole, *The Portable Queen* 30.
68. Frye, *Elizabeth I* 61.
69. Marie Axton, *The Queen's Two Bodies* 62.
70. Susan Doran, *Monarchy and Matrimony* 67.
71. Jean Wilson, *Entertainments for Elizabeth I* 22.
72. The Anjou courtship of 1578 is usually regarded in this light. While it is true that it was the final opportunity for marriage, it is unlikely, given that Elizabeth was forty-five years old at the time, that it was realistically regarded as an opportunity for Elizabeth to produce an heir.

73. See Milton Waldman, *Elizabeth and Leicester* (London: Collins, 1944); Alan Kendall, *Robert Dudley: Earl of Leicester* (London: Cassell, 1980); R. C. Strong and J. A. Van Dorsten, *Leicester's Triumph* (Leiden: Leiden University Press, 1964); Susan Doran, *Monarchy & Matrimony* 40–73.

74. Berry, *Of Chastity and Power* 99.

75. Hackett, *Virgin Mother* 89.

76. George Gascoigne, *The Princely Pleasures at the Courte at Kenelwoorth. That is to saye, The Copies of all such Verses, proses, or poetical inventions, and other Devices of Pleasure, as were there deuised, and presented by sundry Gentlemen, before the Quene's Majestie ...* , in Nichols, *Elizabeth I*, 1:485–523; Robert Langham, *A Letter* ed. R. J. P. Kuin Medieval and Renaissance Texts (Leiden: E. J. Brill, 1983). The latter has been reproduced as *A Letter: Whearin, part of the Entertainment, unto the Queenz Majesty, at Killingworth Castl, in Warwik Sheer, in this Soomerz Progress, 1575, iz signified: from a freend officer attendant in the Coourt, unto hiz freend a Citizen, and Merchaunt of London*, in Nichols, *Elizabeth I*, 1:420–84. According to Muriel Bradbrook, Langham was in fact an actor in Leicester's Men, and was named John rather than Robert; see Muriel C. Bradbrook, *The Rise of the Common Player: a Study of Actor and Society in Shakespeare's England* (London: Chatto and Windus, 1962) 143(fn). David Bergeron finds Bradbrook's thesis questionable; see *English Civic Pageantry* 30(fn). David Scott goes as far as to say that the *Letter* is in fact an elaborate joke played upon Robert Langham by William Patten, a retainer of Lord Burghley. Scott believes that Langham was regarded as both pompous and meddlesome at court and that the letter, a kind of 'in-joke' exaggerates this pomposity; see David Scott, 'William Patten and the Authorship of "Robert Laneham's *Letter*" (1575)', *English Literary Renaissance* 7 (1977) 297–306. Susan Frye goes even further than Scott, stating that, as a jest, the letter 'provides a view of court unique to texts of this period', showing that 'the Elizabethan court seethed with disagreements' (*Elizabeth I: The Competition for Representation* 65). For my purposes, this last point is interesting in itself – the possibility of ambiguity and contingency in the reception of the entertainments – but does not form part of my critique of this event.

77. Gascoigne, *The Princely Pleasures* in Nichols, *Elizabeth* 1:486.

78. Ibid., 490.

79. His grandfather was executed in the reign of Henry VIII and his father became embroiled in the plot to put Lady Jane Grey on the throne.

80. Both Dudley and Elizabeth were regarded as having been connected to the above plot.

81. Robert Langham, *A Letter* 39.

82. Ibid., 40.

83. Gascoigne 491.

84. Langham, *A Letter* 41.

85. Ibid., 45.

86. Ibid., 45.

87. Berry, *Of Chastity and Power* 90.

88. Langham, *A Letter* 49–50.

89. Ibid., 50.

90. Frye, *The Competition for Representation* 70–72.

91. Langham, *A Letter* 52.

92. Ibid., 57.

93. Gascoigne 515.

94. This is true of traditional studies of Elizabethan progresses identified earlier.

95. Gascoigne 515.

96. Helen Cooper, 'Location and Meaning in Masque, Morality and Royal Entertainment', *The Court Masque*, ed. David Lindley (Manchester: Manchester University Press, 1984) 135–48:142.

97. In this other cancelled device, Elizabeth is cast as Zabeta and is lectured on the virtues of marriage by the goddess Iris. See Gascoigne 501–15.

98. Frye, *The Competition for Representation* 65–72.

99. Matthew Woodcock, 'The Fairy Queen Figure in Elizabethan Entertainments', *Elizabeth I: Always Her Own Free Woman*, eds Carole Levin, Jo Eldridge Carney and Debra Barrett-Graves (Aldershot: Ashgate, 2003) 97–115:100.

100. *CSP (Spanish)* Elizabeth 2:498.

101. Conyers Read, *Lord Burghley and Queen Elizabeth* (New York: Knopf, 1961) 70.

102. Ibid., 70–71.

103. Frye, *The Competition for Representation* 57.

104. Haigh, *Elizabeth I* 156. These rumours were founded in the belief that the Queen was sexually insatiable.

105. *CSP (Dom)(1547–80)* 157.

106. *CSP (Dom)(1601–03) with Addenda (147–65)* 534. Many of these records are valuably contained in Levin, *Heart and Stomach* 66–90.

107. Levin, *Heart and Stomach* 78. Levin in fact reproduces many records written by various ambassadors regarding Dudley, Elizabeth and possible pregnancy: see 78–81.

108. *CSP (Spanish) (1558–67)* 520.

109. Carole Levin, '"We shall never have a merry world while the Queene lyveth": Gender, Monarchy, and the Power of Seditious Words', *Dissing Elizabeth: Negative Representations of Gloriana* (London: Duke University Press, 1998) 77–95:78.

110. See Levin, *Dissing Elizabeth* 87. See also Retha Warnicke, *The Rise and Fall of Anne Boleyn* (Cambridge: Cambridge University Press, 1989).

111. *Calendar of Assize Records: Essex Indictments* 195.

112. Levin, *Dissing* 89.

113. *Calendar of Assize Records: Essex Indictments* 259.

114. *Calendar of Assize Records: Essex Indictments* 220. An important article in this present context is Joel Samaha, 'Gleanings from Local Criminal Court Records: Sedition amongst the "Inarticulate" in Elizabethan Essex', *Journal of Social History* 8 (1975) 61–79.

115. *CSP (Dom) (1598–1601)* 136–7.

116. *Calendar of Assize Records: Kent Indictments* 246.

117. Yates, *Astraea* 106.

118. Bergeron, *English Civic Pageantry* 63.

119. Ibid., 63.

120. *CSP (Dom.) (1595–97)* 345.

121. Strong, *The Cult of Elizabeth* 191.

122. In *Entertainments for Elizabeth I* Jean Wilson writes that what occurred at Rycote 'is more in the nature of a *divertissement* arranged for a family friend than a lavish spectacular ...' (52). Wilson reproduces the whole perfomance (47–52). Nichols also reproduces this entertainment in *Elizabeth* 3:168–72. The original, written by Joseph Barnes, exists as *Speeches delivered to her Majestie this last progresse, at the Right Honorable the Lady Russels, at Bissam, the Right Honorable the Lord Chandos at Sudley, at the Right Honorable the Lord Norris, at Ricote* (Oxford: BL C33e7 (19), 1592).

123. Harry H. Boyle, 'Elizabeth's Entertainment at Elevetham: War Policy in Pageantry', *Studies In Philology* 68 (1971) 146–66:156.

124. Reproduced in Jean Wilson, *Entertainments for Elizabeth I* 49.

125. Jean Wilson believes that the likely intended author is Henry, surmising (though without any evidence) that John was present at the time of the Queen's visit.

126. However, it does not undermine the interpretive process I conduct here if it were not John but one of the other brothers. As commanders, the conclusions I reach apply to them all.

127. *CSP (Foreign) (July–Dec 1588)* 166.

128. Ibid., 166.

129. Ibid., 322.

130. Reproduced in Jean Wilson, *Entertainments for Elizabeth I* 49.

131. Breight, *Surveillance* 183.

132. The text of the Ditchley entertainment is reproduced in Nichols, *Elizabeth* 3:193–8, though the original documents he used have been lost. Chambers reproduces a combination of Nichols' text, sections of the *Petyt Manuscript* at the Inns of Court (Inner Temple Petyt MS 538/43), and the *Ferrers Manuscript*, a collection of ten pieces made by Henry Ferrers: see Chambers, *The Elizabethan Stage* 3:404–7. The fullest account is reproduced in Wilson, *Entertainments for Elizabeth I* 126–42; the text that shall be used in this chapter.

133. He may well have been one of her favourites because Lee was never a threat to Elizabeth in an emotional sense. Unlike Leicester, or most famously Essex, Lee never seems to have sought her affections in terms of possible marriage. For an excellent survey of his life and career see E. K. Chambers, *Sir Henry Lee: An Elizabethan Portrait* (Oxford: Clarendon Press, 1936).

134. Wilson and Helen Hackett argue for Woodstock as a rejection of Leicester's advances, with Lee emphasising duty as the courtier's chief virtue with regard to his sovereign. Philippa Berry, on the other hand, sees it as a continuation of (gendered) chivalric content: see Wilson, *Entertainments for Elizabeth I* 119–20; Hackett, *Virgin Mother* 153–4; Berry, *Of Chastity* 100–108.

135. Berry, *Of Chastity* 93. See also Frances Yates, *Astraea* 106.

136. Wilson, *Entertainments for Elizabeth I* 120.

137. Berry, *Of Chastity* 100.

138. Wilson, *Entertainments for Elizabeth I* 123.

139. Ibid., 123 and 167.

140. Hackett, *Virgin Mother* 154.

141. Berry, *Of Chastity* 108.

142. Wilson, *Entertainments for Elizabeth I* 132.

143. George Steiner, introduction, *The Origin of German Tragic Drama*, by Walter Benjamin 16.

144. Fletcher, *Allegory* 272.

145. Ibid., 333–41.

146. Ibid., 273. Fletcher believes that 'Spenserian ambivalence is not simple. We find it throughout the poem: Book 1, the ambivalence resulting from the sense of sin, the archetypal Christian *taboo*; Book II, the ambivalence of appetite and will; Book III, the ambivalence of the fear of sexual impurity; Book IV, a continuation of Book III, centring, officially, on the conflict of loyalties, or conflicting friendships; Book V, the ambivalence ... between idea and law; Book VI, perhaps the least openly ambivalent of the six (though even here ... the final vision of Serena is a depiction of *sparogmos*, the ripping apart of the goddess)'(269).

147. Ibid., 272.

148. Stone 454.

149. Mary Hill Cole, *The Portable Queen* 90.

150. Wilson, *Entertainments for Elizabeth I* 131.
151. Ibid., 131.
152. Chambers, *Sir Henry Lee* 151.
153. Wilson, *Entertainments for Elizabeth I* 126.
154. Ibid., 126.
155. Ibid., 126.
156. *CSP (Dom.) (1595–97)* 345.
157. Ibid., 342–5.
158. K. J. Allison, *The Deserted Villages of Oxfordshire* (Leicester: Dept. of Eng. Local History Occasional Papers 17, 1965) 36–45.
159. Chambers, *Sir Henry Lee* 92–3; see also A. Ballard, *Chronicles of the Royal Borough of Woodstock* (Oxford: Alden & Co., 1896) 25–6.
160. Walter, 'A Rising', *Past and Present* 114.
161. *CSP (Dom.) (1595–97)* 344.
162. See, for example, *Acts of the Privy Council (1596–97)* 88–9, 94–6 and 112–13; Walter, 'A Rising', *Past and Present* 108–19.
163. *CSP (Dom) (1595–97)* 98; *Acts of the Privy Council (1596–97)* 437–8, 447–51 and 455.
164. *Acts of the Privy Council (1596–97)* 483.
165. Wilson, *Entertainments for Elizabeth I* 136.
166. Walter, 'A Rising,' *Past and Present* 90–91.
167. Wilson, *Entertainments for Elizabeth I* 141–2.
168. Strong, *The Cult of Elizabeth* 116.
169. Ibid., 116.

Conclusion

'The true picture of the past flits by': Re-reading a Procession Painting

> From my childhood, one picture has always summed up for me the Elizabethan age: the canvas attributed to Robert Peake called *Queen Elizabeth going in Procession to Blackfriars in 1600.*[1]

The picture (see Fig.1) that has played such a large part in the life of Sir Roy Strong is an interesting artefact, not only because it depicts a procession that insinuates the material complexion of both Elizabethan royal entries and progresses, but also because it seems to delineate for so many scholars of the Elizabethan period precisely the essences that allow the summing up of that age.[2] The picture as a text to be read can represent the material and textual realities of pageantry, not because it produces identical effects, but because it produces similar ones through a related medium. What the picture also represents and which is most important for this study is what Walter Benjamin has theorised as an image of the past that 'flashes up'.[3] He writes:

> The true picture of the past flits by. The past can be seized only as an image which flashes up at the instant when it can be recognised and is never seen again ... . For every image of the past that is not recognised by the present as one of its own concerns threatens to disappear irretrievably ... (247).

As such, to 'articulate the past historically ... means to seize hold of a memory as it flashes up at a moment of danger' (247). Such a materialist practice was integral to Benjamin's desire to wrest history from a historicism that he believed constructed it as the 'great story of the past', and such a practice can be used in order to re-read the painting now, treating it as a 'concern of the present' (247). For the picture is the only existent painting of Elizabeth I on procession, and must therefore be regarded as important evidence in any attempt at analysis of such public events. It is a condensed scenario, a microcosm of a material practice that mirrored the effects of the painting itself. Display is the painting's central metaphor, one that it shared with that of processional pageantry. My desire in this conclusion is to apply the same kind of methodology to an analysis of this picture and its critical history as has been applied throughout this book, in order to demonstrate the pervasive nature of conventional ways of looking at Elizabethan processions. As well as reading the actual painting itself this analysis will consist of the various attempts at

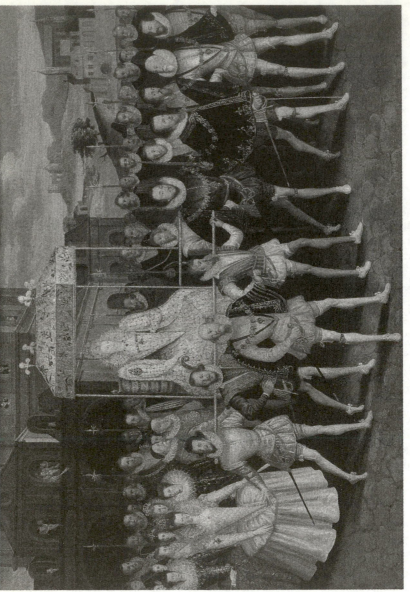

Figure 1. The Procession of Queen Elizabeth I (attributed to Robert Peake the Elder). By kind permission of Mr J. K. Wingfield Digby, Sherborne Castle, Dorset.

interpretation that have been made of the painting up to the present. This analysis will show that, just as with other texts concerning Elizabethan processions, these interpretations tend to consider only the various powerful individuals present and ignore almost completely the presence of the common people. For, though their presence is certainly marginal in the painting, it is apparent and therefore needs to be taken seriously. In order for this analysis to reach the conclusions it seeks, it is necessary to track the painting's confused history and delineate and investigate the various attempts to uncover its origins.

The picture is discussed at some length by John Nichols in his study of Elizabethan pageants and progresses, where he attempts to ascertain its origin by considering everything that had been written about it up until his moment of writing in 1823. He eventually names the picture *The Royal Procession of Queen Elizabeth to Visit Lord Hunsdon*, though he seems far from happy with this decision. He writes:

> It is much to be admired, that in this picture, so large and historical, there should be no date on it, nor arms, nor other insignia, unless the story was then so well known and remarkably public, that the Nobleman who caused it to be done, and to whose honour the ceremonial was performed, might believe it would never be forgot in his family, or to posterity.[4]

This last is precisely what did happen, and is the source of Nichols' and all subsequent scholars' problems with regard to the picture's origins. Thus Nichols' conclusions regarding the picture are, as he freely admits, conjecture based upon previous research. In a move that attempts to enlighten his discussion but which conversely confuses it, Nichols reproduces a copy of an engraving that itself attempted to copy the original painting, the original being, according to him, the supposed work of Marc Gerrards.[5] The engraving was done by George Vertue, the antiquarian, the copy of this engraving by one J. Bouvier, and this in turn was printed by P. Simonass.

Nichols' conjecture is in fact based upon the work of George Vertue, who wrote in 1740 that, in his opinion, the picture was indeed a representation of a procession at Hunsdon House, commissioned by Lord Hunsdon (the fourth Garter-Knight from the left), and painted by Marcus Gheeraerts (the Elder) in 1571. Vertue's investigations were nothing if not thorough, yet today all of his conclusions have been dismissed as incorrect. George Scharf, the first director of the National Portrait Gallery, published findings in the *Archaeological Journal* of 1866 stating that the picture is in fact a portrayal of the marriage of Lady Anne Russell to Henry Somerset, Lord Herbert, at Blackfriars on 16 June 1600.[6] These findings were based on research carried out by Vertue himself, who unfortunately died before he could make these further conclusions public. These findings naturally pointed towards Edward Somerset (the central, fore-grounded figure) as the person responsible for commissioning the painting. The problem with such a theory however, according to Roy Strong, who devotes a large section of his study of Elizabethan portraiture and pageantry to this picture,[7] is that Scharf, and indeed all subsequent commentators on the Procession picture, have wrongly identified the majority of the persons represented in it. Strong writes that the 'Procession Picture is really one of the great visual mysteries of the Elizabethan age, and for nearly two hundred and forty years successive generations of scholars have tried to unravel its secret' (17). He summarises in what ways these successive generations of scholars have erred in their attempts to unravel its secret, his intention being to pronounce his own verdict regarding the painting's origin and depicted event.

Strong believes the defining error made by previous scholars to be a literal one, in that they all sought to find in the painting the depiction of a specific material event. All prior readings had tried to tie the painting to an actual historically verified procession, deeming it to be a celebratory snapshot of a real incident. Strong, however, states that the picture portrays neither Hunsdon nor Blackfriars, as they simply bear no resemblance to the landscape depicted. Thus the topography represented is not that which it had previously been held to be. Similarly, the human topography. Strong insists that of the Garter-Knights pictured, only one, Lord Cumberland (third from left) was present at the wedding of 1600, and only Lord Hunsdon present at the 1571 procession. Furthermore, at both processions the Queen was carried in a litter, while in the picture Strong believes that she is being pushed along 'on some sort of triumphal car with a chair of state upon it' (36). Such a car was used for the Victory procession of 1588 to commemorate the defeat of the Spanish Armada. What Strong thus begins to make clear is that all previous attempts to situate the painting have been wrong because they have been misconceived. For the painting is not the depiction of a specific material event, but rather an allegorical representation of the relationship and power of Queen Elizabeth and Edward Somerset, Fourth Earl Of Worcester.

Reading the picture in this way enables Strong to make certain compelling suggestions. He believes that the painting was indeed commissioned by the figure in the lower foreground, Edward Somerset, who became the Queen's Master of the Horse in 1601, replacing the disgraced and executed Essex. Following a period of apprenticeship in the role while Essex languished in the Tower,[8] Somerset was deemed to be a 'man who clearly had an instinctive feeling for pageantry and ceremonial' (40), subsequently arranging many entries and pageants for James I and Henry, Prince of Wales. He was also the best tilter of his time. Strong uses this information as the instigation for an allegorical reading of the painting, stating that the top left of the picture depicts two buildings in landscapes at variance with one another. This impossible topography is of course not Blackfriars and, according to Strong, nor is it Hunsdon. In fact it is the juxtaposition of two discrete and distant country properties held by the Somerset family at the end of the reign of Elizabeth. The nearest is Chepstow Castle, encircled by the River Wye, and the other is Raglan Castle, both in Monmouthshire. The top right of the picture is filled with a building which, Strong surmises, is in fact another property belonging to the Somerset family, the Worcester Lodge at Nonsuch Palace, Somerset being the Keeper of Nonsuch Great Park at the time.

The impossibility of the topography, together with the prominence of the figure of Somerset and the presence of the combination of the Lords portrayed enables Strong to deduce that the picture is 'something much more than an allusion to the celebrated marriage of 1600' (46). What the picture represents for Strong is an 'historical device', an allegorical celebration of 'Worcester in his role as Queen's favourite and master of ceremonies at the Elizabethan court' (46). In other words, it depicts the centrality of Edward Somerset in that institution of power, demonstrating his wholly pivotal position. And Strong would indeed seem to be correct in his deduction, not because of his detection, or his unravelling of the picture's secrets, but more because the human topography delineates a constellation of power that would be hard to miss. The picture is clearly displaying its subject's power, his allure, his presence. It depicts his family, his property, his affluence, all in proximity to the highest authority, the absolute power, the sovereign.

While Somerset is therefore the subject of the painting, his subjectivity is all in relation to this highest authority, the Queen, who is the painting's greater subject. It is by his relation to the Queen that Somerset is defined, and displaying her allows him to display himself. Roy Strong agrees with this: 'It is Worcester casting himself into his role as the successor of Essex escorting, not the reality of a seventy-year-old woman, but the *idea* – Eliza the sun, the moon, the pelican, the phoenix, the rainbow – fragile like a young girl in virgin white ...' (54).

It is apparent that Strong is correct in his perception that the picture portrays an idea of Elizabeth, or that it at least attempts to. Indeed, for Strong the picture becomes a 'visual statement on the Elizabethan state, on order, the order of the body politic which she animates' (52). The picture thus begins to move outside of itself, and becomes an allegory of order, of discrete though interdependent loci of power, a pictorial display of power on display. The Procession picture is in effect a part of the procession it is depicting, a part of the idea. It attempts to do what the material processions themselves attempted, namely to demonstrate the presence of absolute power through total display. It is a display not merely of affluence, majesty, order and hierarchy, however. It is also a display of distance and of possibility; of potential and arbitrary violence, of the dissymmetry Michel Foucault believes is integral to such a ritual which 'deploys before all eyes an invincible force', and demonstrates 'the unrestrained presence of the sovereign'.[9] And, importantly, it is a display that does not deny the presence of the common people.

Roy Strong has done everything possible to identify those who appear in the Procession picture, and has also made great progress in determining the picture's meaning. He enabled himself to do this by stating a thesis regarding this meaning and then posing himself elementary questions: 'This is Gloriana in her sunset glory, the mistress of the set piece, of the calculated spectacular presentation of herself to her adoring subjects. But who are the other people and where are they going?'[10] The body of his research is taken up in attempting to answer these questions comprehensively. However, his original thesis begs another question (indeed, a series of questions): Where are her adoring subjects? Where are the audience for this spectacular presentation? If this is, as Strong claims, *Eliza Triumphans*, where are all of those sharing in this, acclaiming her, adoring her? Where are the common people who would line the route of such processions, even allegorical ones? Are they simply not present, deemed either unworthy or unnecessary? It is a question that George Vertue asked himself (in the belief that the procession depicted actually took place), and his answer was a very practical one: 'The populace that was there to see this sight are prudently avoided, and not represented, that the most conspicuous part of it without crowd or incumbrance might be seen in the picture, as I presume this Nobleman had appointed and directed the painter'.[11] However, it would seem also to be a totally unsatisfactory answer, as he fails to account for a presence that is definitely there, even if it is not as clearly defined as the central figures. It is the presence of the common people which, when recognised, enables the formulation of a more sceptical reading of the Procession painting. In such a viewing the visual attention is not concentrated upon the two noble figures, but elsewhere, on the margins. It is worth re-examining the picture with a desire to account for this marginal presence.

If we allow our gaze to move away from and behind Elizabeth, her courtiers, and the main body of the procession, we meet a line of uniformed guards, many holding halberds, each wearing a ruff collar and dark tunic. These are the Queen's Gentlemen Pensioners, her personal bodyguards, of whom she had about fifty in 1600.[12] In the picture, these bodyguards form a solid line behind the Queen, though a number of them are standing slightly further back. There seem to be twelve who are forming a front line of defence, with twelve heads inserted between (discernible by their ruffs), filling out this initial line whilst at the same time constituting a further protective boundary. According to J. Nevinson, these twelve secondary heads 'are portraits of the Pensioners who lined the route on the opposite side',[13] sensibly transferred in order to allow the uncontaminated contemplation of the painting's central figures. These individuals appear as stationary figures in the picture, though would of course have walked along beside the Queen in an actual procession. And naturally, these individuals are armed. The numerous halberds that point into the air are not merely there for decoration, but signal what can be termed a threshold of legitimisation where the material centre that is the procession begins to state its own limits, begins to immerse itself in its own centrality in opposition to something else, something that by necessity cannot be central. These weapons, held by the lower strata of the court (minor gentlemen), are the final essential elements or dissymmetrical signifiers of this magnificent spectacle, insisting as they do that the outer limits of magnificence is being reached.

According to Roy Strong, behind these Gentlemen Pensioners are the 'ordinary citizens [who] press forward to gain a glimpse or, more comfortably, lean out of the windows of a house along the route'.[14] It would be easy, given the description 'ordinary citizens' to think that these are in fact the 'adoring subjects' he referred to earlier. However, Strong's use of the term 'citizen' is an unambiguous one, even when undermined by the use of the adjective 'ordinary'. For a citizen in early modern England was not ordinary but was 'next place to gentlemen ... free within the cities, and are of some likely substance to bear office in the same ...'.[15] These were the members of the Trade Guilds, organisations which formed the governments of cities, and who were responsible for the commercial life of these cities. They were respectable business people, merchants, and were, as described earlier, also responsible for the preparation and financing of the processional pageantry that occurred in royal entries. As the financiers of the procession, they can be regarded as very much part of it, of the display, of the power on show, constituting the inner limits of the boundary between centre and margin. Strong is correct in identifying citizens in the Procession picture, and correct too in positioning them both behind the Gentlemen Pensioners, and in the windows (of what is probably Worcester Lodge). However, the painter has also included, in the background, a number of dark, half-faces mostly in the shadows. These are the furthest faces away from the central presence of Elizabeth, ill-defined but perceptibly there. Though difficult to make out (particularly in black and white) they can be seen peeking between heads and over ruffs. These are, I believe, representations of the common people.

It is important to point out (which is indeed the foundation for such a re-reading) that in all interpretations of this painting the common people have only ever been mentioned once (by Vertue), and then only to state that their presence has been 'prudently avoided'. Yet they are present and, given the argument of this book, are a defining presence as the targeted subjects of this spectacular ritual. Traditionally the picture has been regarded as un-problematically representing the radiating Queen surrounded by the splendour of her courtiers. From Vertue to Strong, the Procession picture has been regarded as a glorious dance of state:

> Love created the universe and social order and he invented the dance. Dance cannot exist without music, and the idea of society as musically ordered, of political unity as musical harmony, of ritual and dance as physical expressions of such order are commonplaces of Renaissance thought.[16]

However, Strong's thesis is founded on a conventional topography, a topography of unity, that beholds a central, dominant element and is awe-struck by it. His immersion in Elizabeth-cultism does not allow him to perceive that other presence in the picture. Acknowledging it, the common people become more central, in a topographical inversion that is born from their being the target of these spectacular rituals. These common people – the employed poor, the paupers, the ex-soldiers, the vagrants – become another subject of the painting, become another focus, in their movement towards the centre. That is not to say that they attempted to disrupt this spectacular (and allegorical) event and reject it out of hand. Rather it is to say that, as the general argument of this book states, this presence needs to be taken seriously and needs to be considered in any reading of such an event. Looking at the Procession picture this is the case in two particular ways. First, the common people were, as previously stated, the targeted subject of these rituals and as such, their attitude to them needs to be taken into account. Second, in the painting they are represented as a shadowy, ill-defined and perhaps threatening presence. This would perhaps reflect the ways in which they were perceived by the dominant culture at the time and, given the evidence presented here, probably with good reason. Any analysis of the procession depicted in this picture therefore, as any analysis of a procession undertaken by Elizabeth, should recognise the potential for resistance on the part of the common people, resistance to the normative message of these allegorical representations.

This discussion of the Procession picture therefore demonstrates the effects and results of a re-reading of a cultural artefact that has been reproduced endlessly, in a process that is always seeking to glorify Elizabeth I and, by extension, the golden age she nostalgically represents. What Sir Roy Strong has unravelled therefore is a desire to transmit conventional knowledge, one which both underwrites and constitutes a notion of power that is also conventional. His thesis as discourse joins with the picture and with Elizabethan royal entries and progresses as part of a 'triumphal procession' that parades a dominant ideology. Strong effectively fixes meaning onto a cultural artefact that can then be passed down in a traditionalist manner. But, in the light of Benjamin's theory of images flashing up, and his further claim that all cultural artefacts that have been passed down to the present as such articulations of conventional order are participating in such a 'triumphal procession' which occludes other potential meanings, the important point is not to name the picture, but to investigate this transmission.

The picture and its troubled history therefore articulate Benjamin's belief that such 'cultural treasures' must be viewed 'with cautious detachment', in order for the process of their transmission through time to be analysed both rationally and adequately.[17] The re-reading offered above enables an alternative version of an historical process, but is perhaps not sufficient on its own. This reading, which perceives a haunting common presence in the picture, needs to be placed within a more general 'hermeneutics of suspicion',[18] in which the painting is subjected to various genealogical questionings. Not merely hard facts like, at the time the picture was painted, the Queen was seventy years of age, was partly bald, had blackened teeth and wore a wig. But relevant peripheral facts, such as that the village of Cuddington near Epsom in Surrey was demolished by Elizabeth's father, Henry VIII, in order to build the palace of Nonsuch, a property in the care of the Edward Somerset at the time the picture was painted. Anecdotal evidence too, such as the following, which deals with the actual wedding in Blackfriars that historians thought the picture depicted:

> In 1600 she [Elizabeth] took part in the celebrations for the marriage of Henry Somerset to Anne Russell. The masque afterward represented eight muses in search of the ninth (Elizabeth) to dance with them to the music of Apollo. Mary Fitton begged the Queen to participate, and Elizabeth asking what she represented, was told 'Affection'. 'Affection', said the Queen, 'is false'. It was a sour comment – on the marriage of one of her Maids of Honour, to which as the reign progressed she became more and more violently opposed ... even on Mary Fitton herself, to be dismissed from the court the following year after the disclosure of her affair with the Earl of Pembroke.[19]

Lord Hunsdon, the Queen's cousin, and fourth from the left in the Procession picture, kept a 'bawdy-house of Beasts' in Hoxton, a London suburb.[20] Sherbourne Castle, where the picture now hangs, was confiscated from Sir Walter Ralegh and given to its present owners, the Digby family (into whose hands the painting passed) by James I, Elizabeth's successor. All this is not 'what gives the picture its hypnotic power across the centuries',[21] but rather encourages the evaporation of both the painting's and Elizabeth's aura, tainting it, making it and her more 'approachable'.[22] It clarifies the nature and effect of the triumphal procession, and enables the perception of 'carefully protected identities'.[23]

Notes

1. Strong, *The Cult of Elizabeth* 17.
2. This particular painting appears in many studies of and about Elizabeth and, naturally, of pageants and progresses. See, for example, Strong, *The Cult of Elizabeth*; Roy Strong and Julia T. Oman, *Elizabeth R*; Nichols, *Elizabeth I*, 1:1. Additionally, see the following: Plowden, *Elizabethan England*; Wallace MacCaffrey, *Elizabeth I* (London: Edward Arnold, 1993); Neville Williams, *The Life and Times of Elizabeth I*, introd. Antonia Fraser (London: Weidenfeld & Nicolson, 1972); Philippa Berry, *Of Chastity and Power*.
3. Walter Benjamin, 'Theses On The Philosophy Of History' 247.
4. Nichols, *Elizabeth I* 1:283.
5. Ibid., 282.
6. George Scharf, 'Queen Elizabeth's Procession In A Litter To Celebrate The Marriage Of Anne Russell At Blackfriars, June 16th 1600', *Archaelogical Journal* XXIII (1866) 131–44.
7. Strong, *The Cult of Elizabeth* 17–55.
8. Essex was actually in the Tower at the time of the wedding at which Somerset substituted as the Master of the Horse.
9. Michel Foucault, *Discipline and Punish* 48–9.
10. Strong, *The Cult of Elizabeth* 17.
11. Nichols, *Elizabeth I* 1:289.
12. Strong writes: 'J. Nevinson in his study of the costume of Gentlemen Pensioners ... print[s] the list of almost fifty Pensioners in service of Elizabeth at Michaelmas 1600' (*The Cult Of Elizabeth* 37). Strong is referring to J. L. Nevinson, 'Portraits of Gentlemen Pensioners before 1625', *Walpole Society* XXXIV (1958) 1–13.
13. Strong, *The Cult of Elizabeth* 37.
14. Ibid., 17. Glynne Wickham writes about actual audience arrangements for pageant devices, but his observations are useful in this context in what could be termed a snapshot of a procession: 'the people with "the best seats" were those who occupied rooms in adjacent houses with windows over-looking the street ... . Positions of less vantage were the pavements and the roofs. The former, known as "standings", were allotted to members of the Livery Companies. Those for whom no specific provision was made could scale the roofs ... or take back places on the pavements' (Wickham, *Early English Stages* 1:61).
15. William Harrison, *A Description of England*, eds J. Hurstfield & A. G. R. Smith 18.
16. Strong, *The Cult of Elizabeth* 53.
17. Benjamin, 'Theses On The Philosophy Of History' 248.
18. 'The "hermeneutics of suspicion" ... assumes that the text is not, or not only, what it pretends to be, and therefore searches for underlying contradictions and conflicts as well as absences and silences in the text ...' (Moi, *Sexual Textual Politics* 75–6).
19. Jean Wilson, *Entertainments for Elizabeth I* 13–14.
20. E. J. Burford, *London; The Synfulle Citie* (Brighton: Hale, 1989) 128.
21. Strong, *The Cult of Elizabeth* 54.
22. Benjamin, 'The Work Of Art In The Age Of Mechanical Reproduction', *Illuminations* 236. Walter Benjamin formulated his theory of the aura in this seminal essay, in which he writes: 'The definition of the aura as a "unique phenomenon of a distance however close it may be" represents nothing but the formulation of the cult value of the work of art in categories of space and time perception. Distance is the opposite of closeness.

The essentially distant object is the unapproachable one. Unapproachability is indeed a major quality of the cult image' (*Illuminations* 211–44:236–7).

23. Michel Foucault, 'Nietzsche' 78.

Appendix 1

Procession to St Paul's, 1588

The Proceeding in State of the High and Mightye Prince ELIZABETH, by the Grace of God, Queene of England, Fraunce, and Irland, etc. from Somersett Place to St. Paule's Church in London, Anno 1588.

Messengers of the Chamber.
Gentlemen Harbingers.
Servauntes to Ambassadours.
Gentlemen, Esquires, (her Maiasties servauntes.)
Trumpetes.
Sewers of the Chambers.
Gentlemen Ushers.
The Six Clearkes of the Chauncery.
Clearkes of the Starre Chamber.
Clearkes of the Signett.
Clearkes of the Privye Seale.
Clearkes of the Counsell.
The Queen's Chaplaines having dignities, as Deanes.
Maisters of the Chauncerye.
Aldermen of London.
Knightes Bachelers.
Knightes Officers of the Admiralty.
Judges of the Admiralty.
The Deane of the Arches.
The Soliciter and Atturney Generall.
Sergeante at Lawe.
The Queene's Sergeantes.
Barones of the Exchequer.

| A Pursuivant | (Judges of the Common Pleaes.) | A Pursuivant |
| of Armes. | (Judges of the King's Bench.) | of Armes. |

The Lord Chiefe Baron, and the Lord Chiefe of the Common Pleas.
The Maister of the Roles, and the Lord Chiefe Justice of the King's Bench.
The Queene's Doctor of Phisick.
The Maister of the Tents.
The Maister of the Revells.
The Lieutenant of the Ordinance.
The Lieutenant of the Tower.
The Maister of the Armory.

Knightes that have bin Ambassadors.
Knightes that have byn Deputies for Ireland.

| A Pursuivant | (The Maister of the Great Wardrobe.) | A Pursuivant |
| of Armes. | (The Maister of the Jewelle House.) | of Armes. |

Esquiers of the Bodye, and Gentlemen of the Privie Chamber.
Trumpetes.
The Queene's cloake and hat, borne by a Knight, or an Esquier.
Barones younger Sonnes.
Lancaster Herald. (Knights of the Bathe. Knights Banneretts.) York Herald.
Viscounts younger Sonnes.
Barons eldest Sonnes.
Earles younger Sonnes.
Viscounts eldest Sonnes.
Secretaries to her Majestie.

| Somerset | (Knights of the Privye Counsell.) | Richmond |
| Herald. | (Knights of the Garter.) | Herald. |

The Principall Secretary.
Vice-chamberleine.
Comptroller and Thresorer of the Housholde.
Chester Heralde. (Barons of the Parliament. Bishops.) Windsore Heralde.
The Lord Chamberleine of the House, and the Lord Admirall of England, being
Barons.
Marquesses younger Sonnes.
Earles eldest Sonnes.
Viscounts.
Dukes younger Sonnes.
Marquesses eldest Sonnes.
Norrey King of Armes.
Earles.
Dukes eldest Sonnes.
Marquesses.
Dukes.
Clarencieux King of Armes.
The Almoner. The Maister of Requests.
The Lord High Thresorer of England.
The Archbishop of Yorke.
The Lord Chauncelor of England.
The Archbishop of Canterbury.
The French Ambassador, accompanied with the Lord Buckhurst.

| The Maior | (Garter principal) | A Gentleman Usher of the |
| of London. | (King of Armes.) | Privie Chamber. |

Sergeants at Armes. (The sword, borne by the Lord Marquis.) Sergeants at Armes.

Gentlemen Pens-	(The Queene's Majestie in her	Gentlemen Pens-
ioners, Esquires,	chariot, her Highnes' traine borne	ioners, Esquires,
for the stable footman.	by the Marchiones of Winchester.)	for the stable footman.

The Palfrey of Honour, led by the Maister of the Horse.
The chiefe Lady of Honour.
All other Ladies of Honour.
The Captaine of the Guard.
Yeomen of the Guard.[1]

---

1. Reproduced in Nichols, *Elizabeth* 2:541–2.

Appendix 2

Lord Burleigh's Plan for the Entertainment of Queen Elizabeth at Theobalds, 1583

Of the Roomes and Lodgyngs in the two Courts at Theobalds, 27 May, 1583.
Roomes and Lodgyings in the first Court, beinge the Base Court.

The South side beneathe,
The brewhouse,
The backhouse.
The laundrie.
A chamber for joynores from the steare-foot Eastward.

A chamber next to that Westward from the steare-foot Westward, Chamber. an other chamber next thereto Westward — For the Groomes of the Privie Chamber.

The same syde above at one steares-head.

One chamber over the backhouse towards the brewhouse. — For the Officers of the sellor and pantrye.

One other chamber next to that Westward — For the Queene's Cookes.

The same syde above at an other steares-head on the left-hand.

One chamber at the Easter end of the entrie above the steare. — For Mr. Howard and Mr. Edward Norrice.

One other next to it Westward. — For the Clerk of the Kitchine.

One other next to the steare-head. — For the Squires of the Bodie.

And on the right-hand of the same steare.

One at the Steare-head. — For the Gentlemen Ushers.

One other with a chimney. — For my Lady of Lincolne.

The North syde beneath.

A longe rooffe that served for the Joyners. — For a common hall and a buttery.

A little room that serveth the Paynter. — For the Groome Porter.

Another lardge longe roome that serveth for a storehouse. — One part for the wardrobe, another part for pallets for the Lords servants that lack lodgings.

The same syde above.

Four servants chambers to be distributed by the Usher.

For Mr. Farnham, Mr. Novell, Mr. Bowes, Mr. Bronkard, Mr. Goringe, etc.

Rooms and Lodgings in the Inner Court.
Beneath Southward.

At the entry of the gate.

The Porter's lodge.

In the corner, a chamber with a baye window towardes the Base Court, with an inner roome openinge towards a greate garden.

The robes.

Twoe roomes westward.

One chamber at the East end of the chappell.

The chappell under the withdrawinge-chamber.

The great parlor under the privie chamber, with a wyne cellor under it.

The presence chamber.

On the West syde

The hall.

The pantrye.

The butterey, with a butterye for beare under the hall.

A Winter parlor over the surveying place, openinge Easte and West.

Under the grounde Northwarde.

The kitchin, with bylinge-house scullery, pastry, and larders.

Another kitchin and larder under the ground.

The Steward's chamber at the East end of the court.

A platehouse.

The second stage in the Inner Court.

Over the gate, a gallery painted with the Armes of the Noblemen and Gentlemen of England in Trees.

Southward.

A chamber, named the Lord Admirall's chamber, with an inner chamber openinge towards the garden.

The Lord Admirall.

Another chamber, named the Earle of Warwick's chamber, with

The Erie of Warwick.

a pallett-chamber.
Another chamber, named the Lord
Keper's chamber, under the Queen's   The Ladie Stafforde.
bed-chamber.
Another roome, beinge the closett
over the chapell, and under the
withdrawinge-chamber.
    Upon the same stage, retorninge to the Lord Admirall's chamber,
    there are,
One chamber, with a pallett-
chamber, named the ... having   The Ladie Marques.
a steare downeward towards the
East into a garden.
One chamber, with a pallett-
chamber, named the ... having   For the Lord Howard.
a steare downewards the East into
a garden.
One chamber in a tower next
under the Erle of Leicester's   The Lord Hunsdon.
chamber, with two pallet-
chambers.
And one other chamber, called   The Erle of Leicester's servants.
the Still House chamber.
    The South syde, a third stage.
A Gallery for the Queen's Majestie.
At the South end in a tower one
chamber, with two   The Erie of Leicester.
pallet-chambers.
At the East syde of the same   1. The Gentlewomen of the Privie
gallery, towards the Base Court,   Chamber.
in a garrett two roomes.   2. Theire servants.
    At the North-west end of the Gallery.
Two chambers, whereof one with   The Gentlewomen of the
a chimney.   Bedchamber.
A bed-chamber in a turret.   The Queen's Majestie.
An inner dyneinge-chamber   The Queen's withdrawinge-
over the clossett.   chamber.
A dyneinge-chamber.   The Queen's privie chamber.
    A fourth stage.
A chamber in the uppermost   Mrs. Blanche.
part of the South-east turrett.
A chamber in the turrett, over
the Queen's bedchamber.
A chamber, with a pallet-   Sir Christopher Hatton,
chamber over the privie chamber.   Vice-chamberlaine.
A gallery over the hall, with a

closett vawted with stone for
evidences.

    The North syde of the said Inner Court.

    In the second stage, beginninge at the North end of the painted
    gallery

A chamber over the Steward's chamber, with an inner chamber towards the privie garden, both with chymnyes, and one pallet-chamber.	Mr. Grevell, Mr. Rawley, Mr. Gordge, Mr. Cooke, etc.
A second chamber Westward, with a pallet-chamber over the privie kitchen.	Sir Thomas Henneage.
A third chamber Westward, named the Erle of Rutland's chamber, with a pallet-chamber.	Mr. Secretarie Walsingham.
A fouth chamber, named the Ladie Veare's chamber, with a pallet-chamber and a labbye.	The Ladie Cobhame.

    For the third stage.

A gallerie, named the suitors gallerie, with a roome like a square.	The Lord Treasurer's table.
A chamber at the West end of the Gallery.	
A chamber at the West end thereof, with a pallett-chamber.	The Lord Treasurer's Bed chamber.
At the West end, and terninge Southward towards the hall, two lodgings.	The Lady Burghley.

    For the fourth stage.

A single chamber in the turret, over the East end of the suitor's gallery.	An evidence-house.
Another single chamber in the tower, at the West end of the gallery.[1]	

---

1. Reproduced in Nichols, *Elizabeth* 2:400–404.

Bibliography

Primary Sources

Acts of the Privy Council. Volumes 1558–1604.

Barnes, Joseph. *Speeches delivered to her* Majestie *this last progresse, at the Right Honorable the Lady Russels, at Bissam, the Right Honorable the Lord Chandos at Sudley, at the Right Honorable the Lord Norris, at Ricote*. Oxford: BL C33e7 (19), 1592.

British Library. MS 3320. Egerton.

Calendar of State Papers and Manuscripts. *Domestic Series*. Volumes 1568–1603.

——. *Foreign Series*. Volumes September 1585–December 1588.

——. *Ireland*. Volumes 1596–99.

——. *Spanish Series*. Volumes 1531–79.

——. *Venetian Series*. Volumes 1558–1619.

Cockburn, J. S. *Calendar of Assize Records: Home Circuit Indictments, Elizabeth I and James I*. London: HMSO, 1975–80.

Corporation of London Records Office. *Journals*. Volumes 1585–95.

——. *Remembrancia*. Volumes 1579–1609.

——. *Repertories*. Volumes 1549–83.

Dekker, Thomas. *The Dramatic Works of Thomas Dekker*. Ed. Fredson Bowers. 4 vols Cambridge: Cambridge University Press, 1961.

Ellis, H, ed. *Original Letters Illustrative of English History*. 3 vols London: Triphook & Lepard, 1824.

Gairdner, James, ed. *Letters and Papers of the Reign of Henry VIII*. 13 vols London: Longman & Co., 1882.

Gascoigne, George. *The Princely Pleasures at the Courte at Kenelwoorth. That is to saye, The Copies of all such Verses, proses, or poetical inventions, and other Devices of Pleasure, as were there deuised, and presented by sundry Gentlemen, before the Quene's Majestie … . The Progresses And Public Processions Of Queen Elizabeth I*. Vol.1 John Nichols. 3 vols 1823. New York: AMS Press, 1977: 485–523.

Grafton, Richard. *Abridgement of the Chronicles of England*. London, 1562.

Holinshed, Raphael. *Holinshed's Chronicles of England, Scotland, and Ireland*. 6 vols London: J. Johnson, 1807.

Hughes, P.C. & J.F. Larkin, eds. *Tudor Royal Proclamations*. 3 vols New Haven & London: Yale University Press, 1989.

Inns of Court. *Petyt Manuscript*. Inner Temple Petyt MS 538/43.

Jeaffreson, J. C. ed. *Middlesex County Records I: Indictments, Coroners' Inquests, Post-Mortem and Recognizances from 3 Edward VI to the End of the Reign of Queen Elizabeth*. Middlesex: County Records Society, 1886.

Langham, Robert. *A Letter*. Ed. R. J. P. Kuin. Medieval and Renaissance Texts. Leiden: E. J. Brill, 1983.

Lyly, John. *The Complete Works of John Lyly*. Ed. R. Warwick Bond. 3 vols Oxford: Oxford University Press, 1902.

Middleton, Thomas. *The Triumphs of Truth*. London: N. Okes, 1613.

——. *The Triumphs of Love And Antiquity*. London: N. Okes, 1619.

Middlesex County Records. Microfilm Acc. 312/565.

——. Microfilm. Acc. 312/565.

——. Microfilm. SR. 199/4.

Middlesex Standing Joint Committee. *Middlesex in Shakespeare's Day: Exhibition of Records from the Middlesex County Record Office at the Middlesex Guildhall, Westminster*. London: The Committee, 1964.

Mulcaster, Richard. *The Passage Of Our Most Drad Soveraigne Lady Quene Elyzabeth Through The Citie Of London To Westminster The Daye Before Her Coronacion London 1558–9. The Progresses And Public Processions of Queen Elizabeth I*. Vol.1 John Nichols. 3 Vols. 1823. New York: AMS Press, 1977: 38–60.

——. *The Passage of our most drad Soueraigne Lady Quene Elyzabeth through the citie of London to westminster the daye before her coronacion. Anno 1558. Cum privilegio. Imprinted at London in flete strete within Temple barre, at the signe of the hand and starre, by Richard Tottull, the .xxiii. day of January*. London: Richard Tottill, 1558.

Nichols, J. G., ed. *The Diary of Henry Machyn, Citizen And Merchant-Taylor of London: From A.D. 1550 To A.D. 1563*. London: Camden Society, 1848.

Nichols, John. *The Progresses and Public Processions of James I*. 4 Vols. 1828; New York: AMS Press, 1977.

Osborn, James M., ed. *The Quenes Majesties Passage Through The Citie Of London To Westminster The Day Before Her Coronacion*. New Haven: Yale University Press, 1960.

Public Record Office. *Records of the Lord Chamberlain and other Offices of the Royal Household, and the Clerk of the Recognizances*. LC 2 4/3.

——. LS. 13/168/368–71.

——. *MS State Papers* SP 63/167: 6(1).

Puttenham, George. *The Arte of English Poesie 1589. Elizabethan Critical Essays*. Ed. Gregory Smith. 2 Vols. Oxford: Clarendon Press, 1959. 1–193.

Shakespeare, William. *Hamlet*. Ed. T.J.B. Spencer. *The New Penguin Shakespeare*. Harmondsworth: Penguin Books, 1980.

——. *Henry V*. Ed. T. W. Craik. The Arden Shakespeare. London: Routledge, 1996.

——. *1 Henry VI*. Ed. Andrew S. Cairncross. The Arden Shakespeare. London: Methuen & Co., 1969.

——. *2 Henry VI*. Ed. Andrew S. Cairncross. The Arden Shakespeare. London: Methuen & Co., 1969.

——. *3 Henry VI*. Ed. Andrew S. Cairncross. The Arden Shakespeare. London: Methuen & Co., 1969.

——. *King Henry VIII*. Ed. R. A. Foakes. The Arden Shakespeare. London: Methuen, 1986.

Sidney, Sir Philip. *The Prose Works of Sir Philip Sidney*. Ed. Albert Feuillert. 4 Vols. Cambridge: Cambridge University Press, 1962.

Spenser, Edmund. *The Works of Edmund Spenser*. Vol. 1. Ed. Rev. H. J. Todd. 8 Vols. London: Rivington, Payne, Cadell, Davies & Evans, 1805.

Stow, John. *Annales*. London: Thomas Adams, 1615.

Sutherland, I. *A Summary Tabulation Of Annual Totals of Burials, Plague Deaths and Christenings in London Prior to 1666*. Bodleian Library, Oxford.

Secondary Sources

Allison, K. J. *The Deserted Villages of Oxfordshire*. Leicester: Dept. of Eng. Local History Occasional Papers 17, 1965.

Althusser, Louis. *Essays on Ideology*. London: Verso, 1984.

Anglo, Sydney. *Spectacle, Pageantry and Early Tudor Policy.* Oxford: Clarendon Press, 1969.

Archer, Ian W. *The Pursuit of Stability: Social Relations in Elizabethan London.* Cambridge: Cambridge University Press, 1991.

Axton, Marie. *The Queen's Two Bodies: Drama and the Elizabethan Succession.* London: Royal Historical Society, 1977.

Ballard, A. *Chronicles of the Royal Borough of Woodstock.* Oxford: Alden & Co., 1896.

Barker, Francis. *The Culture of Violence: Essays on Tragedy and History.* Manchester: Manchester University Press, 1993.

Beauvoir, Simone de. *The Second Sex.* Trans. and Ed. H.M. Parshley. 1953. Harmondsworth: Penguin Modern Classics, 1987.

Beier, A. L. 'Vagrants And The Social Order In Elizabethan England'. *Past And Present* 64 (1974) 3–29.

——. *Masterless Men: The Vagrancy Problem in London 1560–1640.* London: Methuen, 1985.

——, and R. Finlay, eds. *London, 1500–1700: The Making of the Metropolis.* Harlow: Longman, 1986.

Belsey, Catherine and Jane Moore, eds. *The Feminist Reader: Essays in Gender and the Politics of Literary Criticism.* London: Macmillan, 1989.

Benjamin, Walter. *Illuminations.* Trans. Harry Zohn. Ed. Hannah Arendt. 1970. London: Fontana Press, 1992.

——. *The Origin of German Tragic Drama.* Trans. John Osborne. 1977. London: Verso, 1990.

Bergeron, David M. *English Civic Pageantry 1558–1642.* London: Edward Arnold Ltd, 1971.

——, ed. *Pageantry in the Shakespearean Theatre.* Athens, Georgia: University of Georgia Press, 1989.

——. 'Elizabeth's Coronation Entry (1558): New Manuscript Evidence'. *English Literary Renaissance* 8 (1978) 3–8.

Berlin, Michael. 'Civic Ceremony in Early Modern London'. *Urban History Yearbook 1986.* Leicester: Leicester University Press, 1986, 3–30.

Berry, Philippa. *Of Chastity and Power: Elizabethan Literature and the Unmarried Queen.* London and New York: Routledge, 1989.

Birt, David. *Elizabeth's England.* Harlow: Longman, 1981.

Black, J. B. *The Reign of Elizabeth 1558–1603.* The Oxford History Of England. Oxford: Clarendon Press, 1959.

Boyle, Harry H. 'Elizabeth's Entertainment at Elevetham: War Policy in Pageantry'. *Studies In Philology* 68 (1971) 146–66.

Boynton, Lindsay. *The Elizabethan Militia, 1558–1638.* London: Routledge and Kegan Paul, 1967.

Bradbrook, Muriel C. *The Rise of the Common Player: a Study of Actor and Society in Shakespeare's England.* London : Chatto and Windus, 1962.

Breight, Curtis C. *Surveillance, Militarism and Drama in the Elizabethan Era.* London: Macmillan, 1996.

Bristol, Michael D. *Carnival and Theatre: Plebeian Culture and the Structure of Authority in Renaissance England.* London: Methuen & Co. Ltd, 1985.

Bromham, A. A. 'Thomas Middleton's *The Triumphs of Truth*: City Politics in 1613'. *The Seventeenth Century* X: 1 (Spring 1995) 1–25.

Burford, E. J. *London; The Synfulle Citie.* Brighton: Hale, 1989.

Burgon, John William. *The Life and Times of Sir Thomas Gresham*. 2 Vols. New York: Burt Franklin, 1964.

Burke, Peter. 'Popular Culture in Seventeenth Century London'. *London Journal* 3.2 (November 1977) 143–62.

Campbell, Lily B. *Shakespeare's 'Histories': Mirrors of Elizabethan Policy*. 1947; London: Methuen & Co., 1977.

Chambers, E. K. *The Elizabethan Stage*. 4 Vols. Oxford: Clarendon Press, 1923.

——. *Sir Henry Lee: An Elizabethan Portrait*. Oxford: Clarendon Press, 1936.

Clark, Paul and Paul Slack, eds. *Crisis and Order in English Towns, 1500–1700: Essays in Urban History*. London: Routledge & Kegan Paul, 1972.

——. *English Towns in Transition 1500–1700*. Oxford: Oxford University Press, 1976.

Cohen, Hermann. *Ästhetik des reinen Gefühls* II. Berlin: System der Philosophie 3, 1912.

Cook, Ann Jennalie. *The Privileged Playgoers of Shakespeare's London*. Princeton, New Jersey: Princeton University Press, 1981.

Cooper, Helen. 'Location and Meaning in Masque, Morality and Royal Entertainment'. *The Court Masque*. Ed. David Lindley. Manchester: Manchester University Press, 1984: 135–48.

Cruickshank, C. G. *Elizabeth's Army*. Oxford: Clarendon, 1966.

Derrida, Jacques. *Of Grammatology*. Trans. Gayatri Chakravorty Spivak. Baltimore: John Hopkins University Press, 1976.

——. *Writing and Difference*. Trans. Alan Bass. London: Routledge and Kegan Paul, 1978.

Dollimore, Jonathan. *Radical Tragedy: Religion, Ideology and Power in the Drama of Shakespeare and his Contemporaries*. Brighton: Harvester, 1984.

Doran, Susan. *Monarchy and Matrimony: The Courtships of Elizabeth I*. London: Routledge, 1996.

Dovey, Zillah. *An Elizabethan Progress: The Queen's Journey into East Anglia, 1578*. Stroud: Alan Sutton Publishing Ltd, 1996.

Drakakis, John, ed. *Alternative Shakespeares*. London: Routledge, 1985.

Eagleton, Terry. *Walter Benjamin: Towards a Revolutionary Criticism*. London: Verso, 1981.

——. *Marxism and Literary Criticism*. London: Methuen, 1976.

Fairholt, F. W. *Lord Mayors' Pageants*. 2 Vols. London: Percy Society, 1843–4.

——. *Gog And Magog: The Giants In Guildhall*. London: John Camden Hotten, 1859.

Fletcher, Angus. *Allegory: The Theory of a Symbolic Mode*. Ithaca, New York: Cornell University Press, 1964.

Foucault, Michel. 'Nietzsche, Genealogy, History'. *The Foucault Reader*. Ed. Paul Rabinow. Harmondsworth: Penguin Books, 1987.

——. *Discipline and Punish: The Birth of the Prison*. 1975; Harmondsworth: Penguin Books, 1982.

——. *The History of Sexuality: An Introduction*. 1976; Harmondsworth: Penguin Books, 1984.

Frye, Susan. *Elizabeth I: The Competition for Representation*. Oxford: Oxford University Press, 1993.

——. 'The Myth of Elizabeth at Tilbury'. *Sixteenth Century Journal* 23 (1992) 95–114.

Geertz, Clifford. *Local Knowledge*. London: Fontana, 1993.

——. *The Interpretation of Cultures*. 1973; London: Fontana, 1993.

——. *Negara: The Theatre State in Nineteenth Century Bali*. Princeton; Oxford: Princeton University Press, 1980.

Giehlow, Karl. *Die Hieroglyphenkunde des Humanismus in der Allegorie der Renaissance, besonders der Ehrenpforte Kaisers Maximilian I. Ein Versuch.* Vienna: Jahrbuch der kunsthistorischen Sammlungen des allerhösnsten Kaiserhauses, XXXII, 1, 1915.

Goldberg, Jonathan. *James I and the Politics of Literature.* Baltimore: Johns Hopkins University Press, 1983.

Greenblatt, Stephen. *Renaissance Self-Fashioning: From More to Shakespeare.* 1980; Chicago: The University Of Chicago Press, 1984.

——. Introduction. *The Forms of Power and the Power of Forms in the Renaissance. Genre* 15.1–2 (Spring and Summer 1982) 3–6.

Guy, John, ed. *The Reign of Elizabeth I: Court and Culture in the Last Decade.* Cambridge: Cambridge University Press, 1995.

Hackett, Helen. *Virgin Mother, Maiden Queen: Elizabeth I and the Cult of the Virgin Mary.* Basingstoke: Macmillan, 1995.

Haigh, Christopher. *Elizabeth I.* 2nd edition. London: Longman, 1998.

Hegel, Georg Wilhelm Friedrich. *Phänomenologie des Geistes.* Frankfurt: Ullstein, 1973.

Hill Cole, Mary. *The Portable Queen: Elizabeth I and the Politics of Ceremony.* Amherst: University of Massachusetts Press, 1999.

Holderness, Graham. *Shakespeare Recycled: The Making of Historical Drama.* Hemel Hempstead: Harvester Wheatsheaf, 1992.

——, ed. *The Shakespeare Myth.* Manchester: Manchester University Press, 1988.

Holmes, Martin. *Elizabethan London.* London: Cassell, 1969.

Howard, Jean E. and Phyllis Rackin. *Engendering a Nation: A Feminist Account of Shakespeare's English Histories.* London: Routledge, 1997.

Hurstfield, J. and A. G. R. Smith, eds. *Elizabethan People: State and Society.* London: Edward Arnold, 1972.

Irigaray, Luce. *The Sex Which Is Not One.* Trans. C. Porter. New York: Cornell University Press, 1985.

Ivornel, Phillipe. 'Paris, Capital of the Popular Front or the Posthumous Life of the 19th Century'. *New German Critique* 39 (Fall 1986) 61–84.

Kamps, Ivo, ed. *Shakespeare Left and Right.* London: Routledge, Chapman & Hall, 1991.

Kelly, H. A. *Divine Providence in the England of Shakespeare's Histories.* Cambridge, Mass: Harvard University Press, 1970.

Kendall, Alan. *Robert Dudley: Earl of Leicester.* London: Cassell, 1980.

King, John N. 'Queen Elizabeth I: Representations of the Virgin Queen'. *Renaissance Quarterly* 43:1 (Spring 1990) 30–74.

Lacan, Jacques. *Ecrits: A Selection.* Trans. Alan Sheridan. London: Tavistock, 1977.

Leahy, William. 'All would be Royal: The Effacement of Disunity in Shakespeare's *Henry V*'. *Shakespeare Jahrbuch* 138 (2002) 89–98.

——. '"Thy hunger-starved men": Shakespeare's *Henry* plays and the contemporary lot of the common soldier'. *Parergon: Journal of the Australian and New Zealand Association for Medieval and Early Modern Studies* 20.2 (July 2003) 119–34.

——. 'Propaganda or a Record of Events? Richard Mulcaster's *The Passage Of Our Most Drad Soveraigne Lady Quene Elyzabeth Through The Citie Of London Westminster The Daye Before Her Coronacion*'. *Early Modern Literary Studies* 9.1 (May 2003) 1–18.

——. '"You cannot show me": Two Tudor Coronation Processions, Shakespeare's *King Henry VIII* and the Staging of Anne Boleyn'. *Renaissance Renegotiations.* Eds William Leahy and Nina Taunton, *EnterText* 3:1 (Spring 2003) 132–44.

Levin, Carole. *The Heart and Stomach of a King: Elizabeth I and the Politics of Sex and Power.* Philadelphia: University of Pennsylvania Press, 1994.

——, Jo Eldridge Carney and Debra Barrett-Graves, eds. *Elizabeth I: Always Her Own Woman*. Aldershot: Ashgate, 2003.

Logan, Sandra. 'Making History: The Rhetorical and Historical Occasion of Elizabeth Tudor's Coronation Entry'. *The Journal of Medieval and Early Modern Studies* 31:2 (Spring 2001) 251–92.

MacCaffrey, Wallace. *Elizabeth I*. London: Edward Arnold, 1993.

Macherey, Pierre. *A Theory of Literary Production*. 1978; London: Routledge & Kegan Paul, 1989.

Manley, Lawrence. *Literature and Culture in Early Modern London*. Cambridge: Cambridge University Press, 1995.

Manning, Roger B. *Village Revolts: Social Protest and Popular Disturbance in England 1509–1640*. Oxford: Clarendon Press, 1988.

Moi, Toril. *Sexual Textual Politics: Feminist Literary Theory*. London: Methuen, 1985.

Montrose, Louis. '"Eliza, Queene of shepheardes," and the Pastoral of Power'. *English Literary Renaissance* 10.2. (Spring 1980) 153–82.

——. 'Professing the Renaissance: The Poetics and Politics of Culture'. *The Forms of Power and the Power of Forms in the Renaissance*. *Genre* 15.1–2 (Spring and Summer 1982) 15–36.

——. 'Renaissance Literary Studies and the Subject of History'. *English Literary Renaissance*. 16.1 (Winter 1986) 5–12.

——. 'The Purpose of Playing: Reflections on a Shakespearean Anthropology'. *Helios*. 7 (1980) 51–74.

Neale, J. E. *Queen Elizabeth I*. 1934; Harmondsworth: Penguin, 1971.

Nevinson, J. L. 'Portraits of Gentlemen Pensioners before 1625'. *Walpole Society* XXXIV (1958) 1–13.

Nichols, J. G. *London Pageants*. London: J. B. Nichols & Son, 1831.

O'Callaghan, Evelyn. *Woman Version: Theoretical Approaches to West Indian Fiction by Women*. London: Macmillan Caribbean, 1993.

Orgel, Stephen. *The Illusion of Power: Political Theatre in the English Renaissance*. Berkeley: University of California Press, 1975.

——. *Impersonations*. Cambridge: Cambridge University Press, 1996.

Parker, Patricia and Geoffrey Harman, eds. *Shakespeare and the Question of Theory*. London: Methuen, 1985.

Pearl, V. 'Change and Stability In Seventeenth Century London'. *London Journal* 5:1 (Spring 1979) 3–34.

——. 'Social Policy in Early Modern London'. *History and Imagination: Essays in Honour of H. R. Trevor-Roper*. Eds H. Lloyd-Jones, B. Worden and V. Pearl. London: Duckworth, 1981, 115–31.

Plowden, Alison. *Elizabethan England: Life in an Age of Adventure*. London: Reader's Digest, 1982.

Rackin, Phyllis. *Stages of History: Shakespeare's English Chronicles*. London: Routledge, 1991.

Rappaport, Steve. *Worlds Within Worlds: Structures of Life in Sixteenth-Century London*. Cambridge: Cambridge University Press, 1991.

Read, Conyers. *Lord Burghley and Queen Elizabeth*. New York: Knopf, 1961.

Roberts, Julian. *Walter Benjamin*. London: Macmillan, 1982.

Said, Edward. 'Representing the Colonised: Anthropology's Interlocutors'. *Critical Inquiry* 15 (Winter 1989) 205–25.

Samaha, Joel. 'Gleanings from Local Criminal Court Records: Sedition amongst the "Inarticulate" in Elizabethan Essex'. *Journal of Social History* 8 (1975) 61–79.

Scharf, George. 'Queen Elizabeth's Procession In A Litter To Celebrate The Marriage Of Anne Russell At Blackfriars, June 16th 1600'. *Archaelogical Journal* XXIII (1866) 131–44.

Scott, David. 'William Patten and the Authorship of "Robert Laneham's *Letter*" (1575)'. *English Literary Renaissance* 7 (1977) 297–306.

Sharpe, R. R. *London and the Kingdom*. 3 Vols. London: Longman, Green and Co., 1894.

Sinfield, Alan. *Faultlines: Cultural Materialism and the Politics of Dissident Reading*. Oxford: Clarendon Press, 1992.

——, and Jonathan Dollimore, eds. *Political Shakespeare: Essays In Cultural Materialism*. Manchester: Manchester University Press, 1985.

Slack, Paul. *Poverty and Policy in Tudor and Stuart England*. Harlow: Longman, 1988.

Smuts, R. Malcolm. 'Public Ceremony and Royal Charisma: the English Royal Entry in London, 1485–1642'. *The First Modern Society: Essays in English History in Honour of Lawrence Stone*. Eds A. L. Beier, David Cannadine and James M. Rosenbaum. Cambridge: Cambridge University Press, 1989, 65–93.

Stone, Lawrence. *The Crisis of the Aristocracy 1558–1641*. Oxford: Clarendon Press, 1965.

Strong, Roy. *The Cult of Elizabeth: Elizabethan Portraiture and Pageantry*. Wallop: Thames and Hudson, 1977.

——. *Splendour at Court*. London: Weidenfield and Nicolson, 1973.

——, and Julia T. Oman. *Elizabeth R*. London: Secker & Warburg, 1971.

——, and J. A. Van Dorsten. *Leicester's Triumph*. Leiden: Leiden University Press, 1964.

Tanner, L. E. *The History of the Coronation*. London: Pitkin, 1952.

Tennenhouse, Leonard. *Power on Display: The Politics of Shakespeare's Genres*. London: Methuen, 1986.

Tillyard, E. M. W. *Shakespeare's History Plays*. 1944; London: Chatto and Windus, 1966.

Turner, Victor. *The Ritual Process: Structure and Anti-structure*. Ithaca: Cornell University Press, 1969.

Tuve, Rosamund. *Allegorical Imagery: Some Medieval Books and Their Posterity*. Princeton: Princeton University Press, 1966.

——. *Elizabethan and Metaphysical Imagery: Renaissance Poetic and Twentieth-Century Critics*. Chicago: Chicago University Press, 1947.

Unwin, George. *The Gilds and Companies of London*. 1908; London: Methuen, 1925.

Veeser, H. Aram, ed. *The New Historicism*. London: Routledge, 1989.

Venezky, Alice S. *Pageantry on the Shakespearean Stage*. New York: Twayne, 1951.

Vickers, Brian. *Appropriating Shakespeare: Contemporary Critical Quarrels*. New Haven & London: Yale University Press, 1993.

Waldman, Milton. *Elizabeth and Leicester*. London: Collins, 1944.

Walker, Julia M. ed. *Dissing Elizabeth: Negative Representations of Gloriana*. Durham & London: Duke University Press, 1998.

Walter, John. 'A "Rising Of The People"? The Oxfordshire Rising Of 1596'. *Past And Present*. 107 (May 1985) 90–143.

Warnicke, Retha. *The Rise and Fall of Anne Boleyn*. Cambridge: Cambridge University Press, 1989.

Weber, Max. *The Theory of Social and Economic Organisation*. Trans. A. M. Henderson and Talcott Parsons. Ed. Talcott Parsons. New York: Oxford University Press, 1947.

Wickham, Glynne. *Early English Stages 1300–1660*. 4 Vols. London: Routledge & Kegan Paul, 1959.

Wilders, John. *The Lost Garden: A View of Shakespeare's English and Roman History Plays*. Totowa, New Jersey: Rowman & Littlefield, 1978.

Williams, Neville. *The Courts of Europe: Politics, Patronage and Royalty 1400–1800*. Ed. A. G Dickens. London: Thames And Hudson, 1977.

——. *Elizabeth I*. London: Weidenfeld & Nicolson, 1972.

——. *The Life and Times of Elizabeth I*. Introd. Antonia Fraser. London: Weidenfeld & Nicolson, 1972.

Williams, Shelia. 'The Lord Mayor's Show In Tudor And Stuart Times'. *The Guildhall Miscellany* 10. London: The Malone Society, 1959.

Wilson, E. C. *England's Eliza*. London: Frank Cass & Co., 1966.

Wilson, Jean. *Entertainments for Elizabeth I*. Woodbridge: D. S. Brewer, 1980.

Wilson, Richard. *Will Power: Essays on Shakespearean Authority*. London: Harvester Wheatsheaf, 1993.

Wilson, Scott. *Cultural Materialism: Theory and Practice*. Oxford: Blackwell, 1995.

Withington, Robert. *English Pageantry: An Historical Outline*. 2 Vols. Cambridge, Mass: Harvard University Press, 1918–20.

Woodworth, Allegra. 'Purveyance for the Royal Household in the Reign of Queen Elizabeth'. *Transactions of the American Philosophical Society* 35 (1945) 1–89.

Wynne-Davies, Marion, ed. *The Renaissance: From 1500 to 1660*. London: Bloomsbury, 1992.

Yates, Frances. *Astraea: The Imperial Theme in the Sixteenth Century*. London and Boston: Routledge & Kegan Paul, 1975.

Index